STAGED

Staged

SHOW TRIALS, POLITICAL THEATER,
AND THE AESTHETICS OF JUDGMENT

Minou Arjomand

Columbia University Press
New York

Columbia University Press wishes to express its appreciation for assistance given by the President's Office at the University of Texas at Austin in the publication of this book.

Columbia University Press
Publishers Since 1893
New York   Chichester, West Sussex
cup.columbia.edu
Copyright © 2018 Columbia University Press
Paperback edition, 2022
All rights reserved

Library of Congress Cataloging-in-Publication Data
Names: Arjomand, Minou, author.
Title: Staged : show trials, political theater, and the aesthetics of
judgment / Minou Arjomand.
Description: New York : Columbia University Press, [2018] | Includes
bibliographical references and index.
Identifiers: LCCN 2018008518 | ISBN 9780231184885 (cloth) |
ISBN 9780231187794 (pbk.) | ISBN 9780231545730 (e-book)
Subjects: LCSH: Theater—Political aspects. | Legal drama—History and
criticism. | Political plays—History and criticism. |
Aesthetics—Political aspects.
Classification: LCC PN2051 .A75 2018 | DDC 792223
LC record available at https://lccn.loc.gov/2018008518

Cover image: Stage model for *The Investigation* at the Freie Volksbühne, West Berlin (1965). Courtesy of the Akademie der Künste Archive, Berlin

In memory of Kathryn Arjomand

Illumination may well come less from theories and concepts than from the uncertain, flickering, and often weak light that some men and women, in their lives and their works, will kindle under almost all circumstances and shed over the time span that was given them on earth.

—HANNAH ARENDT, *MEN IN DARK TIMES*

CONTENTS

LIST OF ILLUSTRATIONS   xi

ACKNOWLEDGMENTS   xiii

Introduction
Show Trials and Political Theater   1

Chapter One
Hannah Arendt: Judging in Dark Times   22

Chapter Two
Bertolt Brecht: Poetic Justice   56

Chapter Three
Erwin Piscator: Theater After Auschwitz   93

Chapter Four
Trials in Nuremberg   139

Conclusion
Archives, Law, and Theater Today   171

x

CONTENTS

NOTES   181

BIBLIOGRAPHY   213

INDEX   227

ILLUSTRATIONS

FIGURE 0.1   *The Exonerated* at the Culture Project, New York City (2012)   17

FIGURE 0.2   Heinar Kipphardt's *In the Matter of J. Robert Oppenheimer* (1964)   19

FIGURE 2.1   Courtroom scene, *The Caucasian Chalk Circle* (1954)   72

FIGURE 2.2   Ernst Busch as the singer in the prologue of *The Caucasian Chalk Circle*   76

FIGURE 2.3   The Picasso debate in the program of *The Caucasian Chalk Circle*   80

FIGURE 2.4   Propaganda photo in the program of *The Caucasian Chalk Circle*   82

FIGURE 3.1   Trial scene in *§218*, directed by Erwin Piscator (1929)   97

FIGURE 3.2   Photograph of the audience at *§218*   98

FIGURE 3.3   *The Crucible*, directed by Erwin Piscator in Mannheim (1954)   105

FIGURE 3.4   Chronology of atrocities in the Essen program for *The Crucible* (1958)   106–7

FIGURE 3.5   Holocaust survivor Peter Edel testifies at the Globke trial (1963)   117

FIGURE 3.6   Peter Edel as a witness in *The Investigation* in East Berlin (1965)   117

FIGURE 3.7   Ernst Busch reading at *The Investigation* in East Berlin   119

FIGURE 3.8   *The Investigation* at the Rostock Volkstheater (1965)   120

FIGURE 3.9   Martin Berliner testifies, on the Freie Volksbühne holiday card   122

FIGURE 3.10   Inside of the Freie Volksbühne holiday card, holiday greetings from Erwin Piscator   123

FIGURE 3.11   *The Burning Bush* at the Dramatic Workshop (1949)   126

FIGURE 3.12   *The Investigation* at the Stuttgart Staatstheater (1965)   130

FIGURE 3.13   Berliner testifying in *The Investigation* at the Freie Volksbühne   133

FIGURE 4.1   Schacht on the stand in *Trial in Nuremberg* at the Deutsches Theater (1967)   157

ACKNOWLEDGMENTS

This book is about what it means to spend time sitting beside other people, sometimes learning from them or arguing with them, but other times simply sharing space and then leaving changed. So many people have sat with me and with this book and left their marks.

This book may never have gotten off the ground without the immense generosity and support of my dissertation adviser, W. B. Worthen. Attending Columbia University for both college and graduate school meant desperately trying to emulate and impress the same people for a decade. Thank you all for putting up with me. Nicholas Dames first made me want to become an academic; Sarah Cole made it happen. Andreas Huyssen's integrity as a scholar and teacher served as a model from early on, as did his ability to always ask the best, and shortest, question in the room. There are few people who get the big picture so right but also line edit the small stuff—Bruce Robbins has been there for everything. Whenever I felt like my manuscript was finally falling into place, Lydia Goehr was ready to remind me to be more dialectical. Finally, thank you to Judith Butler, who is really good at debunking common sense—above all, that you should never meet your heroes. As for my small but incredible cohort, Darragh Martin and Annie Holt: I would not have made it more than a year without you two and our shared projects. You both inspire me endlessly.

As this project transformed into a book, it benefitted from the feedback and insight of so many smart and generous people. Thank you to Craig Calhoun and Richard Sennett and all the members of the NYLON working group for letting a humanist experiment with social theory. My colleagues at Boston University and the University of Texas at Austin brought me into the fold and gave this project both the space and sustenance to grow. Thank you in particular to my faculty mentors, official and unofficial: Julia Prewitt Brown, Bill Carroll, Liz Cullingford, Alan Friedman, Heather Houser, James Loehlin, Lisa L. Moore, and Carrie Preston. Emily Barman, Julian Go, Joseph Rezek, and Ash Anderson made Boston home, often quite literally, giving me—and my furniture—a place to stay during years of my transcontinental commuting. Through many conversations, Andrés Fabian Henao Castro, Joseph Cermatori, Shonni Enelow, Jonathan Foltz, Martin Harries, Julia Jarcho, Rebecca Kastleman, and Freddie Rokem gave new energy and ambition to the project. In the final hour, Bonnie Honig helped me figure out what I was trying to say about Arendt. Martin Puchner has been part of this project from the very beginning; his generous reading and suggestions for the final manuscript were only the tip of the iceberg.

Of course, it is not only individuals but also institutions that enable research. I am deeply indebted to the archivists at the Akademie der Künste Archive, the Deutsches Theatermuseum, and the Harry Ransom Center for guiding me through their collections, and to the DAAD (Deutscher Akademischer Austauschdienst) German Academic Exchange Service and Harry Ransom Center fellowships that made those research trips possible. The Bertolt Brecht Archive houses the most precious resource of all: Erdmut Wizisla, whose support and friendship have meant so much. The Boston University Center for the Humanities and the American Academy of Arts and Sciences bought me the time to finish this project; thank you especially to James Winn and Larry Buell for fostering interdisciplinary exchange through those programs. A publication subvention from the President's Office at UT Austin made it possible to include the photographs in this book. Rachel Rosenthal, Rolf Schneider, and Marianne Simon generously shared their memories with me and brought life to the archives.

Thank you to Columbia University Press and especially to Wendy Lochner, Eric Schwartz, Lowell Frye, and Kathryn Jorge for supporting this project and turning it from a manuscript into a book. Abby Graves rescued you readers from some truly clunky language, for which we should all be grateful.

Parts of chapter 3 were originally published in *Modern Drama*: I am grateful for their permission to reprint this material as well as to R. Darren Gobert for his suggestions at that early stage.

The central argument of this book took shape on the uptown local train: Alix Rule, there is no way to thank you enough for missing your stop in order to continue our conversation, much less for thirty-odd years of everything else. Amy Delfyett has put up with lawyer questions for years and is the source of endless strength. Thanks to Kristen Fallica, Victoria Kocian, Karoline Raeder, and Emily Stolfo for the time I spent not working on this book.

Among many other things, my brother, Noah Arjomand, is an unparalleled editor—the best prose in this book is the result of his suggestions. My father, Saïd Arjomand, cultivated in us the life of the mind, and it stuck.

Harel Shapira has read and reread every page of this book, editing out jargon and asking the big questions that are only obvious in retrospect. This book is just one of many things that are so much better because of him.

I learned to read while my family was living abroad in Germany. It was my mother, Kathryn Arjomand, who taught me and went on to read, edit, and encourage me through every subsequent project. Around the time that I began this book, she was diagnosed with ALS and lost her ability to move and to speak. What she taught me during her illness is at the center of this book: that a person, by her presence in a room, changes everyone in that space, even without words or movement. And the way she always saw the world—with dark humor, with joy, and with indignation—continues to shape the world for all of us lucky enough to have spent time with her. It is to her that this book is dedicated.

SHOW TRIALS AND POLITICAL THEATER

Courtroom dramas have been around as long as tragedy itself. The oldest complete trilogy of Greek tragedy, *The Oresteia*, culminates in a trial that is judged by the goddess of justice herself. In this trial, Athena ends the cycle of violence in the House of Atreus and, in doing so, not only inaugurates the jury system but also founds Athens and asserts the power of her generation of gods over the primordial Furies. In the trial, Athena arbitrates between the Furies and Orestes (along with his defense lawyer, Apollo). The Furies claim their right to chase and persecute Orestes unendingly for his crime of matricide. Apollo insists that he has purified Orestes of the crime. The trial that unfolds is certainly a case of victor's justice: the younger gods, Athena and Apollo, triumph over the older Furies through questionable arguments and evidence, and Athena casts the deciding vote. It is ultimately only by bribing the Furies—offering them a degree of power over Athens—that Athena is able to get them to agree to the verdict she gives.

The trial within *The Oresteia* is staged in such a way that the new gods are sure to win (not least because one of them is the judge). But even though the outcome can be guessed in advance, the performance of the trial is essential. Athena's admonitions to the jury are performative; her speeches create the law of the polis Athens:

> Men of Attica, hear my decree
> now, on this first case of bloodletting I have judged.
> For Aegeus' population, this forevermore
> shall be the ground where justices deliberate.[1]

When *The Oresteia* premiered at the Great Dionysia Festival in 458 BCE, Athens was on the verge of civil war. Lower- and middle-class men in Athens were gaining political power as the People's Assembly and Council of 500 wrested power from the ancient senate and courts, which had consisted primarily of nobles. Filled with references to contemporary power struggles, *The Oresteia* calls for a new sort of politics that will replace clan identity (the purview of the Furies) with a political identity of Athenians *as* Athenians.[2]

Within the play, Athena founds Athens in a courtroom. And during the Great Dionysia Festival, Athenian citizens were constituted as a public as they gathered to perform, watch, and judge this play together.[3] As Athena arbitrated the trial onstage, citizens took on the roles of judges as well, not of the trial itself but of the virtuosity with which Aeschylus and the performers turned the trial into theater. The judges of the festival—who were selected in part by election and in part by casting lots—awarded Aeschylus the coveted prize in the competition (*agon*) among tragedies. Within the framework of the Great Dionysia, *The Oresteia* created two different types of publics simultaneously. The first was a public sphere of rational argument and normative practices of judgment, which was represented onstage by Athena and the jury system she creates. The second was an agonist public (a public that embraced conflict as an integral aspect of politics). This agonist public was instantiated by the competition in which citizens judged plays by their virtuosity. Through this theater performance, these two seemingly opposite structures of the public came together.[4]

While all theater has the potential to constitute multiple forms of publics, trial plays have a particular capacity to reflect on how publics are constituted through the act of judging. This book is about a historical moment—the two decades after the Second World War—when public judgment of the past became the central way in which to constitute new postwar societies. The era of postwar trials—the Nuremberg trials, the Eichmann trial, the Frankfurt Auschwitz trial—was also an era of trial plays. In these decades, trial plays not only flourished but also became a way to articulate the role of theater in postwar society.[5] These plays sought to do some of the same work as postwar trials themselves, which were struggling to interrogate, represent, and judge unprecedented crimes.

Post–World War II trials raised both a legal problem of judging unprecedented crimes and also a philosophical problem about the relationship between judgment and law. The most common defense at the Nuremberg, Eichmann, and Frankfurt Auschwitz trials was that defendants were merely following orders. This defense raises fundamental questions about what judgment is: Is judgment merely a matter of knowing how to obey the law? Or are there forms of judgment that can judge the law itself? Observers of these trials, including Hannah Arendt and Bertolt Brecht, confronted the challenge of judging perpetrators who acted in a context where murder was legally sanctioned, even prescribed. While the courts themselves worked to justify verdicts against defendants legally, Arendt and Brecht both focused on how to prevent such crimes in the future. They both saw theater as a place where people could develop their capacities for judging in ethical ways (even if this judgment meant disobedience to the law) and in ways that took other people into consideration.

Postwar trial plays bring together the legal judgments of postwar trials and the aesthetic judgments of the performances themselves. Rationally applying the law to a given situation is an individual practice, but watching a trial performed in a theater is a shared one: you are no longer judging by yourself but in the company of others, aware—sometimes painfully so—of their glee, their boredom, their head colds. Judgment is no longer simply individual. Moreover, in judging a performance to be good, audiences are not determining whether the play follows a set of rules but are rather reflecting on the specific bodies, images, sounds, and stories in front of them. Like the Great Dionysia Festival, these performances link two modes of judgment to two different models of political life: political life based on rational debate and the rule of law on the one hand, and on the other hand, an agonist politics that measures greatness by virtuosity. These postwar productions offer important lessons about how theater—both then and now—can serve as a public institution. Throughout this book, I will use these plays and performances in order to explore two key questions about politics and political theater: How do we judge actions differently when they are staged in a theater rather than narrated in a courtroom? And what can theater teach us about the theatricality that is always present in courts and is integral to political life?

Theatricality in legal and political arenas is more often a cause for concern than celebration.[6] Trial plays foreground the uneasy relationship between law and theatricality. The term "show trial" is a relatively new phrase in the English language. It was first used by journalists covering Stalinist trials in Moscow. The term derives from the Russian *pokazatel'nyi protsess*, which could be translated as either "demonstration trial" or "show trial." This original use of the term "show trial" conveyed two meanings at once: the courtroom as a didactic space (a space *to show* something) and as a theatrical space (a space *for shows*). This initial use was not pejorative; it was the term the organizers themselves used to express the didactic quality of the trials. Journalists evaluated the theatrical elements of these trials in different ways; a reporter for the *New York Times* praised the 1928 Shakhty trial of engineers who had been accused of sabotage and espionage as a "marvelous human drama where lives are at stake" while a United Press correspondent condemned its spectacular, festive quality and "calculated melodrama."[7]

In these early uses of the term "show trial," there is a deep ambivalence about the relationship between law and theatricality. The notion of a show trial posits the courtroom as a stage, a place for performance and show. However, when used pejoratively (as it usually is today), "show trial" conveys a deep mistrust of theatricality and a claim that authenticity and show are mutually exclusive. The pejorative use of the term relies on a distinction between legal judgment and aesthetic judgment. Legal judgment is presumably objective, fact and evidence based, and unmoved by the atmosphere of the proceedings and the acting skills of those testifying. To experience and judge a trial aesthetically, by contrast, would mean to judge the case based on the virtuosity of the acting, on your immediate impressions and emotions while watching, and on the atmosphere in the courtroom. Legal and aesthetic judgments are not mutually exclusive, though. The legitimacy of a trial relies, to an extent, on how spectators perceive the trial. As Hannah Arendt writes in *Eichmann in Jerusalem*, "Justice must not only be done, but must be seen to be done."[8] In order to show justice being done, courts inevitably need to use theatrical devices. The question is not so much whether a courtroom employs theatrical devices but which ones they employ and to what end.

The history of early twentieth-century Europe and America is characterized by highly publicized and debated public trials and hearings, among them the Dreyfus affair, the Moscow trials, the Nuremberg trials, the House Un-American Activities Committee (HUAC) hearings, the Emmett Till trial, and the Eichmann trial. In each of these trials, the stakes were greater than the individual defendants. Each trial corresponded to political efforts to define national belonging as well as the rule of law.

Some of these trials targeted individuals as proxies for groups that were either already marginalized or feared as subversive or both. The Dreyfus affair galvanized political anti-Semitism in France, perpetuating the myth of an international Jewish conspiracy, which only grew when Dreyfus was finally cleared (thus proving in the minds of the anti-Dreyfusards that Jews secretly controlled the Third Republic). The Moscow trials staged public confessions of counterrevolutionary plots, legitimizing Stalin's purges of the old guard of the Bolsheviks, prominent artists, and intellectuals as well as ethnic minorities, clergy, and peasants. The House Un-American Activities Committee hearings were a far less brutal method of justifying paranoia about subversive influence. HUAC and McCarthyism targeted individuals from groups deemed "Un-American": recent immigrants, homosexuals, Jews, and African Americans. Other trials were about law itself. In Post–World War II trials such as the Nuremberg trials and the Eichmann trial, the law of the Third Reich was deemed criminal; the defendants in these trials were convicted not because they broke the law but because they followed the murderous laws and orders of the Third Reich. Trials could also reveal the radical injustice of courts, such as when Emmett Till's murderers were unanimously acquitted by all-white jury in Mississippi.

All these trials led to public debates about how justice could be done and about how it could be *seen* to be done; each of the trials—in some cases fairly, in others unfairly—was accused of being put on *for show* rather than to effect justice. These trials also inspired plays, some of which were greeted with the same controversy as the trials themselves. Arendt describes the 1931 French premiere of *The Dreyfus Affair* by Hans Reyfisch and Wilhelm Herzog as reviving the atmosphere of the trials themselves, complete with "stink-bombs in the stalls" and "the shock troops of the Action Française standing around to strike terror into actors, audience, and bystanders."[9] These plays also extended the process of judgment beyond both the physical and discursive boundaries of the courtroom. Plays like Rolf Schneider's *Trial in Nuremberg* and Peter Weiss's *The Investigation* restaged the proceedings of the International Military Tribunal at Nuremberg and the Frankfurt Auschwitz trial in order to present modes of testimony and historical analysis that would have been inadmissible in a court of law. By doing so, their adaptations moved away from the questions of individual moral and legal culpability that shaped the trials themselves and toward political questions about the structural factors that allowed for the rise of Fascism and the perpetration of genocide.[10]

While legal judgment can only address the past, theater can teach judgment as a continual process. This capacity to foster judgment is not unique to postwar documentary trial plays. But because these plays were written in an era of public trials and at a time when the capacity of courts to enact justice was seriously questioned, they offer particularly useful cases for thinking about the relationship between theater, law, and politics.

The trial plays that I focus on in this book are all situated in a very particular historical context: German and German American theater between the First World War and 1968. But their significance extends well beyond that relatively narrow frame. The plays pick up on models of judgment and politics that link the theater and philosophy of classical antiquity with the German Enlightenment, the historical avant-garde, and the Frankfurt school. These plays were written in response to Fascism, genocide, and the threat of a Nazi resurgence and continue to resonate today with the rising ethno-nationalism in the United States and Europe. The project of this book, then, is to understand the intertwining relationships between philosophy, theater, and law at one historical moment in order to apply the lessons of that moment to the present. In this sense, I follow Hannah Arendt's historiographical method, which she calls "pearl fishing" (*Perlenfischerei*): this is an attempt to reach back to the past to draw out valuable insights for use in the present without collapsing the distance between the past and the present or explaining the present as an inevitable outcome of transhistorical processes.[11]

This book is primarily organized around three central figures—Hannah Arendt, Bertolt Brecht, and Erwin Piscator—rather than by chronology, concepts, or works. Arendt and Brecht described their lifetimes as "dark times," times that were dark not only in the sense that they were violent, but also in the sense that at such moments, the world itself became opaque. As Arendt puts it, in dark times, the "space of appearances" in which people can show "who they are and what they can do" ceases to exist.[12] The dark times in which they lived, as well as the public trials that they followed closely, inspired Brecht and Arendt to develop theories of judgment that do not rely either on the individual application of moral rules or on obeying the law. As one of Brecht's characters famously sings, "First comes grub, then comes morality."[13] To Brecht, morality is a tool deployed by the powerful against the poor; to speak in the name of morality means you already have enough to eat. For Arendt, too, judgment is not a question of applying moral laws to given political debates. Instead, Arendt offers what Linda Zerilli has termed "a democratic theory of judgment" in which it is the judging itself that comprises politics.[14] For Brecht and Arendt, in other words, judgment that changes the world is political rather than moral: it is something that people do together. They both argue that theater, more so than other art forms or public institutions, reveals how people act and teaches them to judge. Piscator was not a theorist like Brecht and Arendt, but through his work, he, too, sought to turn theater into a space for judgment and politics. He called his postwar work a theater of "knowledge, recognition, and avowal" (*Kenntnis, Erkenntnis, Bekenntnis*).[15]

As they lived through times of statelessness and war, Arendt, Brecht, and Piscator struggled to find ways of judging the world and acting in it. It is by studying their works and performances that we might understand the dark times in which they lived, and in doing so, we might also illuminate our own times. Here, too, I follow Arendt's claim that the illumination we might expect from dark times "may well come less from theories and concepts than from the uncertain, flickering, and often weak light that some men and women, in their lives and their works, will kindle under almost all circumstances and shed over the time span that was given them on earth."[16]

Born in the mid-1890s, Brecht and Piscator belonged to what Arendt calls the first of the twentieth century's "three lost generations": the generation whose first experience of the world was in the trenches of the First World War. Piscator served in the trenches at Ypres before being reassigned to a theater company that performed for fellow soldiers. Five years younger, Brecht escaped the trenches. As a medical student, he was able to defer conscription several times before serving as a medical orderly for the final months of the war. Arendt, born in 1906, was of the "second lost generation," for whom "the effective lesson of inflation and unemployment at once taught it the instability of whatever had been left intact after the preliminary destruction, as it were, of the European world." Along with Brecht and Piscator, she experienced the defining events of the subsequent third lost generation: "The choice of being educated by Nazism, or the Spanish Civil War, or the Moscow trials." Any differences between these three generations, Arendt writes, were ultimately reconciled by their shared experience of the Second World War.[17]

Coming of age in the first decades of the twentieth century meant finding a place in a world on the cusp of radical change. The First World War ended with revolutions, first in Russia and then in Germany. One year after the October Revolution of 1917 brought the Bolshevik party to power, sailors in the German navy began a revolt that turned into the November Revolution of 1918. The first phase of that revolution led to the abdication of Emperor Wilhelm II, Germany's declaration of unconditional surrender, and the creation of a parliamentary democracy in Germany led by the Social Democratic Party (SPD). For members of left-wing groups like the Spartacus League (which later became the Communist Party of Germany), the SPD was not doing enough to overthrow the ruling elites and stamp out nationalist militarism. Therefore, just months after the November Revolution, the Spartacus League attempted their own revolution, the January uprising. This revolution was a failure, and the league's leaders, Rosa Luxemburg and Karl Liebknecht, were both murdered by paramilitary groups with the tacit support of the SPD. These murders marked a definite breaking point between the Socialist and Communist Left that would ultimately allow for the rise of the National Socialist Party.

Piscator was in Berlin during the January uprising and describes the time as one of energy and civic participation as well as violence: "Wild confusion in the streets. Debating clubs on every street corner. Massive demonstrations of workers and fellow travelers."[18] Piscator joined the Communist Party in response to the murders of Luxemburg and Liebknecht. In the south of Germany, Brecht served as a representative on the Augsburg Workers' and Soldiers' Council during the revolution, though without the strong political convictions of Piscator. Piscator's adherence to Communism was a practical matter: he joined the party out of support for the work it was doing and left the party when he saw its shortcomings, especially its inability to account for and counter the rising anti-Semitism in Germany. Brecht, by contrast, became a fellow traveler philosophically, through his readings of G. W. F. Hegel, Karl Marx, and Vladimir Lenin. Though he would carry Lenin's collected works to the Unites States with him and back, he never joined the party.

While the Communist International and the German Communist Party sought to bring proletarian revolution to Germany, Fascism was gaining power across Europe. In 1922, Benito Mussolini marched on Rome and inspired Adolph Hitler to attempt a coup in Munich the following year. Though the coup failed and Hitler was imprisoned, the National Socialist Party continued to rise. The ideological stakes of class struggle were heightened by widespread economic devastation. In order to finance the First World War, Germany relied on selling war bonds and printing money. These policies, combined with the punitive conditions of the Treaty of Versailles, brought about financial ruin for the country. In 1922–23, Germans experienced rapid hyperinflation that rendered currency almost worthless: a loaf of bread that had cost less than one Reichsmark in 1914 would cost twelve hundred Reichsmark by the summer of 1923. Just a few months later, in November 1923, one loaf cost 428 billion Reichsmark.[19] Hyperinflation was brought under control in 1923, but six years later, the stock market crash of 1929 and Great Depression led to mass unemployment and poverty. The impact on both the middle and working classes was profound, and any sense of stability and faith in public institutions was severely undermined. Throughout the 1920s, politics in the Weimar Republic became increasingly polarized. In 1932, the last free election before the Nazi seizure of power saw the Nazi Party win the highest number of seats in the Reichstag (196) while the Communist Party took one hundred, coming in third after the SPD.

Economic instability and class conflicts were only part of the tumultuous politics of the Weimar Republic. It was also a time of culture wars that were interwoven with but not reducible to class politics. The culture wars of the Weimar Era resonate with those of the present. The Nazi Party claimed its guardianship of Germanic heritage against such threats as cosmopolitanism and Jewish influence, Communism, immigration, feminism, and homosexuality (all of which were often conflated). Though not Jewish, Piscator was the target of a smear campaign in the late 1920s, which spread rumors that his real name was Samuel Fischer and that he was an *Ostjude*

(Eastern Jew), which is a pejorative term for Jewish immigrants from Eastern Europe.[20] While the Nazi Party prized Nordic myth and pagan ritual, it
also claimed to be the heir to classical antiquity and the German Enlightenment, eventually appropriating not only Richard Wagner and Friedrich
Nietzsche but also Johann Wolfgang von Goethe, Friedrich Schiller, and
Gotthold Ephraim Lessing as its own.

The culture that the Nazi Party tried to claim was the culture that had
shaped Arendt, Brecht, and Piscator. They had all grown up in middle-class
households that emphasized their education and cultural cultivation (the
German Enlightenment ideal of *Bildung*). Arendt, as a Jew and as a woman,
faced prejudices that Brecht and Piscator did not. Nevertheless, they were
all educated in some of the more prestigious institutions of their day in
fields—philosophy, medicine, literature, and theater—that were central to
a national sense of German identity. Piscator and Brecht both studied at
the Ludwig Maximilian University in Munich, where they attended the
famous seminars on theater taught by Artur Kutscher, one of the founders
of the field of Theater Studies in Germany. Arendt was a star pupil in Martin Heidegger's seminars at the University of Heidelberg. Both Kutscher and
Heidegger would go on to join the Nazi Party, revealing not simply personal
moral failings, but even more seriously, the alignment of representatives of
German *Kultur* with the Fascists rallying at Nuremberg.

In their work during the 1920s and '30s, Brecht, Piscator, and Arendt,
each in different ways, questioned the promises of liberal humanism. Arendt
began a biography of Rahel Varnhagen, a Jewish *salonnière* who lived during the height of Weimar classicism. In the biography, Arendt begins to
make her argument—continued in *The Origins of Totalitarianism*—that the
liberal foundations of the nation-state did not become bulwarks of toleration but rather gave rise to political anti-Semitism. Piscator and Brecht came
to see that the plays and acting techniques of the previous two centuries
were, at best, ill suited to engaging with contemporary politics and, at worst,
complicit in oppression and exploitation. In the interwar years, Piscator
became one of Berlin's most prominent directors, beginning with scrappy
agitprop performances in union halls and working-class neighborhoods
but eventually operating multiple theaters in which he staged both plays
and mass rallies that blurred the distinction between art and politics. In
this sense, Piscator's work exemplified the historical avant-garde movements
across Europe that were challenging the boundaries of the autonomous

aesthetic realm celebrated by German Enlightenment philosophers. These movements sought to draw art into the political realm, closing the distance between institutional theater and nonartistic public performance. In the effort to collapse art and life, theater and performance played an especially pronounced role and became the art form of choice for avant-gardists with otherwise disparate politics and styles.

Walter Benjamin's essay "The Work of Art in the Age of Mechanical Reproduction" frames the opposition between the right-wing and left-wing avant-gardes as one of different approaches to the relationship between aesthetics and politics. Both want to demolish the boundaries between art and politics, but in opposite ways. Italian Futurism, Benjamin argues, supports Fascism by "render[ing] politics aesthetic," turning even war and human destruction itself into an object of aesthetic contemplation. In response to this aestheticization of politics, Benjamin calls on Communism to respond by "politicizing art."[21] It was not in Piscator's but rather in Brecht's epic theater that Benjamin saw the promise of this political art. Brecht began his career working in Piscator's theater collective before becoming a successful playwright and director in his own right. Both Brecht and Piscator worked to develop a genre of theater they called "epic theater," though they took it in different directions. For Piscator, epic theater was theater that dispensed with conventions such as psychologically realistic characters, a dramatic arc, and even individual authorship. His epic theater was created through collective dramaturgical efforts, often radically editing and cobbling together plays with documentary materials (indeed, sometimes creating plays solely out of documentary materials). Piscator also pioneered the use of new stage technologies, building massive sets and incorporating film and conveyor belts into performances. While Piscator's theater was more oriented toward spectacle and affect, Brecht's epic theater used the model of courtroom testimony to appeal to and strengthen the rational, critical capacities of his audience members. Arendt lived in Berlin during the height of this radical experimentation in new forms of theater. While she did not yet know Brecht or Piscator personally, Arendt's husband at the time, Günther Anders, was in Brecht's close circle of friends.

In February 1933 the Reichstag was set on fire, and Hitler declared a state of emergency. Piscator had already left Germany in 1931 to make a film in the Soviet Union and would not return until after the war. Brecht fled Berlin the day after the Reichstag fire. The Gestapo raided his apartment and found his address book containing information about his friends, prompting Anders to flee as well. Arendt remained in Berlin after Brecht and Anders left, working with the Resistance until she was arrested. As soon as she was released, she made her way to Paris. It was in Paris that Arendt met Brecht for the first time, and together they spent time with their close mutual friend Walter Benjamin. The conversations between Arendt, Benjamin, and Brecht that began in Paris were cut short. Brecht settled for a time in Denmark while Arendt and Benjamin remained in France and soon joined the thousands of refugees making their way west across Europe, desperate to secure exit permits out of France and visas to the United States. Arendt was able to escape to New York, but Benjamin was not so fortunate. His suicide, while awaiting deportation on the French-Spanish border, devastated Arendt and Brecht, whose subsequent communications were entirely about posthumous publications of Benjamin's work.

Brecht and Piscator were pushed into exile not only by the rise of Nazism in Germany but also by the rise of Stalinism and changes in the cultural policy of the Soviet Union and Communist International. Starting in 1929 their cultural policy shifted from supporting experimental projects like those of Brecht and Piscator to mandating socialist realism. When Piscator was on what he thought would be a short trip to Paris, he received a telegram from friends in the Soviet Union, warning him not to risk returning. The turn in Soviet cultural policy toward socialist realism meant that with the rise of Hitler, Communist and Communist-sympathizing theater artists, who a decade before would have gone into exile in the Soviet Union, instead came to the United States. Although neither wrote publicly about it, both Piscator's and Brecht's hopes in the Communist Party were fading. They followed the plight of their friends who were murdered in Stalin's purges. Piscator also became increasingly concerned with anti-Semitism and the party's failure to account for the racial as well as the class politics of Nazi Germany. Unlike Brecht, Piscator saw very early on that anti-Semitism was central to the Third Reich in a way that could not be fully explained by an understanding of Fascism as the apex of capitalism. During the first stages of his exile, Piscator hoped to work specifically in Jewish theaters, first seeking to be hired as a director for the Moscow Jewish Theater and later attempting to set up a *"théâtre populaire juif"* in Paris.[22] Over the following decades, Piscator also became increasingly concerned with anticolonial struggles and the civil rights movement in the United States, issues that Brecht (and indeed Arendt) never completely grasped.

With the Soviet Union no longer an option, Brecht and Piscator both fled to the United States. Brecht headed to California, and Piscator was hired to lead the Dramatic Workshop at the New School for Social Research, a university that famously hired scores of European refugees. In the postwar years, leftist German theater artists were forced to confront the fact that the interwar avant-garde had failed to stem the tide of Nazism in Germany. The twin specters of Fascism and Stalinism led them to reconsider the interwar avant-garde's ideal of collective transfiguration and their ambition to dissolve the boundaries between art and life. The challenge was greater for Piscator than for Brecht. Brecht's work, even his didactic plays praising the Communist Party, still focused on cultivating the capacities of individual actors and audience members to think critically about the world. Piscator, though, had sought to create mass audiences in his theater who would be transformed into a collective by the power of spectacle and shared energy. Piscator's and Brecht's different trajectories after the war were also influenced by their experiences of exile. While Brecht remained mostly aloof from the American theater scene, Piscator worked closely with New York artists and students at the Dramatic Workshop, adapting his style to incorporate the Method-acting techniques of colleagues like Stella Adler. Their new home, however, was only temporary. Brecht and Piscator became refugees a third time over during the McCarthy era. Brecht was called to testify before the House Un-American Activities Committee in 1947 and fled to Europe the day after testifying. Piscator was not called, but fled preemptively in 1951, and with good reason. His eighty-eight-page FBI file details multiple investigations into him as well as deportation proceedings that had begun in 1947.[23] Brecht eventually settled in East Berlin and encouraged Piscator to join him there, though Piscator ultimately moved to West Berlin.

Brecht died in 1956, and though everyone knew of the destruction of the European Jewry, neither a popular nor a critical discourse about the Holocaust had yet fully emerged in either East or West Germany. Although Piscator was slightly older, he lived longer, and he shifted his theories and practices of theater more profoundly than Brecht had, creating a bridge between the interwar generation and the generation of 1968. Central to this change was a shift from economically focused Marxism to a concern with genocide, ethnic cleansing, and colonialism. This shifting concern had implications for art as much as for politics. Starting in the 1940s, Piscator looked back to the German tradition of aesthetic philosophy as well as to canonical German plays (Lessing's *Nathan the Wise* in particular) in order to develop a new form of political theater, one that did not seek to dissolve the boundaries between stage and audience or between theater and politics. Instead, this new theater would rely on the traditions of theater in order to engage with politics in ways that were different from a town hall meeting or a public demonstration.

Piscator sought to find a new form of documentary political theater at a moment when the inadequacies of theatrical representation were keenly felt. The Holocaust raised a new set of questions about representation and theatricality as philosophers and artists wondered how art could represent—or even continue to exist after—atrocity. In his essay "Cultural Criticism and Society," first published in German in 1951, Theodor Adorno offers the first iteration of his famous dictum that "to write poetry after Auschwitz is barbaric."[24] Adorno, like Benjamin in "The Work of Art in the Age of Mechanical Reproduction," feared that human destruction itself could become the object of aesthetic contemplation. Adorno's essay "Commitment" lays out the impossible situation of art after Auschwitz. Describing Arnold Schoenberg's *Survivor of Warsaw*, Adorno writes:

The aesthetic principle of stylization, and even the solemn prayer of the chorus, make an unthinkable fate appear to have had some meaning; it is transfigured, something of its horror is removed. This alone does an injustice to the victims; yet no art which tried to evade them could stand upright before justice. Even the sound of despair pays its tribute to a hideous affirmation.[25]

For Adorno, justice demands that art not ignore the victims of the Holocaust, yet any artistic portrayal of the Holocaust does them an injustice by representing—and thus minimizing—the horror they experienced and making sense of (affirming) a senseless genocide. The fear that representation—especially mimetic and theatrical—of the Holocaust perpetrates injustice against its victims has strongly influenced art, literature, and theater about the Holocaust.[26] The questions that genocide raised for the law were also questions for the theater: Are there crimes so heinous that they cannot be narrated or represented? Can recounting and reenacting past events in a public place change the way people think and act, for better or for worse? In the theater, though, these questions were posed to the audiences as questions of aesthetic as well as legal and moral judgment.

At the New York Dramatic Workshop, Piscator staged the first postwar trial play that sought to address the history of anti-Semitism in Europe, *The Burning Bush*. Postwar trial plays like *The Burning Bush* respond to the problem of representing atrocity by representing atrocity through diegesis rather than mimesis. In a courtroom play, atrocity is often narrated by witnesses and lawyers rather than visually reproduced or reenacted onstage. But favoring a diegetic over a mimetic representation of atrocity does not make a trial play less theatrical or aesthetic. Indeed, diegesis brings the play closer to the barbarism that Adorno sees in lyric poetry. Central to this book is how and why, at the very moment when aesthetic representation of the Holocaust seemed most unthinkable, directors like Piscator looked to the German tradition of aesthetic philosophy to develop a theater that could forestall future genocide. Piscator turned to Lessing and Schiller after the war to reconsider how theater might function as a moral and political institution. At the same time, Arendt looked back to Kant to understand how, through aesthetic judgment, people learn to respect human plurality, "the fact that men, not Man, live on the earth and inhabit the world."[27] In their turn toward Kant, Lessing, and Schiller, Piscator and Arendt at once reaffirmed a distance between aesthetic judgment and political action and established a foundational link between the aesthetic realm and the possibility of a public sphere. In this sense, Arendt's understanding of the relationship between aesthetics and politics differs significantly from those of Adorno and Benjamin. Susannah Young-Ah Gottlieb makes this distinction in her introduction to Arendt's collected writings on literature and culture: "If political judgment is always already akin to aesthetic judgment, then there is no sense in looking for the conditions in which politics somehow becomes aestheticized."[28] Rather, the task is to uncover how the practice of aesthetic judgment and the institutions in which such judgment takes place might create publics that support freedom and affirm plurality. As I will argue, the theater—both as a physical space and as an art form—has a particular capacity to support politics in Arendt's sense of the word.

Arendt's democratic theory of judgment offers a way to reconsider the work of political theater and what it means to claim that theater is a public institution. It is possible to classify contemporary political theater in a few different ways. The most common and popularly recognizable form of political theater (especially in the Anglo-American context) is defined in terms of content. This approach often takes the form of documentary theater that provides information about a particular case or topic (for example, Chelsea Manning's imprisonment or the death penalty) and asks the audience to apply moral rules to judge these facts.[29] A second way to define political theater—one that is more popular in the art world and continental Europe—is by process. This approach (often called relational or participatory art) enacts a prefigurative politics, that is, the rehearsal process and/or performances enact the new political configurations it seeks to promote. This type of participatory art performance often takes place outside of theater buildings and even eschews the term "theater": the project *becomes* the public it seeks to create rather than a mere representation of it. This form of political theater at times promotes a liberal model of politics in which participants reach a shared judgment through conversation and debate, but almost as often performances demonstrate the impossibility of this liberal model (as, for example, in the work of Christoph Schlingensief). A third way of defining political theater is in terms of reception: theater is political when it creates a space where audience members judge a work or performance in the company of others, even when the work does not offer a specific claim about justice. This form of political theater, I will argue, is most closely aligned with Arendt's theory of judgment. It is also the form of political theater in which political significance is most closely bound to theatricality, by which I mean its deep connection to art institutions and to the historical traditions of theater practice.

In English-speaking countries, current documentary theater is a genre in which, as a reviewer for the 2004 play *Guantanamo: Honor Bound to Defend Freedom* put it, "Given the material, . . . [t]he facts literally speak for themselves."[30] Understood in this way, the political intervention of documentary theater is to disseminate information, often information that stirs moral outrage, with as little recourse to theatricality as possible. These works emphasize the *documentary* over the *theater* for the sake of political efficacy.[31] Another genre of documentary theater is exemplified by artists like Rabih Mroué and Hans-Werner Kroesinger, who use documentary materials to reflect on how the audience's understanding of reality is created, especially through mass media.[32] In other words, most contemporary documentary theater either frames the performance as a direct expression of reality or questions how reality is framed by theater and other media. Either way, theatricality is viewed with suspicion.

To clarify with an example, in September 2012, I went to see the play *The Exonerated* with a friend (figure 0.1). Created by Jessica Blank and Erik Jensen, the play weaves together interviews, letters, and court transcripts to tell the story of six former death row inmates who were eventually exonerated. During the performance, actors sat and sometimes stood in a line across the stage, reading from text on music stands. There was no set, and the actors appeared to be wearing their street clothes. In the final moments of the play, it was revealed that one of the actors was one of the exonerated, Sunny Jacobs, telling her story. This final reveal highlighted the truth of what was being told. As the show ended, the other actors all crowded around, hugging and applauding Jacobs, not for her acting performance but for her resilience and suffering.[33]

As we left the theater, my friend and I talked about the death penalty, her job as an assistant DA, the terrible story of Sunny Jacobs, and whether the play would have been more effective had it focused on systemic injustice rather than individual innocence. These were the sorts of questions we were supposed to be asking. The publicity material on the theater's website included blurbs from the founder of the Innocence Project, Senator Patrick Leahy, and Janet Reno, all emphasizing the political significance of the play.[34] We would have missed the point of the play if we had spent the rest of the night discussing how skilled the actors were, whether we liked the

FIGURE 0.1 *The Exonerated* at the Culture Project, New York City (2012). Copyright © Carol Rosegg.

lighting design, or what we thought of the costumes. In this sense, then, the reception of documentary plays like *The Exonerated* is designed to be primarily a reasoned process based on the facts presented. To the extent that emotional affect comes in, it is directed at the real experiences of a real person, not toward a character in a fictional world. From this example, I want to draw out two key elements of how we watch and understand documentary plays like *The Exonerated*. First, we are primarily concerned with content (facts, historical background, political intervention) rather than presentation. Second, the experience is more pedagogical than aesthetic: it is a means to an end (greater understanding, political engagement) in which immediate sensory experience and judgments of artistic quality are far less important than rational cognition.

But this was not always true of documentary theater. Documentary theater from the 1940s through the 1960s drew very different conclusions about the relationship between politics and aesthetics. Postwar playwrights and directors like Piscator and Weiss are so instructive today because, for them, theatricality and aesthetic experience were essential to the political message of the play. At first glance, it may seem that the turn to trial transcripts as source material and courtroom proceedings as a model of acting and spectatorship is necessarily an antitheatrical move, forsaking the aesthetic qualities of theater and turning the stage into a legal tribunal. But, in fact, directors and playwrights like Weiss and Piscator created transcript-based courtroom plays in order to highlight the differences between courtrooms and theaters and to make a claim for the importance of aesthetic as well as legal judgment.

Postwar trial theater also offers a radically different approach from the relational aesthetics that has become increasingly popular in the past decades. Relational aesthetics focuses on the production side of art making, inspiring participatory projects that claim to be public and democratic (or to reflect on what it means to be public and democratic) by taking shape as a collaboration between the artist and people outside the art world.[35] Claire Bishop has shown how this understanding of political art risks forfeiting aesthetic judgment for the sake of moral smugness; a work of art is deemed "good" not because of its aesthetic quality but because it incorporates the talents of underprivileged children from a bad part of town.[36]

Over the past two decades, theaters and arts institutions have become increasingly invested in creating events that foster public discourse by

FIGURE 0.2. Heinar Kipphardt's *In the Matter of J. Robert Oppenheimer*, directed by Erwin Piscator (1964). Courtesy of the Akademie der Künste Archive, Berlin.

moving art out of art institutions. Christopher Balme begins his recent book *The Theatrical Public Sphere* with a description of an event held outside of the Munich Kammerspiele. The theater sent out invitations, asking people to join in a "town hall meeting, a centre for public debate, which asks: what does it mean to be poor and rich in Munich? How and at whose expense are wealth and resources allocated in education, politics, and culture?"[37] The theater stated that it planned to include participants from a range of social, economic, religious, and national backgrounds. But presenting the space outside the theater—incidentally on Munich's most expensive shopping street—as an accessible public space where people could participate equally in decisions about the allocation of resources was naïve at best. The theater was certainly not *actually* asking people whether it should give away its twenty million euros of public funding to institutions more attuned to marginalized members of society. Instead, it was justifying its public funding in a way that kept the "public" outside the

theater, playacting at democracy.[38] Aside from being politically questionable, such projects are ultimately self-defeating. They forfeit the idea that
theater itself is a public space. If engaging the public requires leaving the
theater, that begs the question of why we should think of (and fund) theater
as a public institution in the first place.

In valorizing projects like the Munich Kammerspiele's "town hall" as the
primary way for art to engage the public, we risk forgetting what it is that
theater does best. Making a claim for publicly funded art requires articulating what theater *does* that other public institutions do not do. If we are
honest, newspapers are more effective at disseminating information, Twit-
ter can stir up moral indignation faster than a play about Guantanamo, and
if you want to go to a town hall, you should probably go to the actual
town hall. This isn't to say, of course, that there should not be plays that
disseminate information, educational theater projects, or participatory
art. Many of these projects are deeply committed to social justice, impact
people positively, and do not share the problems of the Munich Kammerspiele event. But at the same time, making theater more like social
work can be self-defeating in that it undermines theater's political potential. What I am arguing, then, is that justifying theater as a public institution means articulating what theater can do that is not redundant with
other media, social institutions, and corporations. What sort of justice and
judgment can we find in a theater? How can theater *as theater* reflect on what
it means to be public?

This book offers two answers based on postwar theater practice and
Arendt's political philosophy. First, the very architecture of the proscenium
stage and theater building offers a frame to reflect on the principles and
machinery of inclusion and exclusion: Who gets to appear on the stage?
How does infrastructural machinery (spotlights, curtains, stairs) determine
who stands in the light and who remains in the dark? Art projects taking
place outside the theater run the risk of obscuring their own exclusions and
the ways that not all participants can participate equally. Developing more
equitable forms of public life requires engaging with the ways that bodies,
gestures, and social idioms are valued unequally. Theater, because it calls
for a constant valuing and revaluing of how people speak and perform,
offers the possibly of reflecting on how different voices are heard and evaluated. The bodies that appear on the theater stage and in the auditorium
and the roles in which those bodies are cast can challenge the distribution

of roles on the world stage. This challenge, furthermore, does not need to come from the actors onstage or the intentions of the director or playwright. Rather, as Jacques Rancière argues in *The Emancipated Spectator*, it might come from spectators themselves, whose emancipation begins "when we understand that viewing is also an action that confirms or transforms [the] distribution of positions."[39]

Second, theaters do not have the coercive power of the law. When a trial is staged within a theater, the justice that can be pursued is justice that relies on the copresence of people in a space, not on the state's use of violence. This is a different sort of justice entirely and one that, I argue, implies a continual process of judging in the company of others rather than a single act of legal judgment. It is a form of judgment that does not require following a moral precept or law; in fact, theater may teach audiences to judge the law itself when the law is unjust. This may sound utopian, but it is not. Theater is simply a place where people can sit together without trying to kill each other and where they judge what is happening by taking other people's experiences into consideration. This shared experience is as often a nuisance as a pleasure: the fidgeting of a bored person next to you, the gentle snoring from a few rows back, the slamming door as people stomp out of a controversial staging. It might also be an experience of discomfort and concern: watching *Oedipus* with your mother or realizing that the stranger in front of you is being triggered by a depiction of sexual violence. Certainly, the presence of other people can disturb your enjoyment. It is harder to laugh at ableist humor onstage if you are seated next to someone in a wheelchair; a blackface routine resonates differently in a multiracial audience than an all-white one. Unlike in the cinema, the energy of the room and the behavior of the audience also, in turn, influence the live performers onstage, creating what Erika Fischer-Lichte has called the "auto-poetic feedback loop."[40] Of course, not all experiences of theater resonate politically, and unequal access to theater limits the diversity of audiences. But *some* theater does make you reflect on how the person next to you might be seeing what you are seeing. And the possibility that theater might create publics while giving us a space to reflect on the ways in which roles are distributed, who is allowed to appear, and how performance can resist the scripts of the past make it an institution worth fighting for.

Chapter One

HANNAH ARENDT

Judging in Dark Times

The Eichmann trial was held in a courtroom that was also a theater, the auditorium of the newly built home of Beth Ha'am (the People's House) in Jerusalem.[1] The People's House had begun in 1904 as a program of cultural events and public discussions, inspired by European community centers founded in the late nineteenth century to promote proletarian culture and class consciousness. The Jerusalem People's House, socialist and Zionist in orientation, sought to build a national popular culture united through the Hebrew language. Theater was a central part of its project to create a national public out of ethnically and culturally diverse immigrants from Europe and Asia as well as older Jewish communities living in Palestine. Plans for a permanent People's House building developed in the late 1920s but moved slowly. The complex was not completed until 1960, when the People's House was chosen as the venue for the Eichmann trial and was subsequently quickly finished. The symbolic importance of the People's House was paramount because it incorporated the Eichmann trial and testimony about the Holocaust into Israeli national identity. The Beth Ha'am building was thus transformed into Beth Hamishpath (the House of Justice). The 750-seat theater was turned into a courtroom, and a second building, intended as an adult-education center, became Eichmann's jail.[2]

The theatrical design of the auditorium was not lost on visitors to the trial. Hannah Arendt's *Eichmann in Jerusalem* begins with a description of the auditorium's "orchestra and gallery, with proscenium and stage, and with side doors for the actors' entrance."[3] It is a suitable location for a "show trial," she remarks, with David Ben-Gurion hovering backstage as the "invisible stage manager of the proceedings."[4] The question of whether the Eichmann trial was a show trial immediately became a matter of debate, but not always in the ways we might expect. Susan Sontag provocatively celebrated the trial as "the most interesting and moving work of art of the past ten years." For Sontag, the trial expressed "a great outcry of historical agony," and its function "was that of the tragic drama: above and beyond judgment and punishment, catharsis."[5] Arendt's description of the trial's theatricality in *Eichmann in Jerusalem* is equally provocative, though often misunderstood.[6] For Arendt, the problem with the trial was not that it was too theatrical, as many have supposed, but rather that it failed to follow the demands of dramatic form. She writes that even though the setting and political context may have seemed prime for a show trial, "the play aspect of the trial . . . collapsed." This, she claims, is because the trial did not follow the structure of a play: "A trial resembles a play in that both begin and end with the doer, not with the victim. A show trial needs even more urgently than an ordinary trial a limited and well-defined outline of what was done and how it was done."[7]

Where Arendt and Sontag differ is not so much in how they perceive the trial, but in how they understand theater. This may seem like a trivial difference, but it is not. The theater, both as a metaphorical model and as a set of historical institutions and practices, is at the center of Arendt's understanding of politics and the public realm. Politics and trials alike will inevitably incorporate theatrical techniques and offer moments of drama. The real question is more precise: Which theatrical techniques are best suited to politics?

EICHMANN IN JERUSALEM AS EPIC THEATER

Sontag describes the Eichmann trial as theater in the mode of Greek tragedy. According to Aristotle's *Poetics*, tragedy induces pity, fear, and finally catharsis in its spectators, who leave the theater cleansed of their emotions and newly committed to their community (which, in Athens, was the polis). Arendt agrees with Sontag that the trial was meant to evoke pity, fear, and catharsis, but she criticizes Sontag's assessment in two ways. First, she argues that the trial did not achieve its aim to be a tragic drama. Second, and more significantly, she demonstrates that the attempt to stage the trial as tragic drama was itself misguided, not because it brought theater into the courtroom but because it brought in the wrong *type* of theater.[8]

Tragedy is about the actions of a tragic hero. This hero experiences a reversal of fortune that stirs pity and terror in the audience, who fear that the hero's fate could also be their own. With this reversal of fortune comes the possibility of discovery and self-knowledge. If the Eichmann trial was to be a tragic drama, who was its hero? Arendt argues that the lead prosecutor, Gideon Hausner, attempted to stage the trial as—in Hausner's own words—"the tragedy of Jewry as a whole." But casting millions of people, living and dead, as a tragic hero contradicts the rules of tragedy. Arendt writes, "In the center of a trial can only be the one who did—in this respect, he is like the hero in the play—and if he suffers, he must suffer for what he has done, not for what he has caused others to suffer."[9] This does not mean, however, that Arendt believed the trial should have cast Eichmann as its protagonist. Casting Eichmann as a tragic hero would have been obscene for obvious political and ethical reasons. But it would also have been impossible. His inability and unwillingness to think for himself—which, for Arendt was at the core of his criminality—meant that he could never have gone through the process of recognition that defines tragedy.[10]

Arendt rejects the elements of the trial that she likens to Greek tragedy: an emphasis on fate, the introduction of pity into the public realm, and the goal of catharsis. Her strongest objection to the trial is that it presented the story of the Holocaust as a tragedy bound to an inexorable historical narrative that was redeemed only by the foundation of Israel. The trial, she argues, sought to prove not only Eichmann's guilt but also the constant hostility of the rest of the world to Jews and therefore the need for the Diaspora to immigrate to Israel and for Israel itself to become a military power. To demonstrate this constant danger and hostility, the trial presented the Holocaust as the climax of millennia of anti-Semitism. This, for Arendt, is problematic for a number of reasons. First, it undermined the Nazis' culpability: If it was fate, how could Eichmann be held accountable? Second, it cast the death of millions of Jews as a necessary step in Israel's creation. Third, it instrumentalized the suffering of Holocaust victims to promote Ben-Gurion's nationalist policies. Fourth, and most controversially, Arendt believes that an acceptance of tragic fate and inevitable persecution contributed to the devastation of the Holocaust. She writes that only a belief in this persecution as tragic fate can explain the willingness of the German Jewish community to negotiate with Nazi authorities during the early years of the regime. At the same time, it was only by convincing the German population that World War II was the "battle of destiny" that the Nazis induced ordinary Germans to believe that their only choice was to "annihilate their enemies or be annihilated."[11]

For Arendt, pity and catharsis support this "bad history and cheap rhetoric" by overwhelming people with emotions that make it impossible for them to think critically about the history that the trial presented and its relation to contemporary politics.[12] Arendt is generally skeptical about pity and compassion in the public realm. In *On Revolution*, written at the same time as *Eichmann in Jerusalem*, Arendt describes pity as an excess of compassion, "the passion of compassion."[13] Arendt credits Brecht with discovering a fact that "cannot be found in any history book of modern times . . . , namely, that all revolutionaries of the last centuries from Robespierre to Lenin, acted out of the passion of compassion."[14] It was this pity, Arendt argues, that led Maximilien Robespierre and the men of the French Revolution astray as they focused on assuaging the suffering of the poor instead of establishing the political conditions for freedom.[15] In Jerusalem, pity for Eichmann's victims threatened to overwhelm the spectators' capacity to think critically about how men like Eichmann were able to perpetrate such crimes.

Arendt did not see the possibility of any sort of healing catharsis for survivors at the Eichmann trial but rather the danger that Nazi criminality would be forgotten and obscured in all the commotion. She warns about the impact that the Eichmann trial might have in Germany, where Nazi perpetrators still occupied positions of power. The "normal reaction to this state of affairs," Arendt writes, is "indignation." But indignation can be inconvenient when power brokers have Nazi pasts, and so instead, the postwar generation used opportunities such as "all the *Diary of Anne Frank* hubbub" and the Eichmann trial to "escape from the pressure of very present and actual problems into a cheap sentimentality." In Arendt's analysis, pity leads to apolitical catharsis, "hysterical outbreaks of guilt feelings" that purge German youth of their rightful indignation. Such catharsis only serves to maintain the status quo and allow perpetrators to emerge unscathed.[16]

Although Arendt rejects the attempt at an Aristotelian dramaturgy of fate, pity, and catharsis that she sees in the trial, she does not reject theater or theatricality in the trial or the public realm per se. Arendt's account of the Eichmann trial gestures toward the promise of a new sort of dramaturgy, the epic dramaturgy of Brecht, whose poem "O Germany" serves as the epigraph of *Eichmann in Jerusalem*. This dramaturgy is oriented not toward pity and catharsis but toward judgment and action.[17]

To Arendt, Brecht was "beyond a doubt the greatest living German poet and possibly the greatest living European playwright."[18] When Arendt was living in Berlin on and off between 1929 and 1933, Brecht became friends with her husband, Günther Anders. Anders met Brecht after producing a radio segment that was broadcast around 1930 called "Bertolt Brecht as Thinker." Anders's presentation of Brecht in the segment bears a remarkable similarity to the essays on Brecht that Walter Benjamin, who was Anders's second cousin, would write over the following years.[19] In 1933, Arendt, Anders, Benjamin, and Brecht all fled to Paris, where they were part of the same circle of German refugees.[20] After Arendt and Anders separated, Arendt and Brecht's strongest connection was through their close mutual friend Benjamin. In 1934, Arendt attended Benjamin's famous lecture on Brecht, "The Author as Producer," in Paris.[21] The conversations between Benjamin, Brecht, and Arendt lasted for decades, long after Benjamin's and then Brecht's deaths, through Arendt's writing and editorial work. After the war, Arendt sought Brecht's help in assembling a collected volume of Benjamin's essays and proposed publishing Benjamin's "Conversations with Brecht."[22] She included Benjamin's "What Is Epic Theatre" in *Illuminations* and wrote two essays of her own about Brecht's poetry and plays, "Beyond Personal Frustration: The Poetry of Bertolt Brecht" and "What Is Permitted to Jove . . . Reflections on the Poet Bertolt Brecht and His Relation to Politics."[23]

Brecht and Arendt developed similar conceptions of theater within a particular historical context (the rise of Nazism and Stalinism) in relation to a particular historical tradition (the German tradition of theater as a national institution) as part of a particular theater scene (one that challenged the dominance of realist literary theater) and social milieu (anti-Fascist artists and intellectuals who fled Germany in the 1930s). It is no surprise, then, that their understandings of theater were similar. What is surprising, though, is that while scholarly work on Brecht always contextualizes his theories of

theater historically, work on Arendt generally does not.[24] Without this historical contextualization, her understanding and use of theater can be misunderstood—as is the case with the scholarship on *Eichmann in Jerusalem*
that sees the book as a rejection of all theatricality in the court and does
not understand that Arendt is criticizing one mode of dramaturgy while
elevating another. What interests me here is not tracking Brecht's influence
on Arendt, or Arendt's influence on Brecht, but rather investigating the way
that each of them responded to Fascism by linking philosophy with theater. For Arendt, the result was a theatrical philosophy, for Brecht, a philosophical theater. Combining theater and philosophy was, for Brecht and for
Arendt, a way to preserve humanity in dark times.

The term "dark times" is one that Brecht uses in his poem "To Those
Born After," which begins, "Really, I live in dark times!"[25] "Dark times"
describes not only the experience of a generation who lived through two
world wars but also an epistemic condition: dark times are times when it is
impossible to be wise.[26] "I would like to be wise, too," the poem goes, but
then describes the wisdom of the "old books":

> To keep oneself from the strife of the world and to pass the short time
> Without fear
> To get by without violence
> To return evil with good.

There is no place for that in dark times. In times when wisdom and moral
precepts fail, the only sure way to act is to resist:

> I could do only a little. But the rulers
> Would have sat more comfortably without me, I hoped.[27]

For Brecht, the way out of dark times, then, is not through wisdom but
through dialectics. Incorporating philosophy into his theater thus enabled
Brecht to teach resistance as a way of acting in the world.

Brecht differentiates his epic ("non-Aristotelian") theater from what he
terms "Aristotelian theater," which is a broad category encompassing both
Greek tragedy and psychological realism. Aristotelian theater, Brecht argues,
makes audiences believe that what is happening onstage is inevitable. By
playing on audience members' emotions and evoking identification with

the protagonist, this type of theater teaches audiences to misinterpret structural injustice as tragic fate. Aristotelian theater draws audiences to the edge of their seats and dissolves their energy and passion into catharsis or sentimentality. Audiences leave the theater feeling pity for the hero but remain blind to the unjust system in which they live. Epic theater, by contrast, is designed to teach audiences to judge what happens onstage rationally and to think beyond the plight of an individual protagonist.[28] By forestalling compassion and catharsis, epic theater engages other emotions and energies: anger, indignation, and resistance.[29] This dramaturgy demonstrates exactly "what was done and how it was done." As Arendt describes Brecht's plays, they "concentrate on a logical course of events in which men . . . behave rightly or wrongly and are judged by the objective requirements of the events themselves."[30]

In epic theater, audience members develop their capacity for judgment by watching how the actors maintain a critical distance from the roles they play. The epic mode of acting teaches two things at once: First, it teaches the actor how to step out of the role she plays in order to assess her own actions and the society around her. Second, it teaches both the actor and the audience that events are contingent on human action. When an actor steps out of her role onstage, commenting on her own actions and breaking the fourth wall, she calls the entire world of the play into question. This stepping out of and calling into question are what Brecht calls the *Verfremdungseffekt* (estrangement or alienation effect, depending on translation). The *Verfremdungseffekt*, as Benjamin puts it, reveals "the dialectic at a standstill."[31] Instead of reproducing conditions, epic theater reveals them by interrupting what might otherwise seem like a natural course of events.[32]

For Arendt, the epistemic problem of dark times is even greater: dialectics will not help. Indeed all "theories and concepts," she writes, will likely fail. Instead, the only illumination that we might hope for in dark times is "from the uncertain, flickering, and often weak light that some men and women, in their lives and their works, will kindle under almost all circumstances and shed over the time span that was given them on earth."[33] All we have to illuminate dark times are the stories of people who came before us—*we* are "those who are born after." People's stories can be revealed by poets and historians, but most of all, they can be revealed in theater. Theater, Arendt writes, is "the only art whose sole subject is man in his relationship to others."[34] By presenting the actions of heroes and a web of human relationships onstage, theater also becomes a space for remembrance. In Arendt's conception of action, action does not leave behind physical artifacts (as work does). But theater can restage the actions of the past, and "assures the mortal actor that his passing existence and fleeting greatness will never lack the reality that comes from being seen, being heard, and, generally, appearing before an audience of fellow men."[35] Arendt's own writings are neither theater nor poetry nor academic history but a sort of epic storytelling. Works as different in tone and content as *Origins of Totalitarianism*, *Eichmann in Jerusalem*, and the essays in *Men in Dark Times* all share a method of drawing out individual stories to narrate past events and to illuminate the present. In this sense, her writing mirrors the "web of relationships and enacted stories" that, for her, constitutes the world.[36]

For Arendt, writing philosophy theatrically offers the possibility of writing without settling into one authorial persona. Both across her works and even within individual works, Arendt shifts between personas and voices. By writing in this way, Arendt reflects the multivocalism of thinking itself: thinking requires the ability to consider and describe the world from multiple perspectives. Stepping out of one's role is both a method of acting and a mode of thinking. In her late lecture published as "Some Questions of Moral Philosophy," Arendt describes thinking as a quality of two-in-oneness through which, "as I am my own partner when I am thinking, I am my own witness when I am acting."[37] She writes, "Thinking as an activity can arise out of every occurrence; it is present when I, having watched an incident in the street or having become implicated in some occurrence, now start considering what has happened, telling it to myself as a kind of story, preparing it in this way for its subsequent communication to others, and so forth."[38] Thinking requires narrating an event to yourself, becoming both the storyteller and critic of your own experience. Without this ability to think, people become thoughtless, unreflective about the narratives they are given, and incapable of articulating their own stories.

For Arendt and Brecht alike, the ideal spectator is a cool-headed thinker. And to bring out that quality in a spectator, the actor, too, must keep a cool head rather than appeal to pity.[39] For Arendt, the Eichmann trial would have been better if more of the testimony had been presented in the manner of epic theater. Above all other witnesses, Arendt praises Zindel Grynszpan, the father of Herschel Grynszpan who assassinated a Nazi Party diplomat in Paris in 1938. Arendt writes that Zindel Grynszpan "spoke clearly and firmly, without embroidery, using a minimum of words." His story of being deported from Germany to Poland

took no more than perhaps ten minutes to tell, and when it was over—the sense-less, needless destruction of twenty-seven years in less than twenty-four hours—one thought foolishly: Everyone, everyone should have his day in court. Only to find out, in the endless sessions that followed, how difficult it was to tell that story—at least outside the transforming realm of poetry—it needed a purity of soul, an unmirrored, unreflected innocence of heart and mind that only the righteous possess.[40]

While Grynszpan's story used a minimum of words, it is notable just how verbose Arendt's description is, including repetitions (senseless, needless; everyone, everyone; unmirrored, unreflected) as well as multiple dashes and parentheticals. Deborah Nelson argues that the "hitching syntax" of this passage marks it out from Arendt's colder tone throughout much of the book. This syntax is laden with affect, suggesting a provisional sympathetic identification with the pain of the witness.[41] Just as quickly, though, Arendt draws back, presenting her immediate impulse as foolish. She insists instead that except for rare individuals, it is only through aesthetic transformation that such stories can be told. This passage uses the technique of estrange-ment: the first sentence affectively draws the sympathy of the reader through its style, which offers a mimetic approximation of hitching speech. The sec-ond sentence undermines this sympathy by drawing attention to Arendt's failure as a spectator to adequately judge the proceedings ("one thought, fool-ishly") and then reflecting on the role that "poetry" must have in transform-ing testimony when articulated by those who do not tell their stories the way Grynszpan did. Arendt's delivery of his speech was not actually, if we trust her description of his simplicity, the way Grynszpan himself delivered it. In other words, Arendt evokes sympathy as though through mimetic rep-resentation while then immediately reflecting on the aesthetic techniques required to convey the power of such testimony.

Arendt writes that the "dramatic moment" of the trial came during the testimony of Abba Kovner, a writer and former Resistance fighter. Kovner told the story of Anton Schmid, a sergeant in the German army who helped the Jewish Resistance until he was caught and executed.

Arendt writes that the crowd spontaneously fell silent for two minutes in honor of Schmid:

In those two minutes, which were like a sudden burst of light in the midst of impenetrable, unfathomable darkness, a single thought stood out clearly, irre-futably, beyond question—how utterly different everything would be today in this courtroom, in Israel, in Germany, in all of Europe, and perhaps in all countries of the world, if only more such stories could have been told.[42]

In her account of Kovner's testimony about Schmid, it becomes clear that Arendt is not writing against theater or even against testimony that produces strong emotions and responses in the audience. This passage includes some of the same forms of repetition (impenetrable, unfathomable; clearly, irrefutably, beyond question) and parentheticals that Arendt uses in the Grynszpan passage to evoke a sense of eruption. This "dramatic moment" demonstrates how transformative such testimony can be. Schmid's resistance proves that there were German officers who maintained their capacity to judge for themselves. The political lesson of the story is simple but essential: "Under conditions of terror most people will comply but *some people will not.*"[43]

Arendt's style emphasizes the quality of interruption that accompanied both Grynszpan's and Kovner's testimonies: they each brought something new to the courtroom by rejecting sentimentality and a narrative of inevitable fate. Although she is not as taken with Kovner as with Grynszpan, Kovner, too, followed the model of the cool-headed actor as he "addressed the audience with the ease of someone who is used to speaking in public."[44] Significantly, the most dramatic moment came not when he was telling of his own considerable work in the Resistance but when he told someone else's story. As in many of Brecht's plays, this dramatic moment is narrated in the third person, by the actor stepping out of his own story, rather than being enacted or even narrated in the first person.[45] Presenting testimony through third-person narration distances the audience and forestalls pity and empathy. According to Arendt, it was not a feeling of pity for Schmid that washed over the audience, but a thought about how important his story was to hear. This thought is in turn accompanied by another set of emotions: awe, surprise, and righteous anger. For Arendt, stories of resistance, when narrated with composure and simplicity, trigger astonishment at the circumstances of heroism rather than acceptance of these circumstances as the natural outcome of millennia of anti-Semitism. They do so by establishing a distance between the spectator, the storyteller, and the subject that allows for the possibility of thinking about history counterfactually: What "could have been" had more such stories been told?

During this testimony, spectators experienced the trial as they might a Brecht play in which, as Benjamin writes, "instead of identifying with the characters, the audience should be educated to be astonished at the circumstances under which they function."[46] The theater of the Eichmann trial succeeded when it presented stories of resistance in such a way that it modeled for the audience what it means to judge, and if necessary resist, the world around them. Arendt recounts at least one moment in which the Eichmann trial created a critical audience against the intentions of the prosecutors. When Pinchas Freudiger (a member of the *Judenrat*, a Nazi-imposed Jewish council, in Hungary) was called to the stand, members of the audience disrupted the session, screaming insults at Freudiger and accusing him of complicity with the Nazi regime. As Lida Maxwell argues, critics who read *Eichmann in Jerusalem* as antitheatrical neglect the importance of the courtroom audience in Arendt's account of the trial. Through their actions—falling silent following Kovner's testimony and disrupting Freudiger's testimony—the audience became a cocreator of the event, at times supporting and at times resisting the designs of its producers.[47] The theatrical setup of the trial is what allowed for the audience to judge and at times reject the narratives being presented, changing the meaning of the trials. The architecture of the courtroom itself, with its raked theater seating, allowed for the assembly of this live audience, who could respond to the proceeding not only as individuals but as members of a public.

Despite moments like Kovner's and Freudiger's testimonies, resistance to the prosecution's narrative of inevitability was rarer than Arendt would like. In *Eichmann in Jerusalem*, Arendt goes to great lengths to incorporate evidence that the Holocaust was never inevitable, adding her own epic dramaturgy to the account. The biggest—and most provocative—transformation that Arendt makes is in casting Eichmann as a clown.[48] In her postscript to *Eichmann in Jerusalem*, Arendt responds to the controversy surrounding the phrase "the banality of evil" in her subtitle by emphasizing that Eichmann was no tragic hero or even a villain: "Eichmann was not Iago and not Macbeth, and nothing would have been farther from his mind than to determine with Richard III 'to prove a villain.' "[49] For Arendt, emphasizing Eichmann's thoughtlessness did not mean minimizing his crimes; it meant denying him greatness. In a 1974 interview, Arendt said that one of her main goals in writing *Eichmann in Jerusalem* was "to destroy the legend of the greatness of evil, of the demonic force, to take away from people the admiration they have for the great evildoers like Richard III." After publishing *Eichmann in Jerusalem*, she discovered an essay by Brecht on his play *The Resistible Rise of Arturo Ui* that describes his similar goal of holding Fascists up to ridicule. In her interview, Arendt quoted Brecht at length, supporting his claim that "the great political criminals must be exposed and exposed especially to laughter." Hitler, Brecht writes, "is not entitled to a privileged position in our view of history. That is, the fact that he [was permitted to become] a great crook and that what he does has great consequences does not add to his stature." Brecht then turns his remarks on Hitler into a much broader claim about history and genre: "One may say that tragedy deals with the sufferings of mankind in a less serious way than comedy." This, Arendt remarks,

of course is a shocking statement; I think that at the same time it is entirely true. What is really necessary is, if you want to keep your integrity under these circumstances, then you can do it only if you remember your old way of looking at such things and say: "No matter what he does and if he killed ten million people, he is still a clown."[50]

Comedy deals more seriously with suffering than tragedy because it permits people to think and judge, offering them a viewpoint from outside the immediate and devastating experience of the present. Laughter, Arendt writes, can "help one to find a place in the world, but ironically, which is to say, without selling one's soul to it."[51] Benjamin describes the role of laughter in epic theater in similar terms: "There is no better starting point for thought than laughter; speaking more precisely, spasms of the diaphragm generally offer better chances for thought than spasms of the soul."[52]

It is not only Eichmann that Arendt mocks in *Eichmann in Jerusalem*. She deploys her sarcasm to deflate any presentation she sees as political grandstanding or as being gratuitously emotional.[53] She is unsparing in her descriptions of Hausner and even of the concentration camp survivor

K-Zetnik. When K-Zetnik took the stand, he described how he continued to use the pseudonym K-Zetnik (slang for "concentration camp inmate") because he could still feel Auschwitz's influence on human destiny: "I believe with perfect faith that, just as in astrology the stars influence our destiny, so does this planet of the ashes, Auschwitz, stand in opposition to our planet earth, and influences it."[54] He quickly became distraught and fainted. Arendt's rather snide description of this incident is often used as evidence of her hard-heartedness.[55] Arendt is so critical of K-Zetnik's testimony because he describes Auschwitz as being the result of fate and because he appeals to pity rather than judgment. In bringing irony into her description of this moment, Arendt seeks to create a critical distance in her writing that did not exist in the courtroom.[56]

K-Zetnik's description of Auschwitz as outerworldly, unspeakable, and unthinkable also means that it cannot be judged. For Arendt this is deeply troubling because it is an argument that can be used by perpetrators as well as victims. Arendt compares the controversy surrounding *Eichmann in Jerusalem* to the controversy around Rolf Hochhuth's documentary play *The Deputy* about the Vatican's complicity in the Holocaust.[57] The ad hominem attacks against her and Hochhuth, Arendt argues, are attacks against those "who dared to sit in judgment."[58] Everyone, Arendt insists, has the right to judge: the moment when you demur ("Who am *I* to judge?") you—like Eichmann—have abnegated your responsibility to think and judge for yourself. Judging for yourself, however, is not a purely individual practice. Arendt's understanding of judgment rejects the existence of a single truth or set of moral precepts by which all individuals should judge the world. But she also does not propose that history is solely a matter of personal idiosyncratic interpretation or that there is no such thing as historical fact (a postmodernist position deployed by Holocaust deniers in the 1990s and, more recently, by members of Donald Trump's administration). Rather, judging, like thinking, requires the ability to imagine the world from the perspectives of others and appeal to a common sense that is not just your own.

Arendt concludes *Eichmann in Jerusalem* with a long speech, which shifts out of the narrative voice of the rest of the book. She writes, "If it is true that 'justice must not only be done but must be seen to be done,' then the justice of what was done in Jerusalem would have emerged to be seen by all if the judges had dared to address their defendant in something like the following terms." She then offers a speech, presented entirely within quotation marks, of the lines the judges should have delivered.[59] Judith Butler argues that this speech incorporates the language and voices of the prosecutor, judges, and even Eichmann himself along with Arendt's own voice. Butler proposes that in this passage Arendt theatrically enacts the plurality of judging alongside others whom one has not chosen and with whom one may be in conflict. In other words, Arendt uses "textual theater" to model the very form of cohabitation that Eichmann had worked to eradicate.[60] *Eichmann in Jerusalem* narrates the Eichmann trial theatrically, which is to say, it presents a web of human relations to a public both diegetically (in the narrator's voice) and mimetically (as Arendt mimics the voices of others in the final speech). This "textual theater" is not quite a Brechtian theater. Brecht's theater is a theater of dialectics—people adopt one position but step out of it in order to critique it. In the free indirect discourse of *Eichmann in Jerusalem*, however, the boundaries between identities and positions become more complicated. Thinking, for Arendt, means thinking in the company of others, it includes the perpetual threat of losing one's own voice but also the promise of learning to think for oneself in a way that takes others into account.

Arendt's final speech incorporates not only multiple voices but also citations of trials both from recent history (the Nuremberg trials) and archaic theater (*The Eumenides*). In a complicated play of citations within quotations, Arendt prefaces the speech by asserting, "We refuse and consider as barbaric the propositions 'that a great crime offends nature, so that the very earth cries out for vengeance.' " The quote is from Yosal Rogat's account of the Eichmann trial, which in turn refers to the trial of Orestes in *The Eumenides*. Although this claim precedes the quoted final speech, the identity of the "we" who speaks is already ambiguous: Is it Arendt? The judges? Or a *sensus communis*? Susannah Young-ah Gottlieb argues that this "we" has a distancing effect; it serves "to separate us from who 'we' believe ourselves to be." The "we" who refuses barbarism is yet still the "we" who condemns Eichmann to hang.[61]

For Butler, Arendt's speech is positioned between law and vengeance: "The question, one might say, is whether she seeks to play the role of Athena at the end of *Eumenides*."[62] When Arendt finally sentences Eichmann to death—"you must hang"—is she not, rather, enacting the barbaric justice of the Furies? Ariella Azoulay and Bonnie Honig demonstrate that the

question is actually even more complicated: Arendt is not merely presenting but also seeking to disrupt the binary between law and vengeance
(Athena and the Furies) by offering a third option. This third option is in
the figures of *The Eumenides*'s second chorus. This second chorus, which
appears after the Furies broker their deal with Athena and disappear, is a
chorus of women and children. Azoulay and Honig argue that Arendt
steps into the role of a member of this chorus, rather than a Fury or Athena:
"Like Arendt, this second Chorus chronicles what has occurred and lends
its support to a verdict already issued and a decision already made, all on
behalf of a future that citizens affirm for the sake of their 'loved land.'"[63]

By imbricating the judgments of *The Oresteia* within *Eichmann in Jerusalem*, Arendt calls upon a form of judgment that is neither strictly about
law nor about vengeance nor even about citizenship but about aesthetics.
As audiences at the Great Dionysia Festival would have known, speeches
like this may be about law and adjudication, but the play must ultimately
be judged for its virtuosity. Arendt asserts that the judges did not show justice to have been done in Jerusalem. Rather, it is through the speech that
she has written that justice will be *seen* to have been done. This is an aesthetic claim and a claim about virtuosity: Arendt wrote a better final speech
than the judges. It is also a claim about how important the *show* of trials is
for justice.

Arendt takes on the roles of both chorus member and judge in the end
of *Eichmann in Jerusalem*, gesturing toward the situation of performance.
Starting in 1953, lectures and speeches became increasingly central to
Arendt's work. Over the coming decades, all her most important books and
essays aside from *Eichmann in Jerusalem* were initially presented as speeches
or lectures, including *The Human Condition* (developed from the Wal-
green Lectures at the University of Chicago, 1956); *On Revolution* (developed from lectures at Princeton, 1959); *The Life of the Mind* (posthumously
published from lectures given between 1970 and 1975); all the essays published in *Between Past and Future: Eight Exercises in Political Thought* (all
originally delivered as speeches between 1953 and 1964); and those in *Crisis of the Republic* (all delivered as speeches between 1968 and 1971, with
the exception of excerpts from a 1970 interview published as "Thoughts on
Politics and Revolution: A Commentary") as well as the Brecht essay
"What Is Permitted to Jove" (originally a speech delivered at Emory University in 1964) and "Thoughts on Lessing: On Humanity in Dark Times"

(originally delivered in German as her acceptance speech for the Lessing Prize in 1959). In the printed versions of key essays on politics, freedom, and thinking, Arendt emphasizes the original form in subtitles: "Revolution and Freedom: A Lecture" (originally delivered in 1961 at Connecticut College); "Freedom and Politics: A Lecture" (delivered in German at Zurich University in 1958, and then in a revised English version in 1959 at Bryn Mawr); and "Thinking and Moral Considerations: A Lecture" (delivered at the New School in 1970).[64] On the one hand, the genesis of major works through lectures is not unusual, especially for the time when Arendt was working. On the other hand, though, because of Arendt's own understanding of speech and politics, the origins of these works in public speeches are especially significant.

Arendt conceives of the public realm as a space where people are both actors and spectators. Action on the world stage is one of the three activities that define the human condition; the other two are labor and work. In Arendt's account, *labor* sustains the biological processes of the human body, and *work* is how humans fabricate the world around them. Both labor and work are part of the private realm, whereas action is what people do in the public realm. Labor and work are means to other ends, but action is an end in itself. While labor and work are activities of the individual, action relies on human plurality, "the fact that men, not Man, live on earth and inhabit the world."[65] Action must be accompanied by speech for it to have meaning: "In acting and speaking, men show who they are, reveal actively their unique personal identities, and thus make their appearance in the human world."[66] Following Arendt's arguments about the revelatory power of speech means understanding her work in connection to live performance. Arendt's speeches, I want to suggest, are not what she calls "mere talk," that is, "simply one more means to an end." In other words, they are not mere rough drafts or working papers for her published works but rather occasions for acting on the world stage.

In her acceptance speech for the Lessing Prize, awarded to her by the city of Hamburg in 1959, Arendt defines "the world" as that which forms "only in the interspaces between men in all their variety."[67] Over the course of the speech, she moves beyond defining that world and toward creating new relations between herself and her audience by insisting on the space between them (German audience members) and herself (a Jewish refugee). Following her understanding of politics, this insistence on plurality and on the interspaces between people is what constitutes the public. In her speech, then, Arendt treads the line between a public lecture and a theatrical performance in order to challenge postwar West German politics. The speech focuses on Lessing's *Nathan the Wise*, and as Arendt's the speech progresses, she shifts from a critical, scholarly assessment of Lessing to a restaging of a key episode from the play itself.

NATIONAL THEATER AND THE GERMAN STATE

Nathan the Wise is a key text for Arendt for historical and philosophical reasons: historically, because it shaped Enlightenment understandings of religious tolerance, and philosophically, because it argues for the power of friendship as well as for a type of judgment that allows for multiple interpretations of truth. The play is set in Jerusalem during the Crusades and offers a parable about truth and judgment. The sultan Saladin calls the Jewish merchant Nathan before him and asks whether Judaism, Christianity, or Islam is the true religion. In response, Nathan tells the story of a wealthy man who possesses a ring that would make whoever wore it beloved by other people and by God alike. The man loves his three sons equally, and so he has copies of the ring made and gives one ring to each son. Each son believes that he has the original ring, and after the father dies, they fight bitterly, each claiming to be the sole inheritor. The brothers bring their dispute to court. After listening to their story, the judge tells the brothers that all three of their rings must be counterfeit: the real ring would make its wearer beloved, but each of the brothers loves only himself. If, he tells them, each one believes he has the true ring, then he must prove this by living his life with the gentleness, goodness, and devotion to God that reveal the ring's power. In thousands of years, when the ring has been passed from one generation to the next, the descendants of the brothers can return to the court, where there will be a wiser judge than he who can give a verdict on which ring is the true one.

Nathan the Wise, who was modeled on Lessing's friend Moses Mendelssohn, uses reason to argue not merely for toleration but also for acting with friendship and generosity. Arendt celebrates Lessing as "a completely political person" who remained committed to the world even in dark times.[68] Arendt describes how the world emerges through human relations and defines "the world" as that which forms "only in the interspaces between men in all their variety." Lessing's commitment is a rejoinder to those who think of freedom as a freedom from politics, a view that Arendt fears has become widespread. Freedom, she insists, is not an individual attribute; it can only exist in the shared world. Withdrawing from the world may not harm an individual, but "with each such retreat an almost demonstrable loss to the world takes place; what is lost is the specific and usually irreplaceable in-between which should have formed between this individual and his fellow men."[69] In dark times, Lessing used theater to teach audiences that without the plurality of human voices and ideas, there could be no world.[70]

Arendt's speech links seemingly abstract metaphors of the world stage to the history of German theater. The idea of theater as a public institution has a particularly strong history in Germany. More than a century before Germany existed as a unified nation-state, theater was a national institution. In the 1760s intellectuals and artists began to call for the development of a national theater that would reflect Enlightenment values.[71] Unlike existing court theaters, these new national theaters would appeal to a broader, bourgeois audience and would teach morality, tolerance, and even justice. As Schiller declares in his famous plea for the support of the theater as a moral institution: "Where the influence of civil laws ends, the stage begins."[72] In 1766 the first national theater was founded in Hamburg, with Lessing in a position that had not hitherto existed: the dramaturge. Lessing envisioned this new position of dramaturge as an intermediary between the theater and its public.[73] Arendt contrasts the place of the audience at the Hamburg Nationaltheater with another foundational theater, the Weimar Hoftheater (Weimar Court Theater), led by Lessing's younger contemporary Goethe. While Goethe stressed the "perfection of the work of art in itself," Lessing "was concerned with the effect upon the spectator, who as it were represents the world, or rather, that worldly space which has come into being between the artist or writer and his fellow men as a world common to them."[74] Lessing's theater, in other words, is not focused on the work itself but rather on its reception and its role in transforming the human relations that create the world.

Lessing's play *Nathan the Wise* came to epitomize the role of theater in advocating for religious tolerance. The play premiered in Berlin in 1783, the beginning of the period (1780–1806) in which Jewish *salonnières* like Rahel Varnhagen helped to shape public life. *Nathan the Wise* was so central to

Jewish hopes for social integration that, in assimilating, a number of German Jewish families took the name Lessing as a surname.[75] In *The Origins of Totalitarianism*, Arendt writes that *Nathan the Wise* shaped the attitude of the Prussian intelligentsia toward Jews, for better and for worse. The play helped to secure a place for Jews within Prussia's enlightened intelligentsia. But it did so at a price. Arendt argues that a misunderstanding of the play led the Prussians to expect Jews within their circles to be exceptional, both in the sense of being exceptions from unassimilated Jews (who were viewed with contempt) and also as "exceptional specimens of humanity" whose entrance to society required unique gifts.[76] The unanticipated result of this tolerance based on exceptionalism was that with the emancipation of Jews during the Napoleonic Wars, the "exceptional" Jews of Berlin lost the exceptional status that had granted them admission to society. In order to preserve any degree of social respect, "each one of them had to prove that although he was a Jew, yet he was not a Jew."[77]

Arendt's analysis of the decline of Jewish public life during the Napoleonic Wars is closely linked to the rise of anti-Semitism and the Nazi Party in the years when she was writing *Rahel Varnhagen*. The notion of an exceptional Jew was enshrined in Nazi law (for example, in the title of "Honorary Aryan" and in early exceptions to race laws made for frontline veterans of World War I). Even more troubling for Arendt was that the celebration of the exceptional Jew continued, "especially among the cultural elite," after the Second World War. In *Eichmann in Jerusalem*, she writes,

In Germany today, this notion of "prominent Jews" has not yet been forgotten. While the veterans and other privileged groups are no longer mentioned, the fate of "famous" Jews is still deplored at the expense of all others. There are more than a few people . . . who still publically regret the fact that Germany sent Einstein packing, without realizing that it was a much greater crime to kill little Hans Cohn from around the corner, even though he was no genius.[78]

When Arendt was awarded the Lessing Prize for work that the prize committee felt followed and promoted Lessing's Enlightenment values, Arendt worried that she was being cast as an exceptional Jew. To Arendt, the celebration of Lessing and humanism looks suspiciously like an attempt on the part of the prize committee to forget the horror of the recent past. In the beginning of her acceptance speech, Arendt aligns herself with

Lessing, connecting his work to her own conceptions of world and action and accepting her role as heir to the German Enlightenment. But halfway through, Arendt steps out of this role and reminds the audience that she is a Jew:

I so explicitly stress my membership in the group of Jews expelled from Germany at a relatively early age because I wish to anticipate certain misunderstandings which can arise only too easily when one speaks of humanity. In this connection I cannot gloss over the fact that for many years I considered the only adequate reply to the question, Who are you? to be: A Jew. That answer alone took into account the reality of persecution. As for the statement with which Nathan the Wise (in effect, though not in actual wording) countered the command: "Step closer, Jew"— the statement: I am a man—I would have considered as nothing but a grotesque and dangerous evasion of reality.

Lessing's humanism is dangerous because it misleads Jews to think they can defend themselves as humans instead of realizing that "one can resist only in terms of the identity that is under attack."[79] At this moment in her speech, Arendt shifts from describing theater to performing theater. She takes the line from *Nathan the Wise* and restages it: the prize committee asks her to the podium, "step forward, humanist," and she answers, "I am a Jew." At the same time, Arendt counters another possible "misunderstanding," one that would essentialize the Jew as a "special kind of human being." Rather, her insistence on being a Jew is a matter of "acknowledging a political fact," a fact that it is dangerous to obscure.[80] She refuses to play the role of "humanist" demanded by those who would obscure the political fact of her Jewishness. Not only does she refuse, she publicly stages this refusal in front of a live audience who has come to see her play the humanist.

What Arendt does in her acceptance speech is similar to the epilogue of *Eichmann in Jerusalem*; she steps in and out of multiple roles. In the epilogue, this exercise demonstrates the necessity of thinking and judging alongside others with whom you may not agree. In the Lessing speech, Arendt steps between roles to demonstrate how to defend oneself by claiming a political identity that is under attack without essentializing that identity.[81] Both of these theatrical moments have some similarity to Lessing's dramaturgy and his conception of theater as a public institution: Arendt is primarily concerned with her relationship to her readers and spectators and the "worldly space" that her speech creates between them. But at the same time, in the theatrical moments of the Lessing speech and the Eichmann epilogue, it becomes clear that the Enlightenment model of theater does not work. Lessing's theater is theater as a "moral institution"; it is oriented toward morality and social tolerance rather than political emancipation.[82] The theme of *Nathan the Wise*—that "it suffices to be human"—rings false as Arendt looks back on the previous century. Theater as a universalizing "moral institution" of the Enlightenment is not enough. Politics requires new ideas of how theater works as a public institution.

Arendt's years living in Germany were years of radical experimentation in what it meant for theater to be a public institution. Theater was quite literally the foundational institution of the new democratic Germany declared after the First World War. In 1919 the national assembly met to write its constitution at the Weimar Hoftheater (soon renamed the Weimar Nationaltheater), connecting the new democratic Germany with the spirit of the Enlightenment and Weimar classicism. While the national-theater movement of the Enlightenment developed from and sought to forge bourgeois publics, a new *Volksbühne* (people's stage) movement had begun in the 1890s to create publics that included working-class people. Max Reinhardt, the director of the Volksbühne from 1915 through 1918, led the way in using formal experimentation to reconfigure the relationship between the audience and the stage. To create a people's theater, Reinhardt looked to Greek tragedy as well as non-Western (especially Japanese and Chinese) theater and popular entertainment. For Reinhardt, creating a people's theater meant making the audience a part of the action. Reinhardt experimented with using an arena stage (modeled on Greek theater) and a catwalk (modeled on the Kabuki stage) to break the fourth wall of the proscenium stage and disperse action through the auditorium.[83] Reinhardt's productions of *Oedipus Rex* (1910) and *The Oresteia* (1911) took place in a circus arena, which he sought to transform into "A Theater of Five Thousand" that would include members of all social classes.[84]

Reinhardt and his contemporary Leopold Jessner's Weimar-era productions marked the beginning of the German tradition of *Regietheater* (director's theater). Regietheater pushed against the conventions of realist theater that had dominated European stages since the 1870s. Realist theater is oriented toward the individual spectator who sits, as though alone, in the dark to watch a self-contained world onstage. In realist theater, the literary text controls the play, and the staging is expected to reflect the intentions of the playwright. In Regietheater, the staging of a play (the costume and lighting design, the acting, the casting, and in some cases even the way that the rehearsal process is conducted) is just as important as, and often more important than, the script. Regietheater often challenges an audience's understanding of the work itself. At the Krolloper, led by Otto Klemperer, even Wagner was transformed and produced with Bauhaus sets and revised scores, unleashing fury from nationalist Wagner societies across Germany.

In *The Human Condition* and *On Revolution*, Arendt uses the dramaturgy and techniques of Greek theater to support her theory of political action. Describing the role of theater in ancient Athens, she writes, "Of all the arts, only theatre crosses the divide between work and action. Theater is "the political art par excellence; only there is the political sphere of human life transposed into art." Drama, she writes, comes from the Greek verb *dram*, "to act." Theater conveys "the specific revelatory quality of action and speech, the implicit manifestation of the agent and speaker."[85] In this sense, theater calls forth the relations between people, living and dead, who create the world. Arendt is not, however, calling for a return to either Greek theater or the Greek polis.[86] On the contrary, in her use and interpretation of Greek tragedy, Arendt is at her most modernist. Arendt's Greek tragedy is not the tragedy of historical Athens, nor is it the Greek tragedy of Weimar classicism (which was designed to open spectators to the freedom of aesthetic reflection), nor the Greece of the ritualistic music dramas of Wagner (which were designed to forge a nationalist mass audience). Rather, it is the Greek tragedy of the interwar avant-garde.[87]

While Reinhardt insisted that his people's theater was not political, younger directors of Arendt's generation, such as Brecht and Piscator, used elements of Greek tragedy to develop modes of staging and models of audience reception oriented toward revolutionary politics.[88] The term "epic theater" links two different legacies of Greek theories of performance: the narration (diegesis) that Plato sees as the proper mode of poetic expression and the imitation (mimesis) that Aristotle sees as the defining quality of theater.[89] Brecht and Piscator combined diegesis and mimesis in order to contextualize and frame the actions of characters within their historical and socioeconomic circumstances. Like Brecht and Piscator, Arendt saw in Greek theater a model for combining mimesis and diegesis in order to transpose politics into art:

The story's direct as well as its universal meaning is revealed by the chorus, which does not imitate and whose comments are pure poetry, whereas the intangible identity of the agents in the story, since they escape all generalization and therefore all reification, can be conveyed only through an imitation of their acting.[90]

The narration of the chorus is such an important element in Arendt's conception of theater because it is through this form of storytelling that theater can revise existing historical narratives. At the same time, mimetic reenactment offers that spark by which the revelation of a person may illuminate dark times.

Deeply influenced by contemporary theater practice, Max Herrmann founded and developed the field of Theater Studies in Berlin between 1910 and 1930. Herrmann defines "theater" as the shared experience of real bodies inhabiting real space.[91] This contemporary conception of theater underpins Arendt's description of theater's political function in *The Human Condition*. Theater is the political art par excellence not only because it presents action but also because, like the public realm itself, its existence depends on human plurality. In theater and in the public realm alike, action is conditioned by and emerges from a web of other actions, and each story is enacted with others in mind and impinged on in unexpected ways by others.[92] There is no way to control the reception of a play. *Nathan the Wise*, a play that Arendt argues is written to teach friendship and humanity, was misunderstood by the Prussian intelligentsia in such a way that it ultimately had the opposite effect. Similarly, Arendt describes how Brecht's *Threepenny Opera* became wildly successful because its radical message was ignored, and its effect was "exactly the opposite of what Brecht had sought": it made audiences embrace rather than condemn the essential criminality of capitalist enterprise.[93]

Arendt lived in Berlin during the height and quick decimation of interwar modernist and avant-garde theater (1929–33). The central figures of this theater were Jewish, leftist, or both. Reinhardt, Jessner, Klemperer, Brecht, and Piscator were able to flee Germany in time and eventually reached the Unites States. In 1933, following the Reichstag fire, the National Socialist Reichstag began to meet in the abandoned Krolloper. It was at the opera house that the Reichstag passed the Enabling Act, giving Hitler dictatorial powers. The Weimar Republic was founded in a theater and dissolved in a theater, a reminder that it is not the convergence of theater and politics in itself but the convergence of *particular types* of theater and politics that creates conditions for democracy or totalitarianism. At the Krolloper in 1933, the dissolution of the republic, the closure of the theater, and the destruction of human plurality were all intertwined. The meaning of theater as a national institution took a sinister turn. Two months after Hitler took power, Jews working in national theaters were expelled by the Law for the Restoration of the Professional Civil Service. Jewish artists who could no longer work and perform at national institutions organized the *Kulturbund deutscher Juden* (Cultural Association of German Jews).[94] The first performance that they held was a staging of *Nathan the Wise*. Jewish actors performed the classic drama of friendship and toleration for Jewish audiences while perhaps already realizing that enlightened humanism and the claim "I am a man" could not save them.[95]

Starting immediately after the Second World War, *Nathan the Wise* reentered the repertoire in German-speaking countries. Piscator's 1952 *Nathan the Wise* in Marburg confronted audiences with the Holocaust long before it had become a topic of public discourse in Germany, projecting the number "7,000,000" onstage in the second act. His program notes called on his audiences to examine their own complicity with genocide:

Why am I doing Nathan in Marburg? Because, in response to a remark about the Jewish tragedy, a cute little niece of mine said, "Well, this is bad indeed. But we knew nothing about all this. However, I cannot stand them [Jews] in spite of everything." ... Because in Marburg the synagogue also burnt, in this town in which I grew up. Shame covered my face in New York—I did not dare tell it even to my friends, for some who participated were close to me."[96]

Despite spending the Nazi dictatorship as a political refugee, Piscator emphasizes how important it is for him—as for all his audience—not to claim ignorance. Piscator is not advocating for a notion of collective guilt (which, as Arendt argues, could serve to absolve individual perpetrators) but rather for an understanding of collective responsibility. That responsibility means both interrogating one's own relationship to the crimes of the Third Reich and fighting to ensure that such crimes never happen again.

While Piscator's *Nathan the Wise* demanded recognition and responsibility, there were also productions of *Nathan the Wise* that did the exact opposite. At the Vienna Burgtheater, *Nathan the Wise* was staged in 1945 by Lothar Müthel, who was the theater's artistic director during the Third Reich. Only two years before, Müthel had staged an infamously anti-Semitic *Merchant of Venice*, with a Shylock designed to support Nazi propaganda. Yet his production of *Nathan the Wise* was heralded as an appeal for tolerance and was embraced by the public and press. It was performed ninety times, remaining in the repertoire until 1958. Müthel effectively used *Nathan the Wise* to cover for his own part in spreading anti-Semitic propaganda. The Burgtheater promoted guest tours of the play in Switzerland and the Netherlands to promote the "new spirit of the Burgtheater," though it did so without seriously addressing the speed with which the theater had dismissed its Jewish employees and adapted its programming to Joseph Goebbels's demands.[97]

That Lessing's play of tolerance was used both to obscure and to reveal complicity with the Nazi regime shows that theater cannot serve as a moral institution, because the result of a play—like the result of action in the public sphere—cannot be determined in advance.[98] While the meaning of all speech and action is contingent, theater is particularly difficult to enlist in any particular cause or project because its reception depends not only on its audience (as poetry or painting does) but also on its staging. If theater cannot be a moral institution, what can it do? The final two sections of this chapter offer two possible answers. The first is that theater provides models for acting in public as well as criteria by which to judge action. The second is that theater can create publics, even in dark times, by opening space for speech, judgment, and action.

ARENDT'S THEATRICAL MODEL OF ACTION

In Arendt's account of the public realm, action is measured not by its morality or by its result but by the virtuosity of the performance itself. This virtuosity is not a matter of playing an existing role in the best possible way (that is, winning the Mr. Universe competition, getting the highest bonus in your investment bank, or creating a flawless reproduction of the *Mona Lisa*). Instead, virtuosity means exceeding or subverting existing roles and models in order to create something new.

The aesthetic quality of Arendt's theory of action has been criticized for lacking a normative theory of justice as well as rational criteria for evaluating action.[99] But since the mid-1990s, Arendt's agonistic conception of the public realm has gained ground as a way to think about politics beyond liberal models of rational consensus and neoliberal identity politics. Bonnie Honig celebrates Arendt as a theorist of a disruptive virtu politics that resists the formation of obedient subjects.[100] What Arendt offers proponents of agonistic feminism like Honig is a model of resistance based on performativity. Honig and Butler argue that, following Nietzsche, there is no "doer behind the deed" in Arendt's concept of action.[101] This poststructural reading of Arendt is controversial. Seyla Benhabib describes it as an anachronistic reading of Arendt's work, while Amy Allen questions its political efficacy.[102] Turning to Arendt's declaration of "I am a Jew" in her Lessing speech, Allen argues that Arendt's criticism of humanism for obscuring identity could apply equally as a critique of poststructuralism "in the face of the realities of systematic domination the claim 'I am not a member of any repressive identity categories—in fact, I am not even an (identical) I' is no less grotesque and dangerous than 'I am a human being.'"[103] These divergent readings of Arendt are each born out in different writings; the agonist view is supported by *The Human Condition*, and Allen's is supported by the Lessing Prize speech. The difference between these works is less a shift in Arendt's thinking (she delivered the Lessing Prize speech the year after *The Human Condition* was published) and more a matter of how these two works—the first a book that originated in academic lectures delivered in the United States, the second a lecture in postwar West Germany—addressed their audiences and presented a particular speaker (a political philosopher in the first case, a Jew in the second) in relation to that audience. Read together, Arendt's intentional staging of her identity as author and speaker is not just performative but also theatrical. After all, her categories are *actor* and *action*, not *doer* and *deed* as Nietzsche's were.[104] Arendt's central question about politics is not about the status of the subject but rather how actors act in relation to the script they have been given.

Action, by Arendt's definition, is always the beginning of something new. But it also takes place, as Marx would say, under existing circumstances and through inherited narratives. This means that virtuosic acting is difficult. *Eichmann in Jerusalem* and *On Revolution* are both about just how difficult virtuosic action can be. In *On Revolution*, Arendt writes that the problem

has always been the same: those who went into the school of revolution learned and knew beforehand the course a revolution must take. . . . They had acquired the skill to play whatever part the great drama of history was going to assign them, and if no other role was available but that of the villain, they were more than willing to accept their part rather than remain outside the play.[105]

Here Arendt channels the famous opening to Karl Marx's "Eighteenth Brumaire of Louis Napoleon," that all great world historical events occur first as tragedy and then as farce. Marx argues that the French Revolution of 1789 clothed itself in the costumes and rhetoric of the Romans. But the revolutionaries of 1789 always knew that they were not actually Romans; they maintained enough distance between their costumes and critical capacities to find "the spirit of revolution" in the Romans while acting according to their own circumstances. The 1848ers, by contrast, did not maintain this distance. Instead they sought to make the ghost of the 1789 revolution "walk again," embodying the earlier revolutionaries to the extent that they forgot their own historical context.[106]

Marx's "Eighteenth Brumaire" is a common reference point for Brecht and Arendt in their thinking about the relationship between theater and politics. The problem that Marx articulates is not that revolutionaries wear costumes but rather that, in the case of 1848–52, their costumes were outdated and the actors could not think outside the roles they were imitating. In other words, theatricality was not the problem; the problem was bad acting and poor staging choices. Marx, Brecht, and Arendt all share the same concern: How can people begin something new when their actions are circumscribed by their historical context, when they are mere actors in a great historical drama? For Marx and Brecht, the answer is in the dialectic of history itself, a solution that Arendt forcefully rejects. Arendt argues that Marx exemplifies the modern tendency to understand history as a rectilinear process that can be explained and even forecast by theory. Marx sees politics as the work of "making history" and presumes that once history has been made, it will abolish itself. The end of history is also the end of politics: "Whenever we hear grandiose claims in politics, such as establishing a new society in which justice will be guaranteed forever . . . , we are moving into this realm of thinking."[107] This way of thinking is misguided, Arendt argues, because justice is not guaranteed by any political system. Instead of imagining history as a process oriented toward an ideal political system, Arendt proposes that history is composed of "interruptions," those extraordinary "single instances, deeds or events" that interrupt daily life.[108]

Virtuosic action, then, is a matter of interrupting the "great drama of history" by stepping out of one's role and questioning the way the script is supposed to end.

On Revolution and *Eichmann in Jerusalem* both reflect on the disastrous consequences of following a script and uncritically identifying with the role one is asked to play. Arendt's paradigmatic example of an actor who identifies completely with the role assigned to him is Eichmann. Arendt's Eichmann is a sort of extreme Method actor, one who becomes so caught up in his role that he forgets he is acting. Arendt pays particular attention to Eichmann's inability to depart from the script he is given and, moreover, his inability to see the artifice of the Nazi language rules through which he understands the world.[109] By Arendt's account, Eichmann's only language was officialese, and he "was genuinely incapable of uttering a single sentence that was not a cliché."[110] As Arendt understands him, Eichmann had no distance from the role that he played; every line that he was given to speak became truth for him. This inability to think critically about his own role or to question the orders he was given is what Arendt terms his "thoughtlessness."

While Eichmann demonstrates the dangers of completely identifying with the role one is given on the individual level, the French Revolution and the Terror show how this sort of embodiment can lead to the collapse of revolutionary action and, indeed, of the public realm itself. In *On Revolution*, Arendt uses two terms from the theater of classical antiquity—*hypocrite* and *persona*—to differentiate between bad and good types of acting. The hypocrite is the actor who not only plays a role but "who also must identify himself with his role." The hypocrite's identification with his role is directed inward as well as outward: "Not only does he want to appear virtuous before others, he wants to convince himself," and in doing so, he "bears false witness against himself."[111] Arendt contrasts the mask of hypocrisy with the mask of persona. The persona serves two purposes, replacing the actor's face with a new one but also allowing the actor's voice to sound through. Arendt writes that because of this double meaning, the term was appropriated from the theater by legal discourse: "The distinction between a private individual in Rome and a Roman citizen was that the latter had a *persona*, a legal personality, as we would say; it was as though the law had affixed to him the part he was expected to play on the public scene, with the provision, however, that his own voice would be able to sound through."[112] The problem of the French Revolution, Arendt argues, is that in their preoccupation with unmasking hypocrites, the revolutionaries forgot that there was a positive use for the mask of persona. Unlike the mask of hypocrisy, which minimizes the distinction between being and appearance, the mask of persona emphasizes the theatricality of adopting and playing a role in public.

In Arendt's work, the virtuosic historical actor is not measured by the criterion of realism (that is, how well he embodies the role he is asked to play) but by the criteria of epic theater (that is, how well he maintains a critical distance from that role). Existing historical narratives must not determine action, but, as Benjamin describes epic theater, such scripts become the "grid on which, in the form of new formulations, the gains of that performance are marked."[113] In other words, virtuosity is measured not by how well someone plays her role, but by how she departs from the script. Arendt evaluates political action by Brecht's standards and, in this sense, differs from most liberal conceptions of what it means to play a role on the public stage. The most influential liberal conceptions of the public realm ask citizens to suspend their own positions and interests and behave according to Konstantin Stanislavski's *magical if*. In John Rawls's theory of justice, the veil of ignorance is a figure that leads people to act *as if* they did not know their actual position in society. Jürgen Habermas's model of the bourgeois public depends on its participants debating *as if* they were equals. But, as Nancy Fraser argues, the "acting as if" characteristic of liberal models of the public does not actually create an equitable public sphere; instead it merely hides privilege.[114] All this acting *as if* threatens to obscure the theatricality of the whole enterprise. In the epic model of the public, the goal is not to act *as if* you are someone else, or *as if* you have no particular identity, but to maintain a critical distance from any role you adopt and to remain aware of how cultural idioms and performances belonging to different social groups (*Gestus*, as Brecht would call it) are unequally valued.[115]

Even if all social roles are theatrical in the sense of being constructed, inhabiting those roles still has a real effect on one's life chances. The problem with epic acting as a model for action in the public realm is that some roles are particularly difficult to think or step out of.[116] For Arendt, people whose existence is shaped by the urgent biological demands of sustenance and reproduction cannot act politically because overwhelming need binds them to the private space of labor. Arendt attributes the failure of the French Revolution in large part to the entrance of "the multitude of the poor" onto the "scene of politics . . . [whereby] freedom had to be surrendered to necessity, to the urgency of the life process itself."[117] Here, Brecht's materialism offers a useful counterbalance to Arendt. Brecht's theater stresses the material conditions required to enter public life and makes the struggle for these conditions the central political message of his works. The epic stage reveals its own machinery, making the spotlights visible to the audience and having stagehands construct the set with the curtain open. Revealing the machinery of production encourages audiences to question who is able to appear onstage and what mechanisms allow them to appear. It reveals what Seyla Benhabib terms "the secret logic of power, hierarchy, and domination" that lies behind the distinction between public and private.[118] When the machinery of the stage becomes part of the performance, virtuosic acting requires reflecting on and demanding the material conditions that make action possible.[119]

AESTHETIC JUDGMENT IN THE CAMPS

Although Arendt does not explain how people can acquire the material support needed to move from the demands of labor to the freedom of action, she does offer one possible way into public life. This way is not through politics but through art. Arendt argues in *Eichmann in Jerusalem* that there is suffering so profound that it is ineffable. Art can transform this suffering so that it can be articulated and discussed. Arendt approvingly cites the judges' comment at the Eichmann trial that "sufferings on so gigantic a scale were . . . 'a matter for great authors and poets.'"[120] Through art, suffering and personal experience become admissible to the public realm because they are translated into a form that can be communicated.

One of the few times when Arendt writes directly about her own experience of statelessness and incarceration during the war is in the German version of "What is Permitted to Jove." Arendt describes how, while interned in a camp by the French government, Brecht's unpublished poem about Lao Tzu's road into exile spread "like a wildfire in the camps, passed from mouth to mouth like glad tidings [*frohe Botschaft*], which God knows was nowhere more urgently needed than on those straw sacks of hopelessness."[121] She first heard the poem from Benjamin, who had brought it to Paris with him after a visit with Brecht in Denmark.[122] Arendt's messianic description of the poem echoes Benjamin's commentary: "The poem comes to us at a time when such words ring in the ears of men like a promise which has nothing to concede to the promises of a Messiah."[123] The lesson of the poem is a simple one: over time, slowly moving water can erode granite. It is a celebration of resilience in the face of violence; its message is that simply surviving can be an act of resistance. Writing about this poem allows Arendt to speak of her own personal experience during the war. It also shows that even stateless people who are exiled from the political realm are not reduced to mere biological need. The poem became a topic of conversation and speech; it laid a foundation for the emergence of a public even within the camps. Internees performed for each other by reciting Brecht and spoke to each other about what resistance means. While Brecht's epic acting offers a model for political action, his poetry can create public life among refugees who were cast out of the public sphere. Arendt's story about Brecht, in turn, uses Brecht's life and work to illuminate the dark times they lived through.

In a public sphere grounded in aesthetic judgment, action does not depend on following a rule or a law. Aesthetic judgment is Arendt's answer to a central question raised by the Eichmann trial: How can people maintain their faculties to judge when the law condones murder?[124] Arendt is disgusted by Eichmann's claim during the trial that he was acting according to Kant's philosophy. In one respect, though, "Eichmann did indeed follow Kant's precepts: a law was a law, there could be no exceptions."[125] That is to say, Eichmann followed Kant's moral philosophy. The issue here goes beyond the question of obedience to Nazi law. The larger question is whether a universally valid moral law grounds politics or destroys it. Postwar human rights law takes the former position; Arendt takes the latter. For Arendt, it is only because there is no singular truth knowable to all people that freedom, and indeed the world itself, can exist. This, Arendt argues, is what *Nathan the Wise* teaches us:

[If] all men would suddenly be united in a single opinion, so that out of many opinions one would emerge, as though not men in their infinite plurality but man in the singular, one species and its exemplars, were to inhabit the earth. Should that happen, the world, which can form only in the interspaces between men in all their variety, would vanish altogether.[126]

Arendt develops her argument about Kant in her final project, the volumes on thinking, willing, and judging that were published posthumously as *The Life of the Mind*. She argues that Kant's *Critique of Judgment* is more closely connected to politics than his other two critiques. This is because aesthetic judgment is judgment that does not follow a rule or appeal to truth but rather depends on the condition of human plurality. The moral laws articulated in the critiques of pure and practical reason could be deduced by any individual rational being. But the aesthetic judgment that Kant defines in *Critique of Judgment* requires a *sensus communis*, that is, mutual agreement and communicability.[127] There is no rule or law that dictates what is beautiful, but judging something to be beautiful is also not purely subjective. Arendt writes,

When somebody makes the judgment, this is beautiful, he does not mean merely to say this pleases me . . . but he claims assent from others because in judging he has already taken them into account and hence hopes that his judgments will carry a certain general, though perhaps not universal, validity.[128]

Aesthetic judgment is a process of the "enlargement of the mind"—being able to compare one's own view of the world to the viewpoints of others—precisely the faculty that Eichmann lacked.

Theater is essential not because it is a moral institution that teaches laws but because it is a space where people judge in the company of others without recourse to a universal law. In a sense, this is a low bar. Theater does not have to teach people to be moral; it just has to be a place where people share a space with other people and judge alongside them. While the Hamburg Nationaltheater and Jerusalem People's House sought to forge nation-states by producing theater that taught audiences how to act as citizens and subjects, Arendt offers a different vision of public theater. In a 1944 essay on Franz Kafka, Arendt presents a glimpse of what that new public of exiles and refugees might look like. Published on the twentieth anniversary of Kafka's death, Arendt's essay incorporates elements of Benjamin's essay that was written on the tenth anniversary of Kafka's death as well as Benjamin and Brecht's conversations about Kafka during their time as refugees in Denmark (as recorded in Benjamin's "Conversations with Brecht"). Arendt's essay continues a conversation that was broken off too soon. Benji, as Arendt affectionately called him, had died four years earlier while trying to escape to America.

Arendt's essay starts with *The Trial*, which she reads as a call to resist the machinery that makes the "world order" appear to be necessary and inevitable. The story is of a man who is "transformed until he is fit to assume the role forced upon him, which is to play along as best he can in a world of necessity, injustice, and lies."[129] Josef K. comes to fully embody the role forced upon him, eventually believing in his own guilt. He adopts this role because he believes that there is a "divine necessity" to the world order. He does not stop to judge the role that he has been given and therefore also fails to consider whether the world order could be otherwise. The submission of Josef K. is "achieved when the question of guilt or innocence is no longer asked, replaced by the determination to play the role dictated by arbitrariness in the game of necessity."[130] Arendt argues that Kafka wrote the novel to demonstrate the process through which the world is "deified" so that the world order appears inevitable and irresistible. Brecht, like Arendt, argues against the sense of inevitability common in readings of Kafka.[131] In "Conversations with Brecht," Benjamin recounts Brecht's sharp criticism of Benjamin's essay on Kafka for spreading "the darkness surrounding Kafka instead of dispersing it." Brecht insists, "It is necessary to clarify Kafka . . . to formulate the practicable suggestions which can be extracted from his stories."[132] The difference between Brecht and Arendt in their writings on Kafka is that Brecht claims that Kafka himself "never found a solution" to his nightmare visions. Arendt, though, believes that Kafka did see a solution: the new world in the "happy ending" of *Amerika*. After drifting from place to place in a series of strange, unresolved episodes, in the book's final, incomplete chapter, young European immigrant Karl Rossman arrives at the "Nature Theatre of Oklahoma," where "all are welcome."[133]

Benjamin's essay discusses the arrival of Karl Rossman at the Nature Theatre of Oklahoma at length, describing the theater as one whose techniques harken back to Chinese theater. It is a gestic theater, which is to say it is a Brechtian theater. Benjamin goes even further than claiming that the protagonist finds his home in this theater. He suggests that many of Kafka's works themselves "are seen in their full light only when they are, so to speak, put on as acts in the 'Nature Theatre of Oklahoma.' "[134] Benjamin writes:

Kafka's world is a world theatre. For him, man is on stage from the very beginning. The proof of the pudding is the fact that everyone is accepted by the Nature Theatre of Oklahoma. What the standards for admission are cannot be determined.

Dramatic talent, the most obvious criterion, seems to be of no importance. But this can be expressed in another way: all that is expected of the applicants is the ability to play themselves. It is no longer within the realm of possibility that they could, if necessary, be what they claim to be. With their roles these people look for a position in the Nature Theatre just as Pirandello's six characters sought an author.

For those who join the Nature Theatre of Oklahoma, it is both their last refuge and their salvation. It is a space where they do not have to *be* anything in particular; they just have to *play* themselves. During the celebrations for new members, extras from the theater dress up as angels; Benjamin notes, "but for the fact that their wings are tied on, these angels might be real."[135] At the Nature Theatre, actors are able to tie on their own wings. They are theater wings, but they still might open the way for a new beginning.

Benjamin's, Brecht's, and Kafka's stories are among the many stories that Arendt tells of people in dark times. These stories offer illumination because they make meaning of the past without presenting what has been and what might be as inevitable. Benjamin's death while in custody on the French-Spanish border was a result of a tremendous machinery of mass murder and deportation, but it was also a particular case of terrible luck. Arendt tells us, "One day earlier Benjamin would have got through without any trouble; one day later the people in Marseilles would have known that for the time being it was impossible to pass through Spain."[136] Benjamin might have shared Karl Rossman's happy ending: an arrival at Brecht's American home.

Chapter Two

BERTOLT BRECHT
Poetic Justice

On the eve of the Nuremberg trials, judges, attorneys, and dignitaries from the Allied powers gathered for a reception at the city's Soviet headquarters. Years of painstaking planning had gone into ensuring that the trial would not be seen as mere victor's justice. Now, finally, the trial was about to start, and the Soviet Union was hosting the opening festivities. Several drinks in, Iona Nikitchenko, the chief judge representing the Soviet Union, raised his glass and proposed a toast to the defendants: "May their paths lead straight from the courthouse to the grave!" Most of the French, British, and American guests did not wait for a translation before joining in the toast; only a moment later did they realize, abashedly, that they had toasted to executions before the trial had begun.[1]

Meanwhile, in Santa Monica, Bertolt Brecht was having an argument with Lion Feuchtwanger about Feuchtwanger's decision to decline a job writing about the trials for the Associated Press.

"You overestimate the trial," Feuchtwanger told Brecht.

Brecht replied, "For the first time in modern history, a government is standing before a court because of its crimes."

Feuchtwanger remained skeptical: "It's not actually meant seriously."

"That's why you should go," Brecht said, "so that the crimes of this government against its own people are also remembered."

"You're so subjective," Feuchtwanger complained. "At least try to understand my reasons."

"Through luck you find yourself in a position where you are invited to speak, to represent the German anti-Nazis. You have no right to keep writing your novel. Speak badly, stutter, let yourself be gagged, but appear in the arena."

"You know," said Feuchtwanger, "it isn't cowardice."

"I know worse," replied Brecht. "It's complacency."[2]

A decade earlier, Feuchtwanger had watched Nikitchenko and other members of the Soviet Union's legal team for the Nuremberg trials preside over the Moscow trials.[3] The Moscow trials, held between 1936 and 1938, were a series of trials orchestrated by Joseph Stalin to purge the Bolshevik party of hidden Trotskyists (and potential opposition). They were staged to demonstrate the imminent threats of sabotage, assassination plots, and conspiracies among members of the party elite for the benefit of both domestic and international audiences. The trials sparked international debate regarding their legitimacy and, in particular, the veracity of the confessions they extracted. For Hannah Arendt, these trials marked a decisive turning point for the Communist Party, from a revolutionary party to a totalitarian movement. She also saw it as a turning point for Communists and fellow travelers outside the Soviet Union: those who did not publicly break with the party after the trials were complicit in its crimes.[4] In the United States, these trials created a split between liberals, such as John Dewey and members of the Dewey Commission who condemned the trials, and Communists and fellow travelers—among them some of the most important figures in New York's theater and cultural scene, including Marc Blitzstein, Harold Clurman, Lillian Hellman, and Langston Hughes—who published a statement in support of the trials.[5]

In his book *Moscow 1937*, Feuchtwanger defends the Moscow trials against the criticism of most Western observers. While the trials had seemed incredible from the vantage point of western Europe, once he actually attended the trials, he said, "I was forced to accept the evidence of my senses, and my doubts melted away as naturally as salt dissolves in water."[6] All the same, eight years later, Feuchtwanger refused to attend the Nuremberg trials. Perhaps he did not think that seeing the Nuremberg trials in person would melt his doubts. Or perhaps, with the benefit of hindsight, he was concerned that he *would* come to believe in the trials at Nuremberg as he had the trials in Moscow.

Unlike Feuchtwanger, Brecht was relatively unconcerned that the Nuremberg trials might not be "meant seriously" or that the Soviet judge might have toasted to the convictions of the defendants before the trial began. Brecht was less concerned with the impartiality of the judges than with the spectacle of a government on trial for its crimes; after all, as Brecht once wrote, even the verdict of bribed judge can still be just.[7] Brecht and Feuchtwanger understood the relationship between law and performance in very different ways. For Brecht, all trials were shows, but that did not mean they were unjust. For Feuchtwanger, the less like a show a trial was, the better and more authentic it was. In *Moscow 1937*, Feuchtwanger attempts to convince his readers of the fairness of the Moscow trials by indicating how unlike theater they are. He writes that before attending the trials, he felt that "the hysterical confessions of the accused seemed to have been extorted by some mysterious means and the whole proceedings appeared like a play staged with consummate, strange, and frightful artistry."[8] But in the courtroom, he is struck by the lack of theatricality, noting that throughout almost all the proceedings, "judges, public prosecution, and accused all spoke calmly and without emotion, and not one of them ever raised his voice."[9] He remarks that it is "a pity that the laws of the Soviet Union forbade photographs and gramophone records to be made in court. If one could have reproduced for the whole world not only what the prisoners said, but how they said it, their intonations, their faces, I think there would be very few skeptics left."[10]

Feuchtwanger fell hook, line, and sinker for the realist acting of the judges, prosecution, and defendants on the days he attended the Moscow trials. For Brecht, psychological realism was as dangerous in a trial as in the bourgeois theater, and for the same reasons: it tricked audience members like Feuchtwanger into forfeiting their own critical capacities. Brecht wanted spectators to watch and critique trials as they watched epic theater, thinking about the disjuncture between the defendants and the roles they played in a trial, evaluating the evidence, and making their own decisions. To maintain a critical distance from the proceedings, people must understand that all trials are inevitably theatrical and be suspicious of any trial that puts so much energy into appearing realistic. They must, in other words, learn to distinguish between social reality and socialist realism.

Brecht connected the Moscow show trials with the Communist International's adoption of socialist realism as official cultural policy in the late 1930s.
In conversations with Benjamin at the height of the Stalinist purges, Brecht
argued that the Stalinist trials shared the representational strategies of
socialist realism, fetishizing a mode of realist representation whose prime
goal was to convey its own authenticity and earnestness. Brecht rejected the
demand of critics like György Lukács that socialist art must eschew formal
experimentation in favor of realist representation. Brecht redefined the
terms of this debate, insisting that socialist realist representation was *itself*
a "formalism" that obscured the necessary contradictions and conflict of
political life. He interpreted this formalism as an outgrowth of a petrify-
ing bureaucracy that insisted on adherence to strict rules, whether in economic production or in artistic production. In other words, it was not the
arbitrariness of Soviet purges that concerned Brecht the most but the regulations of the Soviet bureaucracy. In Max Weber's terms, Brecht was concerned about a formal rationality that gave primacy to regulations and rules
over the exercise of individual judgment on a case-by-case basis.[11] From the
Stalinist purges until his death, Brecht sought to develop new modes of representation that could foster a new type of justice, a poetic justice that
combined ethical judgment with theatrical performance.[12]

THE COURTROOM AS A MODEL FOR EPIC THEATER

Brecht uses trials in his plays so often that Günther Anders compares him
to Kafka, remarking, "Every Brecht play could also be called *The Trial*."
Brecht creates a judicial world in his works because, Anders writes, he
"wants to make the observer capable of judging."[13] If not all—as Anders
claims—certainly the majority of Brecht's canonical plays could be renamed
The Trial; among them are *The Measures Taken*, *The Good Person of Szechuan*, *Life of Galileo*, *The Caucasian Chalk Circle*, *Man Is Man*, *The Trial of
Lucullus*, and *The Rise and Fall of the City of Mahagonny*. In many of his
plays Brecht includes trial scenes that emphasize the injustice of courtroom
proceedings. Indeed, what is so often put on trial on Brecht's stage is, first
and foremost, the courtroom itself. The trials in *Man Is Man* show the per-
version of justice within a colonial context; the trial in *The Good Person of
Szechuan* portrays the interest that figures of authority have in maintaining the status quo through their legal rulings; the trial in *The Rise and Fall*

of the City of Mahagonny shows that judges and prosecutors ally against defendants out of economic self-interest. In many cases—including *The Rise and Fall of the City of Mahagonny, The Good Person of Szechuan,* and *Man Is Man*—Brecht even includes an onstage audience who behaves as a bad jury, refusing to acknowledge evidence, adopting the claims of those in power without question, and enjoying the trial in direct relation to their intoxication.

Brecht's plays are full of scenes of unjust trials. But at the same time, Brecht uses the courtroom trial as a formal model to develop two different modes of political theater: the learning play and epic theater. The learning plays have no conventional audience and feature amateur performers. The most famous of Brecht's learning plays is *The Measures Taken,* which gained notoriety as a defense of the Stalinist purges (though Brecht had written the play before the purges began). Within the play a mass chorus of workers adopts the role of a people's court. The play begins when four Communist agitators return to the Soviet Union from spreading propaganda in China. They appear before the court to explain and justify killing a young comrade who sought to help them but ultimately let his personal sympathy for individuals undermine the party's work. The agitators reenact what happened in China before the court, each of them stepping into the role of the young comrade at different moments. In this learning play, the four agitators teach the chorus—that is to say, the workers taking part in the production—how to judge.

Brecht also relies on the model of courtroom testimony to articulate his theories of epic theater. Unlike the learning plays, epic theater is designed to be presented on a proscenium stage by professional actors. Nevertheless, Brecht is still concerned that both the actors and the audience develop their critical capacities through the rehearsal and performance process. In the essay "A Street Scene: A Basic Model for Epic Theatre," Brecht compares the epic actor to an eyewitness who is recounting what has just occurred in a car accident to a group of onlookers. In the process, the eyewitness may mime what happened, but there is always an element of distance separating her and the onlookers from the actual accident. When the witness demonstrates the way in which the driver drove, the onlookers don't believe that she herself is the driver. Brecht writes that if brought before a court, the witness's performance would become yet closer to that of an epic actor performing memorized and rehearsed text.[14]

In addition to his learning plays and epic theater, Brecht imagined—though never produced—a third type of theater, what he called the panopticon theater. This panopticon theater would be constructed like an assembly hall and would feature multiple historical trials every evening.[15] One evening of performances would begin with the trial of Socrates followed by a short witch trial featuring a group of armored knights who condemn the witch to be burned at the stake. The knights would remain onstage when the scene changed to a blasphemy case against the artist George Grosz, revealing how contemporary courts used outmoded language and postures and thus condemning contemporary trials for perpetuating the injustices of centuries past.

In all three modes of theater (the learning play, epic theater, and the imagined panopticon theater), the trial model was crucial both to Brecht's articulation of new modes of acting and audience reception (the actor as witness, the audience as jury) and to his ideas about how theater represents history. Whereas realist theater seeks to draw audiences into staged action that is designed to seem contemporaneous with the performance, epic theater signals to its audiences that the staged action is a presentation of a story that already happened and is being offered up for judgment.[16] Instead of becoming caught up in the plot as it unfolds, Brecht hopes this sense of pastness will offer the critical distance that an audience needs in order to consider how the story might have been told differently and might have ended differently. Learning how to judge action within the theater, Brecht believes, also means learning how to reject oppression outside the theater.

THE MOSCOW TRIALS AND THE SWINDLE OF REALISM

Brecht's theater evolved in reference not only to the qualities of bourgeois melodrama and Aristotelian theater that Brecht targeted explicitly but also to the aesthetic debates among leftist artists and critics in the 1930s. This series of debates about politics and aesthetics focused on the historical and political value of formally innovative work and marked the shift of Soviet and Comintern (Communist International) cultural policy from the avant-garde experiments of the Weimar Republic and the early years of the Soviet Union (which were termed "formalist" by their opponents) toward socialist realism. Brecht was closely implicated in these debates. Starting in 1936 he and Feuchtwanger served as editors of *Das Wort* (the Word), a

publication of the Comintern's Popular Front. Brecht's editorship was embattled from the start. Brecht sought to change the tone of *Das Wort* by asking
Erwin Piscator to contribute and by submitting Benjamin's "The Work of
Art in the Age of Mechanical Reproducibility," which was rejected by the
editors in Moscow.[17] Instead, *Das Wort* published a number of essays by
Lukács and others, denouncing formalist experimentation without Brecht's
approval. There was a coordinated campaign among proponents of socialist realism in the Moscow office of *Das Wort* to use these attacks on formalism to goad Brecht into a public break with the Popular Front's cultural
politics.[18] Brecht did not rise to the bait; his essays on formalism were published only posthumously because, as he told Benjamin, he was concerned
that "Lukács' position 'over there' is at the moment very strong."[19]

For Brecht, these debates were about two things at once: first, the capacity of anti-Fascist writers to write for people living under Fascism and, second, the belief that art requires continual formal innovation to respond to
and reflect changing political and social conditions. During his exile in
Denmark in 1934, Brecht wrote about how authors must use *List* (a German
word that connotes both cunning and artifice) when writing for readers living under dictatorship. This cunning, on the part of both the author and
reader, allows the author to cloak the truth in innocuous-sounding prose:
simply using the word "population" instead of "Volk" and "land ownership"
instead of "soil" resists Fascist ideology.[20] A piece of writing could stand
effectively against Fascism by deploying irony rather than direct political
messages. In 1935 the Comintern's general secretary, Georgi Dimitrov, officially promoted a strategy echoing Brecht's position, which Dimitrov termed
the "Trojan Horse" strategy. By 1937, though, Brecht was concerned that
writers and critics within the Soviet Union were turning against this
approach. In response to an attack on his play *Round Heads and Pointed
Heads* (a parable about Nazi race and class politics) submitted to *Das Wort*,
Brecht wrote, "The article is an attack on all camouflage in the theatre. . . .
[W]e must stop [the reviewer] from denouncing and sabotaging literary
attempts to smuggle in the truth about the enemy in camouflaged form."[21]

Camouflage, masking, and smuggling are key motifs in Brecht's essays on
formalism from the late 1930s as well as in the conversations that Benjamin
recounts in his "Conversations with Brecht." Brecht contrasts his own use of
masks (both literal, in his use of theater masks, and figurative, in his use
of irony) to the Comintern's demands for realism and authenticity. In the

essay "Popularity and Realism," Brecht uses masks (worn by the agitators in *The Measures Taken* while they reenact the story of the Young Comrade) as an example of formal techniques that eschew mimetic realism in order to convey deeper truths: "The actors may not use any make-up—or hardly any—and claim to be 'absolutely natural' and yet the whole thing can be a swindle; and they can wear masks of a grotesque kind and present the truth."[22] The masks in *The Measures Taken* reveal the truth in two ways. First, they prevent the audience (who is also the chorus) from identifying with the Young Comrade. The play is about the danger of confusing immediate personal sympathy with awareness of structural injustice: because the Young Comrade tries to alleviate the suffering of a few individual peasants, he imperils the revolution that would help all the peasants. The audience/chorus is likewise taught not to pity the Young Comrade but to consider the good of the party. Second, the masks help the audience to understand that historical action develops through role-playing and that it is always possible to question and step out of the role you may seem destined to play. Much like with the "Street Scene," the audience/chorus never believes that the actor playing the Young Comrade *is* the Young Comrade. The use of masks fosters the critical capacity of the audience/chorus to consider how the agitators and the Young Comrade may have acted differently: What other roles might they have played? How might they have altered the events? People are best able to judge what happened when the occurrences are presented through diegetic narration rather than mimetic reproduction. In "Popularity and Realism," Brecht argues that the claim of the antiformalists that reality can be cohesively and authentically portrayed through mimetic realism is a swindle. Reality is never cohesive, and moreover, we are always performing: there is no such thing as being "absolutely natural."

The formalism debates were simultaneous to and, for Brecht, interwoven with the Stalinist purges and the Moscow trials of the late 1930s. Although the Moscow trials focused on Stalin's political adversaries, the broader purges targeted so-called formalist artists like Vsevolod Meyerhold and ensured a strict adherence to the cultural policy of socialist realism.[23] News and discussions of the Moscow trials appeared in the very same German exile journals as key essays in the formalism debates, most notably *Das Wort* and *Die Neue Weltbühne* (the New World Stage). There was one central question at the heart of discussions of both the Moscow trials and the essays about formalism and expressionism: How do surface appearances reflect or hide deeper truths (whether in a person or in a work of art)? Or, to put it in other words, what is the relationship between form and content?

The Moscow trials elicited deep uncertainty about the authenticity of appearances: Can a seemingly loyal party member actually be hiding treasonous crimes? Are crimes only a matter of action or can thoughts themselves be crimes? During the Moscow trials, the defendants were charged with grave crimes against the Soviet Union (conspiracy, sabotage, espionage, and murder). At the same time, the trials were also about the subjective crimes of defendants (doubting Stalin's policies and the trajectory of the party, having a mechanical rather than dialectical understanding of history, et cetera). The most important defendant of the Moscow trials was Nikolai Bukharin, the Bolsheviks' leading theoretician until he fell afoul of Stalin. In his final plea, as well as in a number of letters to the politburo, Bukharin denied the specific charges against him (that he tried to arrest Lenin and kill Sergei Kirov and Maxim Gorky and that he was conspiring against the Soviet Union with foreign powers). Bukharin did, however, confess to subjective crimes like opposing Stalin's policies during the five-year plan and thus contributing to Soviet "degeneration." He also admitted to defeatism, pessimism, doubt, and—like a number of other defendants—to a "peculiar duality of mind."[24]

Bukharin gave his final plea in March 1938, and in May of that year, Ernst Bloch published an essay defending the trial's proceedings in *Die Neue Weltbühne*. In his defense of Bukharin's trial, Bloch places particular emphasis on his duality of mind as an expression of Hegel's "unhappy consciousness."[25] In Bukharin's final plea, much of which is reprinted in Bloch's essay, Bukharin explains that his long months in prison, suspended between life and death, enabled him to understand his failings, to overcome his duality of mind, and to embrace the Soviet Union. Bloch adds that Bukharin also framed his final plea for both the Moscow courtroom and an international audience. Bloch describes how while writing his final plea, Bukharin studied Feuchtwanger's *Moscow 1937*, which in turn had cited Bloch's earlier essay "Critique of a Trial Critique."[26]

In his final speech, chief prosecutor Andrei Vyshinsky accused Bukharin and the other defendants of having "spent their entire lives behind masks."[27] Here Vyshinsky offers a more commonplace, less Hegelian gloss on Bukharin's own confession of a "particular duality of mind." By claiming that the prosecution was tearing off the masks of the defendants, Vyshinsky posits his role as an antitheatrical one. The defendants had been playacting, and the trials would reveal the reality behind their masks. It was this antitheatricality that convinced Feuchtwanger that the trials were not mere "show." The prosecution was evidently so antitheatrical that it did not provide props like signed documents or surveillance transcripts at the trial. Feuchtwanger suggests that this *lack* of evidence during the trials speaks to the authenticity of the trial and its close connection to the Soviet people; as he puts it, "Details of circumstantial evidence, documents, and depositions may interest jurists, criminologists, and historians," but for ordinary citizens, "the plain confessions were more intelligible to them than any amount of ingeniously assembled circumstantial evidence."[28] Feuchtwanger goes on to insist that the whole proceedings were simply too realistic to be fake, that it would be almost impossible to reproduce the trials as theater: "If a producer had had to arrange this court scene, years of rehearsal and careful coaching would have been necessary to get prisoners to correct one another eagerly on small points and to express their emotions with such restraint."[29]

As I suggest at the outset of this chapter, Brecht approaches the question of theatricality in trials very differently than Feuchtwanger. Since trials are always necessarily theatrical, the earnest performance that Feuchtwanger describes smacks of the "swindle" that Brecht sees in psychological realism (the "claim to be 'absolutely natural'" that he rejects in his essay "Popularity and Realism"). Even more important, the "duality of mind" that Bukharin confessed to in his final plea is not a tragic flaw but an integral part of a person's capacity to understand and judge the world around him. In Brecht's theories of acting, it is essential that an actor never fully embodies a role but rather is always able to step outside that role. This understanding of acting applies even to Brecht himself. In 1934, three years before the start of Bukharin's trial, Brecht confided to Benjamin,

I often imagine being interrogated by a tribunal. 'Now tell us, Mr. Brecht, are you really in earnest?' I would have to admit that no, I'm not completely in earnest. But having said 'no' to that important question, I would add something still more important: namely, that my attitude is *permissible*.[30]

The quality of not being completely in earnest is the foundation of epic theater. It is *only* when the actors are not completely in earnest, when they begin to critique their own actions as they act, that they become epic actors. Here Brecht is defending both his theory of acting and his own presentation of self. This sort of masking was a trick that would come in handy for Brecht later, when he was called before the House Un-American Activities Committee, and again when he moved to East Germany.

Brecht's musings about being brought before a tribunal were prophetic. When he was called before the House Un-American Activities Committee in 1947 on suspicion of being a Communist, his line of defense was just as he imagined: he told the committee he was not completely in earnest. In Washington, DC, Brecht took the opposite tack from the one Bukharin had taken in Moscow. While Bukharin confessed to a "duality of mind" as a weakness, Brecht defended himself by giving an account of both his own politics and his work that was too fragmented for the committee to grasp. Brecht's first tactic was to argue that the meanings of literary works and political positions change according to historical circumstance. When investigator Robert Stripling questioned Brecht about his writings in the 1920 and '30s, Brecht responded by contextualizing his revolutionary writings as part of the "fight against Hitler."[31] As the hearing proceeded, Brecht went even further than insisting that his works be read historically; he suggested that they not be read as *his* at all. Brecht claimed that the meaning of his work was predetermined by the source material. When asked to recite his text for the song "In Praise of Learning," Brecht began by saying that the song was an adaptation from a play by Gorky. He told the committee that *The Measures Taken* was an adaptation of an "old religious Japanese play" that "follows quite closely this old story." In answer to all of Stripling's questions about the death of the Young Comrade, Brecht referred him back to the "old Japanese play," disavowing his own authorship of the story's ending. In doing so, Brecht deployed exactly the kind of *List* he had used when first creating the work. The old stories once again became his Trojan horse. In the face of Stripling's incredulity, Brecht insisted that the play was about China and "had nothing to do about Germany."[32]

Stripling then read aloud from the translation of one of Brecht's poems, but Brecht interrupted him, telling him that it was the wrong translation. Stripling tried a different poem, and Brecht insisted that there, too, the meaning had been changed in translation, so much so that it was not his poem at all:

STRIPLING: Did you write that, Mr. Brecht?
BRECHT: No. I wrote a German poem, but that is very different than this.
   (*laughter*)[33]

By the end of the hearing, none of his texts seemed to have any stable meaning. There was no essential political position behind the guises that Brecht presented (an opponent of Hitler, an adapter of old Japanese stories, a poet dismayed by translation errors). The tactic worked; Brecht was not cajoled into naming names while still appearing to cooperate in his own, naïve way. He was dismissed and complimented on his performance by the HUAC chairman: "You did that very well, much better than the others." Brecht did not waste any time in leaving the United States. Four days later he was in Paris, disapproving of André Gide's adaptation of Kafka's *The Trial*.[34] Brecht eventually settled in East Berlin, where he and Helene Weigel were given control of the Berliner Ensemble. It was at the Berliner Ensemble that Brecht premiered his only trial play that focused specifically on postwar arbitration: *The Caucasian Chalk Circle*.

   In both the HUAC hearings and in his essays during the Moscow trials, Brecht juxtaposed the rigidity of text and law with the flexibility of theater as a performed art, claiming that the meaning of his work is impossible to fully pin down. Because each production interprets a play differently, theater avoids the stasis and rigidity of printed novels. In his essay "On the Formalistic Character of the Theory of Realism," Brecht suggests that in order to understand what is at stake in the term "formalism," we look to the everyday uses of the term:

Let us take the expression: *Formally he is right*. That means that actually he is not right. . . . When I read that the autarky of the Third Reich is perfect *on paper* [*auf dem Papier* perfekt ist], then I know that this is a case of political formalism. National Socialism is socialism in form—that is, another case of political formalism. . . . We are then in a position, if we return to literature (without this time abandoning everyday life altogether), to characterize and unmask as formalistic even works which do not elevate literary form over social content and yet do not correspond to reality. We can even unmask [*entlarven*] works which are real-istic in form. There are a great many of them.[35]

Written two months after Bukharin's final plea, this essay responds both to Lukács and (implicitly) to the Moscow trials. Brecht turns the debate on its head to accuse Lukács himself of formalism, of preserving the style of nineteenth-century novels without paying heed to the changes in historical circumstances that demand new representations of reality.[36] For Brecht, "everyday" formalism means being a certain way *on paper*, but not necessar-ily in reality—that is, in text but not in performance. Brecht returns here to the notion of masking. In contrast to the "grotesque masks" through which works like *The Measures Taken* are able to convey the truth, Brecht speaks here of those masks that are outwardly realistic and yet "do not correspond to reality." Without mentioning the Soviet Union, he encourages the reader to think about other political formalisms aside from the National Socialists and to consider not only the disjuncture between the National Socialists on paper and in reality but also the same disjuncture in the Soviet Union.

The emphasis here on medium—*on-paper* realism versus reality—is sig-nificant. Brecht begins the essay by pointing out that Lukács's conception of realism only refers to one particular genre, the novel, and cannot be so easily applied to lyric poetry or drama.[37] Lukács fails to understand the for-mal characteristics of dramatic literature that gains both form and mean-ing on a stage rather than on paper. By emphasizing the difference between *on-paper* socialist realism and social reality, Brecht aligns written literature with mere realism and theater with reality. In "Popularity and Realism," Brecht points to the production of a play (its staging through a rehearsal process) as the process through which meaning is made. The rehearsals are a collaborative process in which the proletariat can engage with and cocre-ate the work. He describes a discussion with a worker during the rehearsal process of *The Measures Taken* and insists on the importance of the work-er's suggestions to the final version of the work, claiming, "The workers were not afraid to teach us, and they themselves were not afraid to learn."[38] For Brecht, Lukács's celebration of individual authorship is at odds with Social-ist production that takes workers into account. Brecht tells Benjamin that Lukács and his supporters are "enemies of production. Production makes them uncomfortable. You never know where you are with production; pro-duction is the unforeseeable. You never know what's going to come out."[39]

Brecht emphasizes that production is open and does not follow predetermined scripts. In their role as a people's court in *The Measures Taken*, workers are taught to see events critically and to interrogate each particular episode, judging whether actions could have been taken that were different than the ones that were actually taken and even advising Brecht to revise his script. Brecht emphasizes that the key to understanding works like *The Measures Taken* lies in the rehearsal and performance process rather than in the written word.

In *All Theatre Is Revolutionary Theatre*, Benjamin Bennett shows that scholars and critics have long linked Brecht's political dogmatism to the literary quality of his theater. Bennett argues against the tendency for "theorists of literary revolution, or literary theorists who are concerned with revolution," including Susan Sontag, Jacques Derrida, and Julia Kristeva, to prize Antonin Artaud as the revolutionary dramatist par excellence at the expense of Brecht, who is seen as "a mere writer among writers" and who stops short of offering Artaud's "radical rejection of the literary *as such*."[40] Bennett's book asks a crucial question: How does drama contain the seeds of revolutionary action? In the case of Brecht, it is through the capacity of a text to be hidden, masked, smuggled, and saved from an oppressive regime for posterity.[41] At the same time, though, a text is not an autonomous, unchanging artifact—writing gains agency only through performance. We can see this in Brecht's staging of his 1944 play *The Caucasian Chalk Circle* in the aftermath of the East German uprising of 1953. In this staging, Brecht foregrounds his own role as the director (rather than the author) in order to demonstrate the importance of adapting and reinterpreting old scripts within new historical contexts. In stressing the importance of interpretation and contemporaneity, Brecht challenges the East German regime's cultural policy and legal authority. But this challenge is not a direct one: it is masked, hidden, and smuggled, begging the question of whether Brecht was, indeed, a revolutionary at all. Brecht teaches us to judge, but how do we judge Brecht?

THE CAUCASIAN CHALK CIRCLE AFTER THE EAST GERMAN WORKERS' UPRISING

The Caucasian Chalk Circle is structured as a play within a play. It begins and ends with scenes of postwar arbitration in the Soviet Union. The story is about a dispute between two nomadic tribes who were displaced during the Second World War. After their claims are arbitrated by an official from the central government, a singer arrives and performs a play with members of one of the tribes. The inner play they perform is about Grusha, a maid who rescues the son of a governor during a revolution. Years later, the biological mother seeks to get the child back in order to claim his inheritance. The two women appear in the court of Azdak, a common criminal turned judge. Azdak orders that they draw a chalk circle on the floor and each try to pull the child out of the circle. When the maid drops the child's hand, refusing to injure him, Azdak gives the child to her. The moral of this story corresponds to the dispute over the valley; just as the biological mother was not the best person to care for the child, the original tribe was not the most suitable tribe to make use of the land.

This story of the chalk circle, though, is only one part of the inside play. The second part is the story of Azdak himself. When we first meet Azdak, he has taken in a beggar, who turns out to be a nobleman fleeing the revolution. Azdak marches to the court to turn himself in for his counterrevolutionary mistake but quickly realizes that (as Brecht puts it in his journal) with the fall of the old masters, it was not a new era that arrived but an era of new masters.[42] The beginning of Azdak's story has certain parallels with *The Measures Taken*: a character with revolutionary ideals inadvertently damages the revolution and willingly asks for judgment, even execution. Whereas in the earlier play, the execution takes place before the play begins and is retroactively justified by the agitators before the court, in *The Caucasian Chalk Circle*, the man who has acted against the revolution not only lives but because he lives and, crucially, because he gives up on the ideals of the revolution, is able to oversee "a golden time, of something close to justice."[43] Whereas the revolution of *The Measures Taken* has only just begun, the revolution of the inner play of *The Caucasian Chalk Circle* is portrayed as a disappointment from the very beginning. Both plays subvert the expectations of tragic or comic dramatic arcs. In *The Measures Taken*, individual tragedy (the death of the Young Comrade) is necessary to save the possibility of a happy ending (the Communist revolution), though Brecht leaves open the possibility that the sacrifice was in vain. In *The Caucasian Chalk Circle*, it is because of world-historical tragedy (the failure of the revolution) that Azdak and Grusha can have their own happy endings.

This disjuncture emphasizes contingency; if a play need not follow narrative genres, neither does action or history.

Brecht wrote *The Caucasian Chalk Circle* in anticipation of Nazi Germany's defeat, and he chose to premiere it in East Berlin a year after the failed June 17 workers' uprising of 1953.[44] The uprising began as a workers' strike in East Berlin and quickly escalated to insurrection across the German Democratic Republic (GDR). Protestors gained control of radio stations, public buildings, police stations, and prisons. Propaganda was stripped from the walls of public spaces; children threw Russian textbooks out of school windows. The uprising was only quelled through brutal repression and the help of the Soviet army.[45] The play's themes of postwar arbitration and failed revolution were perhaps even more timely in 1954, when Brecht produced the play, than when he had written it ten years before. Although Brecht displaces the disillusion of "a time of new rulers" to the age of imperial Russia, Azdak unmistakably reflects disappointment in the GDR regime. Brecht connects Azdak's experience with those of German leftists. He writes that roles such as Azdak's needed particular actors, in this case Ernst Busch, whose "entire life, from the childhood in proletarian hamburg through the struggles in the weimar republic and in the spanish civil war, through the bitter experiences after '45 were necessary to bring forth this azdak [sic]."[46] Understanding Azdak's disappointment required the experience of a German political exile who had been a Communist Party member in the Weimar Republic and who was bitterly disappointed by the new Communist society.

Just as Azdak is disabused of his hopes for a new, just society, a fat prince arrives with his nephew, whom he hopes to install as the new judge. The soldiers who are guarding the court ask Azdak for his opinion. Azdak explains to the soldiers that judgment is a question of formalized procedure and convention rather than individual reason or morality. He tells them, "A judge's robe and hat are better able to pass a judgment by themselves than a person could without those things."[47] Azdak then suggests that they stage a practice trial with the nephew as judge to test him out. In the practice trial—*People of Georgia v. the Grand Duke*—Azdak plays the role of the grand duke on trial for waging aggressive war. In the role of the grand duke, Azdak rejects the accusation that he is responsible for the failed war with Persia. He blames the war on the lesser nobility (that is, the fat prince himself) for their greedy acquisition of government contracts for soldiers and arms. The fat prince quickly forgets that it is only a "show" trial and loses his temper.

This scene is parenthetical to the play's central narrative. In 1944 the scene—with its clear reference to the war crimes of World War II—shows that trials, and postwar trials in particular, may be theatrical and yet still provide a necessary forum for public dialogue. Although Azdak begins by voicing an antitheatrical skepticism about trials (it is only about props and costumes), he ultimately shows that even a play trial can have real consequences. Azdak convinces the soldiers of the true causes of the war, and he is elected judge instead of the nephew. Soon thereafter, we see the fat prince's head go by on a stake. In 1954 East Berlin, the reference to postrevolutionary trials can also be understood in connection to the GDR's judicial system and the arrests and trials of participants in the 1953 uprising. Although most accounts of the 1953 uprising point to increased work quotas and decreased pay as its primary cause, anger at political repression and harsh sentencing of minor crimes was also a driving force behind the protests.[48] Alongside their material demands, workers quickly began to challenge the regime

FIGURE 2.1. Courtroom scene, *The Caucasian Chalk Circle* (1954). Photo by Gerda Goedhart. Courtesy of Suhrkamp Publishers and the Bertolt Brecht Archive, Berlin.

more fundamentally, insisting on free elections and new leaders. In cities across the GDR, the demonstrators' main targets were police stations, courthouses, and prisons. Between June 16 and 20, there were protests in front of over sixty prisons, and protestors stormed dozens of prisons, detention centers, and courthouses, freeing around fourteen hundred prisoners.[49]

One of the strongest images of the 1954 production is of the courtroom when Azdak enters immediately after the revolution. The former judge is dangling from the gallows directly in the middle of the stage. The image conjures the violent attacks on judges and public prosecutors during the uprising and reflects its carnivalesque reversals in which people came to prosecute and judge their prosecutors and judges. One of the first memoirs to be published about the uprising recounts a judgment scene from the small city of Brandenburg. On the morning of June 17, workers occupied a building containing both the prison and court and released thirty political prisoners from their cells. The "people's judge," Harry Benkendorf—infamous for his harsh sentencing—was seen through the window of the building. He hid, and when found, he begged to be locked in a cell as protection from the protestors. The protestors, however, dragged both the judge and the public prosecutor to the city's marketplace in handcuffs, violently beat them, and then put them on a raised tribune normally reserved for ceremonial occasions and visits from political dignitaries. As the two badly beaten men stood on this stage, five thousand protestors interrogated them about their unjust prosecutions and rulings. The judge used the same defense as the fat prince in *The Caucasian Chalk Circle* (and indeed the Nuremberg defendants): he claimed that he was "in duty bound to act according to instructions from superiors." The crowd demanded that both the judge and prosecutor be hanged, but this proved unnecessary as both died of their injuries.[50]

Azdak embodies this carnivalesque practice of judgment. He is a common criminal who has been made judge for the day. He goes almost naked under his robes and metes out seemingly arbitrary justice. He makes a show of sitting on his law books, singing and leering at female defendants. Azdak is a bad judge. He is full of prejudices, he is selfish, and he asks defendants for sexual favors and bribes. He eschews the rules and rational categories of the law, and in order to emphasize this to the audience, Brecht makes him "the most degenerate of judges."[51] Yet he provides the protection of the law to those who need it most. Azdak is what Weber classifies as a "kadi" judge, one who stands outside a bureaucratized system of justice. Instead of following a law's code to the letter, kadi justice is a form of charismatic authority that follows the schema, "It is written. . . . But I say unto you."[52] King Solomon is the prototypical kadi judge; indeed the *Chalk Circle* parable is a version of Solomon's judgment from the Bible. It is because he abandons the letter of the law that Azdak is able to help the poor through his judgments. In Weber's analysis, the practice of ethical (rather than formal) justice embodied by a kadi judge has an ambivalent relationship to democracy. On the one hand, democracy is predicated on equality before the law and freedom from arbitrary rulings. On the other hand, Weber argues that the masses might themselves take up a stance on a particular individual (or question) that is opposed to formal adjudication and equality. The poor are not served by formal equality before the law or the rational adjudication demanded by bourgeois interests. Rather, the poor can only be compensated for their limited "economic and social life opportunities in the face of the propertied classes" insofar as "justice and administration . . . assume an informal character to a far-reaching extent. It must be informal because it is substantively 'ethical.' "[53]

Azdak is not the first kadi judge to make an appearance in German drama: his forbear is the judge within the ring parable of Lessing's *Nathan the Wise*, who does not issue a legal judgment over which brother has the right to inherit their father's property but rather issues an ethical judgment about the way that they should lead their lives and a philosophical judgment on the nature of truth. When Arendt analyzes *Nathan the Wise* in her acceptance speech for the Lessing Prize (discussed in the previous chapter), she is primarily concerned with the implications of his philosophical judgment: if all people were to agree on a single truth, we would lose the human plurality that creates the world. For Arendt, then, the kadi judge offers a model of judgment akin to aesthetic judgment, one that focuses on particulars and affirms the multiplicity of truths and positions instead of applying a single rule to every situation. In other words, the kadi judge, for Arendt, can issue the sort of judgments that constitute the public realm. For Brecht and Weber, by contrast, the kadi judge is a figure who ensures social and economic justice. Brecht's understanding of justice, as opposed to Arendt's notion of aesthetic judgment, follows the same lines as his and Weber's understanding of kadi judgment: it is concerned primarily with addressing and rectifying the inequality of material conditions.

The problems of economic injustice were foremost in Brecht's writings during his time in the Weimar Republic and when he wrote *The Caucasian Chalk Circle* in the United States. In postwar East Germany, though, the failure of democracy and of the rule of law under "real existing socialism" added a new level to Brecht's understanding of justice, moving from economic justice to what I call poetic justice: justice that takes economic inequality into account (and thus affirms the ideology of the GDR), while also addressing the shortcomings of a merely economic notion of justice and the GDR's legal system. In a program essay for the 1954 production, Brecht's longtime collaborator Elisabeth Hauptmann asks the most pressing question of the play: "Must judges be this way? Is justice always against the law?" The essay, like the play, displaces this tension to Azdak's feudal realm, but in the wake of attacks on judges in the streets, the contemporary relevance is clear. Hauptmann describes how Azdak, despite being protected by the oppressive new regime, uses his power as a judge against the interests of the new regime and for the poor and oppressed. How, Hauptmann asks, "can [Azdak] distribute justice in a society where injustice is legal?"[54] The question brings a central problem of post–World War II trials together with the challenges of the 1954 uprising: How do we judge the judges? And what does personal responsibility mean under dictatorship?

These are, of course, the same questions that we must ask about Brecht himself. Azdak, after all, stages his trials much like Brecht stages his plays. Just like in Brecht's panopticon theater, Azdak always tries two cases at once and will conflate the two cases in his judgment. Azdak is, as the Russian writer Ossip Brick described Brecht, "an adept and cunning casuist,"[55] who rejects universal laws and instead delves into the complexities of individual historically and socially situated cases that have no simple resolution. By framing the story of Azdak within Soviet postwar arbitrations, Brecht reveals how the kadi judge of a folkloric past might be resurrected in a contemporary socialist country. If ethical justice falls within the purview of a kadi judge in the inner play, it is the singer—not the party bureaucrat—who enacts ethical justice in the postwar world of the play's frame. Brecht stages this transformation by casting Ernst Busch both in the role of the singer of the outside narrative and as Azdak (suggesting that the kadi judge of feudal regimes will become the singer of Soviet ones).

There are two ways to read Azdak's transformation into the Soviet singer (and by extension, into Brecht himself). We might say that Brecht

FIGURE 2.2. Ernst Busch as the singer in the prologue of *The Caucasian Chalk Circle*. Courtesy of the Bertolt Brecht Archive, Berlin.

is offering his services to the GDR regime, demonstrating how his theater can work with the regime to stem dissatisfaction with the undemocratic legal decisions of the government. But it is also possible to read this transformation as a criticism of the GDR: Brecht's theater is the only true judicial institution in a land where injustice is legal. The trial format of the play allows Brecht to have it both ways. Brecht's theoretical writings and *The Measures Taken* may suggest that the trial format is for the benefit of the audience—a didactic practice that will help them to think critically. But *The Caucasian Chalk Circle* reveals how the trial format of a play is of greatest benefit to Brecht himself, allowing him to evade the critical position that he seeks to instill in his audience when it comes to the GDR. In *The Caucasian Chalk Circle*, Brecht enacts his fantasy of being brought before a tribunal. And, of course, he stages the trial to issue the verdict he desires: that not being completely in earnest is permissible.

Brecht turned the rehearsal process of *The Caucasian Chalk Circle* into a sort of learning play. Brecht's rehearsals at the Berliner Ensemble were open to members of the public, including students, journalists, interns, and visiting actors. There were 125 days of rehearsal for *The Caucasian Chalk Circle*, and these rehearsals were themselves performances, opportunities for Brecht to play himself—to show what a director is and how a director interprets a script, highlighting that it is the director's interpretation and not the playwright's intention that gives the play meaning (even when they are the same person).[56] During the rehearsal process, Hans-Joachim Bunge, a dramaturge at the Berliner Ensemble, kept a detailed diary in which the tension between text and authorial intentions and the stage director's interpretation appears again and again. In the diary, Bunge seems rather confused about stage-director Brecht's subordination of both playwright Brecht and theorist Brecht. As a good dramaturge, Bunge had closely read the play and Brecht's theoretical writings and seemed dismayed at how quickly Brecht dismissed this sort of dramaturgical work, commenting sarcastically, "The playwright had, incidentally, stipulated [certain things], but this was not taken into account during the staging."[57] As in his conversations with Benjamin, Brecht still believed that production was an unpredictable endeavor: "We want to begin now, and then see how everything develops," he told the cast.[58] At times Bunge remarks on how little Brecht the director remembered about the intentions of the author. In the evening after the first day of rehearsals, a coworker brought Brecht a note he had written about *The Caucasian Chalk Circle* years before, discussing the ways in which the play is not a parable.

BRECHT: Yeah, so what?
WORKER: This morning you said in your introduction: "The play is a parable!"
BRECHT: Did I say it was a parable? Really? Well, naturally that was wrong . . . let's set the parable aside.[59]

As the rehearsals continued, Bunge remarks, "Brecht seems to have forgotten that he wrote the play himself," giving an example from a particular staging question in one of Azdak's scenes. It was unclear from the stage directions when the lawyers were supposed to hand their bribes to Azdak. Brecht asked Busch what he thought, and Busch replied, laughing, "I don't know that. I'm not the poet." To this, Brecht answered, "You can't always turn to the poet."[60] While staging the trial scenes, Brecht urged the actors to consider the relationship between text and performance in both a law court and in the theater. Strikingly for a playwright, Brecht was eager to dismiss all the various sorts of texts that are presented in these scenes. The books that appear onstage are always counterrevolutionary. Only the expensive lawyers write and then memorize their speeches. Instead of consulting the law books, Azdak sits on them. Azdak's good judgments are not given in spite of his sitting on the law books but *because* he sits on the law books and departs from the letter of the law. In one scene, Azdak and his assistant, Schauwa, sing a subversive song together. Busch suggested that Schauwa should read the text of the song while singing to show that he is learning the song as he sings. Brecht hated the idea:

BRECHT: No, he can't do that, he [Schauwa] is too inexperienced in reading and writing.

BUSCH: Of course he knows how to read and write. He's transcribing the cases for me.

BRECHT: Yes—but this here is an illegal song. You don't let it out of your hands.

BUSCH: But Azdak says: "Don't be scared, you can listen, it has a popular refrain!"

BRECHT: Yes—but why should you write it down then?[61]

In subsequent rehearsals, Schauwa would learn the song by listening to it rather than by reading the book. Although Schauwa transcribes cases from the oral speeches in the court, he cannot learn a subversive song from a book.

In his staging, Brecht is concerned with three different conceptions of *form*. First is the *art form* of theater as an art whose meaning is created through staging rather than written text. Second is *formal law*, in Weber's sense, as rational, codified law (as opposed to informal, ethical justice). And third is *formalism* as Brecht defines it against Lukács—as a preoccupation with an outwardly realistic style over commitment to reality (that is, socialist realism). Brecht's staging collapses these three concepts of form to create a binary between written text/codified law/socialist realism and staging/ethical justice/social reality.

The Caucasian Chalk Circle premiered at a moment when East German cultural policy had turned away from the relative artistic freedom of its early years and toward a consolidation of party control over artists and writers. In 1948 a series of articles published in the *Tägliche Rundschau* (the paper of the Soviet Occupation Forces and second most widely circulating East

German paper at the time) inaugurated a second round of debates on formalism and realism.[62] The attacks on formal experimentation, carried out in part by party functionaries, drew heavily on the same terms that National Socialists had used to condemn contemporary art—*entartet* (degenerate) and *volksfeindlich* (hostile to the people)—and aimed to bring the arts under party control and to align the cultural policy of the GDR more closely with that of the Soviet Union. These aims were realized in 1951 at the Fifth Congress of the Central Committee of the Socialist Unity Party (Sozialistische Einheitspartei Deutschlands or SED, East Germany's single party), which issued a resolution bringing all arts under the control of the party and laying the groundwork for the Staatliche Kommission für Kunstangelegenheiten (State Arts Commission, abbreviated as Stakuko). Brecht himself was a target of attacks on formalism from 1948 on. In 1953, Stakuko hosted a conference on Stanislavski that was conceived as a direct rebuke of Brecht's epic theater.[63] Brecht faced the party's condemnation and censorship of works like *The Mother* and *The Trial of Lucullus*. As Brecht rehearsed for *The Caucasian Chalk Circle*, he was simultaneously trying to gather support from other artists and allies to shut down Stakuko. The premiere of *The Caucasian Chalk Circle* revealed a moment of deep division between GDR cultural policy and GDR audiences: the premiere was greeted with over fifty curtain calls from the audience while it was condemned as a failure in the press.[64]

The program book of the *Caucasian Chalk Circle* served as a platform for the Berliner Ensemble to engage in the formalism debates. But it does so obliquely and with *List*—not by defending Brecht but by defending Pablo Picasso. Since 1949, the Berliner Ensemble had used Picasso's "Dove of Peace," designed for the Paris International Peace Conference, as its emblem. When the ensemble moved into the Theater am Schiffbauerdam in 1954, they displayed the *Dove of Peace* on the front curtain, and for their 1954 season-opening poster, they used the image from the scarf Picasso had designed for the World Festival of Youth in East Berlin in 1951.[65] The scarf's famous design features a dove surrounded by faces representing four races, and on the edge the phrase "peace for all peoples" is written in multiple languages. At once a Communist and a modernist, Picasso had long been a contentious figure in the GDR. In the early years of the GDR (1946–48), Picasso was praised in the East German press for his political engagements. But in an article that launched the GDR attacks on formalism, Alexander

Dymschitz—one of the very same bureaucrats who obsequiously recruited Brecht back to the GDR—targets Picasso in particular, calling him the "idol of Western-European formalism."[66] Yet Dymschitz has to account for the seeming contradiction between Picasso's formalism and his Communism. Picasso's art, Dymschitz claims, is at odds with his politics: "The tragic character of creative opposition between the fighter Picasso and the artist Picasso should serve as a first warning for the uncritical imitators of Picasso."[67] Picasso's tragedy demonstrated that artists—even those who were Communists—could seriously err in their art and presumably needed strong guidance. By bringing art under party control, the SED could prevent tragedies like that of Picasso.

Picasso-Plakat im Meinungsstreit

THEATER *dienst* vom 3. April 1954

Eröffnungsplakat des BERLINER ENSEMBLES am Schiffbauerdamm mit einem Motiv von Picasso und den Worten "Friede allen Völkern" in den wichtigsten Weltsprachen. Dieses Plakat ist zum Anschlag auf den S-Bahn-Stationen der Westsektoren nicht zugelassen worden, da auf dem Plakat eine Friedenstaube zu sehen ist. Das ist also die Freiheit der "freien Welt"!

BZ am Abend vom 3. April 1954

Das "BERLINER ENSEMBLE" Helene Weigels ist uns allen zu einem Begriff bester Schauspielkunst geworden. Wenn man sich jedoch sein neues Plakat anschaut, kann man nur kopfschüttelnd sagen: "Ich weiß nicht, was soll es bedeuten." Diese vier halben Gesichter in einem bunten Durcheinander verschiedener Farben haben meines Erachtens nach keine Beziehung zu dem Schaffen des Ensembles. Was meinen die anderen Leser, und was meint vor allem Helene Weigel selbst dazu? Horst Jacob, Lichtenberg

Das umstrittene Plakat bedeutet: Die vier halben Gesichter sind die vier Menschenrassen, die auf der Erde leben. Die Friedenstaube von Picasso soll alle Menschen in Frieden verbinden. Das ist Sinn und Zweck der Arbeit des "BERLINER ENSEMBLES". So denke ich mir das. Und ich glaube, ich habe recht.

Willy Klauke, C 2

An die "Berliner Zeitung"

Als ich vor einigen Tagen auf meiner täglichen Fahrt in die Stadt auf meiner S-Bahnstation ein sehr formalistisches Plakat sah, mußte ich an die Entwicklung unserer Kunstschaffenden in der Deutschen Demokratischen Republik denken, die einen harten, aber auch erfolgreichen Kampf um eine neue, gesunde, realistische Gestaltung geführt haben. Ich selbst habe 1947 bis 1950 an einer Kunsthochschule studiert und habe mich intensiv mit diesen Problemen auseinander gesetzt. Du glaubst nicht, Bärchen, wie groß mein Erstaunen war, als ich gestern feststellen mußte, daß dieses Plakat, nicht, wie ich annahm, ein westliches Produkt war, sondern das Symbol des BERLINER ENSEMBLES, das von dem bekannten französischen Maler Picasso entworfen wurde. Mir ist bekannt, daß der Maler Picasso ein fortschrittlicher Mensch ist und ich schätze ihn als Friedenskämpfer. Dennoch

Willkommen beim

BERLINER ENSEMBLE

am Schiffbauerdamm

vi kvinder

Liebe Kollegen vom Berliner Ensemble!

Habt Ihr genug von den schönen Picasso-Plakaten? Wenn Ihr uns welche überlassen könntet, könnten wir sie für 10 Kronen das Stück verkaufen und so Geld für unsere Friedensarbeit beschaffen. Mit vielen Grüßen und Dank für die guten Theaterabende, welche die Delegation des Friedensrates im Berliner Ensemble verbracht hat. Erna Watson, Redaktion "Wir Frauen"

FIGURE 2.3. The Picasso debate in the program of *The Caucasian Chalk Circle*. Courtesy of the Bertolt Brecht Archive, Berlin.

The Berliner Ensemble's decision to use Picasso's images as their emblem and on their season-opening poster directly challenged official cultural policy. The program book for *The Caucasian Chalk Circle* reprinted this poster as well as material related to the controversy it occasioned. The program features a letter to the *Berliner Zeitung* written by Inge Schmidt-Tewes from the *Zentralhaus der Jungen Pioniere* (Central Headquarters of the Young Pioneers) that condemns the Berliner Ensemble's use of a formalist like Picasso. Schmidt-Tewes writes that she "cannot understand why such a poster would be used as a signboard for a progressive theatre." Newspaper articles, also reprinted in the program, defend the poster by claiming that the poster is forbidden in the subway stations in West Berlin because of the West's fear of the poster's message of peace. For good measure, the program also includes stories about Picasso that showcase his anti-Fascist credentials.[68]

The Caucasian Chalk Circle is at once about legal arbitration (formal versus ethical justice) and about aesthetic policy (socialist realism versus epic theater). The staging linked formal arbitration to socialist realism and ethical justice to epic theater through the respective backdrops of the outside frame and inside story. The backdrop of the prologue looked rather unepic, portraying a mountain range of the Caucasus in a socialist realist style. The backdrops of the inside play provided a sharp contrast to this socialist realist style: the image of the city on the backdrop was, in fact, almost cubist. Through these two backdrops, Brecht emphatically connected and juxtaposed the socialist realism of the party (connected to formal law) with his own epic theater (connected to ethical justice). As an epic actor, Ernst Busch portrayed the character of the singer while also presenting his own attitude and carrying with him his own biography. In other words, the figure onstage was both a Soviet singer and the actor Ernst Busch, whom the SED had removed from his own publishing house in 1948, accusing him of "sectarian, proletkult tendencies and right-wing opportunism."[69]

An essay in the program, "Realism and Stylization" (signed simply "b."), attacks the principles of socialist realism and reiterates the claims of Brecht's unpublished articles against Lukács. Here Brecht does not use the word "formalism" but instead "stylization," arguing that purportedly realist artists have distanced themselves from "the unique, particular, contradictory, coincidental," and instead simply imitate other styles. They end up presenting not reality but rather "copies of copies." The program slyly demonstrates what a "copy of a copy" might look like. The program features a reprint of a propaganda photograph of a Caucasian village from the Soviet Union. The socialist realist backdrop of the prologue was almost a copy of this propaganda photograph. In contrast, Brecht concludes "Realism and Stylization" with the suggestion that the actor playing Katja Grusha should study the beauty of Pieter Bruegel's *Tolle Grete* and includes an image of the painting. The inclusion of this painting sharply differentiates the techniques of epic theater from the "stylization methods" that would produce a copy of a copy. It is clear that the actor cannot simply mimic the painting but must instead study and interpret it before using it as inspiration for a performance.

FIGURE 2.4. Propaganda photo in the program of *The Caucasian Chalk Circle*. Courtesy of the Bertolt Brecht Archive, Berlin.

Following the uprising, the relationship between artists and the government became a source of greater unease for Brecht. Immediately after the uprising, Brecht wrote a notorious note to the leader of the GDR, Walter Ulbricht, stating,

History will respect the revolutionary impatience of the Socialist Unity Party of Germany. The great debate with the masses about the rhythm of socialist construction will help to inspect and secure our socialist achievements. It is necessary for me, at this moment, to articulate to you my solidarity with the Socialist Unity Party of Germany.[70]

The final sentence of this letter was reprinted in the SED newspaper *Neues Deutschland*. While offering the regime this public statement of solidarity, Brecht also wrote a seemingly critical poem about the collusion of artists with repression. The poem "The Solution" begins,

> After the uprising of the 17th June
> The Secretary of the Writers Union
> Had leaflets distributed in the Stalinallee.

The leaflets encouraged workers to win back the confidence of the party after the uprising by increasing their productivity. The poem concludes,

> Would it not be easier
> In that case for the government
> To dissolve the people
> And elect another?[71]

Here Brecht does not explicitly condemn the party or the government for its actions on June 17, but he does mock the Writers Union for speaking in the language of the party. The Writers Union evidently no longer produces literature, according to Brecht, but instead writes propaganda flyers. While internal party memoranda suggest that the intelligentsia for the most part supported the regime during the uprising, a report by the top Soviet officials in Berlin recorded demands for greater artistic freedom: "Among workers in art, an aspiration is noted to review the earlier decision of the party on the question of art, and under the banner of 'creative freedom' to liquidate any party and state leadership in the area of art and literature and to give freedom to formalistic trends."[72]

The framing structure of *The Caucasian Chalk Circle* demonstrates Brecht's ideal of the proper relationship between artists and bureaucrats. The story of Grusha is told to legitimate the formal arbitration of the prologue. The final scene returns to the frame of postwar arbitration, and the singer concludes by telling his audience,

> What is there should belong to those that are good for it, so
> The children to the motherly, so that they thrive
> The wagons to the good drivers, so that they are driven well
> And the valley to the irrigators, so that it bears fruit.[73]

By recounting the story of the chalk circle, the singer helps to lay a foundation for the new, Soviet society. The singer does not tell the tribes anything they don't already know; in fact, the displaced tribe concedes its rights to the valley before the song even begins. Yet the story is still necessary. From the beginning, it is clear that the dispute cannot be adequately settled through purely rational considerations. The government official articulates this difficulty:

THE OFFICIAL: Comrades, why does one love one's homeland? Because: the bread tastes better there, the sky is higher, the air is fresher, voices sound more powerful there, the ground is easier to tread there. . . . It is correct that we must see a piece of land as a tool, with which once can produce something useful, but it is also true that we must recognize love of a particular piece of land.[74]

The dispute cannot be easily solved through rational application of the law because the feeling of a homeland defies rational calculation: the sky is higher there, the ground easier to tread. Resolving the dispute requires more than a party bureaucrat. It requires a singer. While Azdak is a figure of ethical justice in the inside narrative, Brecht is very clear that he is not a model to emulate in the present. For all his mistrust of party bureaucrats, Brecht is not advocating a nostalgic return to traditional modes of authority. Instead, Brecht stages justice as a collaboration between two complementary figures: the government official who adjudicates rationally and the singer who is able to reconcile opposing sides poetically.

The singer and the official represent two separate modes of authority, each crucial to constituting a new postwar society. Upon first mention of the singer, one of the tribesmen suggests to the official that the government should ensure access to singers:

THE OLD MAN, LEFT: You in the planning commission should take care that he comes to the North more often, Comrade.

THE OFFICIAL: We are actually more concerned with the economy.

THE OLD MAN, LEFT: (*smiling*) You bring order to the redistribution of grape-vines and tractors, why not of songs?[75]

The old man suggests that songs are as important a part of the new soci-ety as grapevines and tractors. Here the government official and singer appear to work in close collaboration. But can we reconcile this collabora-tionism with Brecht's revolutionary theories of theater? When the purpose of theater is to provide support for the regime by speaking to the emotions of individuals, it starts to sound a lot like the Aristotelian theater that Brecht so harshly condemned.

In the prologue and epilogue, Brecht seems to be making a plea directly to the SED about the usefulness of his theater to their regime. The program even includes a request for the government to allocate more resources to the theater. In a statement in the program entitled "Difficulties with Mate-rials," the costume designer Kurt Palm describes the difficulties of work-ing with the cheap materials available to the theater. Echoing the old villager who requests that the central planning commission pay more attention to the distribution not only of grapevines and tractors but also of songs, Palm's purpose is to "draw the attention of public authorities to a problem that remains partly unsolved," that is, the distribution of quality fabric to the-aters.[76] The program supports its plea by demonstrating how the theater can supplement the efforts of the government (as the singer does with his song). Even this complaint about the lack of material resources is couched in ingra-tiating euphemism: the problem is only "partly unsolved."

Brecht promotes artistic freedom on two levels: first, the freedom of an artist vis-à-vis the government and, second, the freedom of a director vis-à-vis the text. But this freedom has its limits on both levels. The program uses Picasso to show that in order to best support the party, theater needs its artistic freedom. The program does not stress the importance of artistic freedom for its own sake but instead claims that Picasso's poster is useful to East Germany because West Berlin is afraid of its promotion of peace. The message of the program is clear: party bureaucrats must give artists their freedom if they want the artists to do their job supporting the regime. The artistic freedom of a director to interpret a play also has its limits. The *Caucasian Chalk Circle* was one of many plays for which Brecht created a "model book." These books, composed of photographs from each scene and notes on body postures, movements, directorial instructions, suggestions, and conversations from the rehearsal process, were designed to help stage revivals at the Berliner Ensemble and were also lent to other theaters to aid their rehearsal processes. While Brecht was so ostentatious about bucking the authority of the play's author during rehearsals, he was simultaneously creating a model book that would offer other theaters the authoritative staging of the work. Despite director Brecht's downplaying of playwright Brecht and theorist Brecht, it was still all Brecht all the time. The model books suggest that when it came to a different director interpreting one of Brecht's plays, Brecht might have seen the relationship between playwright and director somewhat differently. In such cases, the other directors would be beholden not only to the script but also to its exegesis at the Berliner Ensemble.

Although Brecht's essays on formalism emphasized production as an unpredictable process, that does not mean that he saw staging as a democratic process. The 1954 program features a blurb about the rehearsals entitled "With Astonished Eyes," attributed to a journalist ("W. G.") who claims to have known nothing about theater before sitting in on rehearsals for *The Caucasian Chalk Circle*. W. G. describes with astonishment, "In this theatre, everyone is allowed to join the conversation. The actors make all sorts of recommendations to the director. The director is all ears, and praises the suggestions a great deal. But then, it is done how the director wants." A democracy this certainly is not, the journalist ends ironically: "In constitutional law, one would call this the separation of powers."[77] This "separation of powers" sounds a lot like the arbitration in the prologue of the story: all the villagers know before the hearing begins that the decision has already been reached by the central government. But they are still allowed to make their recommendations. The dramaturge's notes on the rehearsal tell how Brecht conveyed the principle of arbitration between the tribes: "Everyone knows the decision from the start, but it first needs to be found."[78] Brecht's rehearsals mirrored the arbitration of the prologue (everyone can give his or her input even though the conclusion is predetermined) as well as the "separation of powers" in the GDR (the people voluntarily vote to accept decisions already made by the government). The blurb makes this connection clear and asks audiences to compare the false democracy of Brecht's staging process with the false democracy of the GDR.

Did the journalist W. G. actually exist? The W. G. blurb might have come from a journalist with a critique of Brecht and GDR policy, or it could have been Hauptmann's own dig at Brecht, challenging his authoritarian and patriarchal control over the theater. Or is it possible that W. G. was, in fact, Brecht himself, encouraging his audiences to critique his own rehearsal process? If W. G. was just one more of Brecht's masks, we might think about the entire rehearsal process as an exercise in estrangement. Brecht the director and Brecht the poet were just masks that Brecht put on in order to smuggle a disturbing truth to the audiences: it was not only socialist realist art but also epic theater that served as a handmaiden to the regime. Might Hauptmann, Brecht, Bunge, or one of the other house dramaturges have been estranging epic theater itself?

BRECHT ON TRIAL

Brecht's relationship to the East German regime is not only a subject of critical dispute but has also become the subject matter of plays, including Frank Castorf's *Die Maßnahme/Mauser* (Volksbühne am Rosa-Luxemburg Platz Berlin, 2008) and Günter Grass's 1966 play *The Plebeians Rehearse the Uprising*. In *The Plebeians Rehearse the Uprising*, Brecht (referred to only as Boss) is rehearsing his adaptation of Shakespeare's *Coriolanus* when workers burst in from the street. They ask him to sign a document in support of the uprising. Instead of taking the side of the workers, though, the Boss uses them to help him stage the plebeian uprising in the play. He records them and steals their slogans to put onstage. Refusing to help them politically, he turns their struggle into theater. The first acts of the play suggest that Brecht's practice of staging and his use of estrangement are tools to distance himself from current political contention and from his own personal responsibility. The actress playing Volumina, who has a penchant for revising and deploying her old lines, tells the Boss: "There's too much method in your method."[79]

In the final act of Grass's play, the revolution has been suppressed, and a party functionary comes to demand a statement of solidarity with the SED. The Boss writes a letter that so disgusts Volumina that the audience never gets to hear it:

VOLUMINA: Why read this pussyfooting document aloud? Three succinct paragraphs. The first two are critical; you say the measures taken by the government, in other words the Party, were premature. In the third and last something makes you proclaim your solidarity with the same people you attacked in the first two. . . . They'll cross out the critical paragraphs and trumpet the solidarity until you die of shame.[80]

This is the very letter that Brecht did write. Indeed, only the final sentence of solidarity was printed in Brecht's lifetime, but the full letter was finally printed in *Theater Heute* in 1965. The Boss knows the full statement will eventually be published and assures his friends that he has a carbon copy of the letter. For his assistant, this is not enough: "Those things are locked up in archives; they get published with your posthumous papers when it's too late." The Boss knows this well, but he is looking to the future to judge. He sends his carbon copies and unpublished essays to the archives, dreaming that his case will be tried again and again. Grass suggests in his play, though, that this is not enough and that Brecht has turned his theater into a reactionary force.

In her essay "What Is Permitted to Jove," Arendt argues that Brecht "offers a kind of case history of the uncertain relationship between poetry and politics." The case of poets like Brecht "concerns all of us, not only critics and scholars; it concerns us in our private lives and also insofar as we are citizens."[81] Arendt's essay is about the difficulty of judging poets. She takes the title of her essay from the phrase "What is permitted to Jove is not permitted to an ox," suggesting her own affinity with Brecht's "casuistry," the argument that judgment and forgiveness must take place on a case-by-case basis. She starts with a key problem: What do we do with poets who write beautifully but lend their support to barbaric politics? This question gets to the heart of what it means to judge action and art in terms of virtuosity rather than morality. Arendt does not want to claim that aesthetic judgment incorporates moral judgment (that is, that poetry praising outrage is bad poetry because it is morally wrong). But she also cannot abide

the thought that praise of totalitarianism within poetry should escape condemnation. As she puts it, "A poet is to be judged by his poetry, and while
much is permitted him, it is not true that 'those who praise the outrage have
fine-sounding voices.'"[82] To explain how we can judge poetry aesthetically
rather than morally, she makes a curious claim: that poets who "praise outrage in their poems" will lose their gift of poetry. According to Arendt, Brecht
ceased to write in the final years of his life as punishment for what she saw
as his dogmatic support of Soviet policies from the 1920s until his death.
But who made this judgment against Brecht and issued this punishment?
Arendt stages a deus ex machina. Apollo enters the essay, and he is the one
who doles out the punishment: "The faculty of writing a good line is not
entirely at the poet's command but needs some help. . . . [T]he faculty is
granted him and he can forfeit it." Brecht lives not under the laws of the rest
of us but "under the laws of Apollo."[83] These laws are in some sense more
permissive than ours, but if the poets sin gravely enough, they are deprived
of their "divine gift." Worse writers than Brecht can sin without being
punished by a loss of talent, because "no god leaned over their cradle, [and
therefore] no god will take revenge."[84]

Arendt points to *The Measures Taken*, which she calls Brecht's only truly
Communist play, as the moment in which he praised the outrage and
"sinned." Although Brecht wrote the play before the Moscow trials, Arendt
argues that it was written just after Stalin had announced the beginning of
the liquidation of the old guard of the Bolsheviks during the Sixteenth
Congress of the All-Union Communist Party: "Brecht felt that what the
Party needed right then was a defense of killing one's own comrades and
innocent people." In her essay, Arendt gives the year of the Sixteenth Congress as 1929, but in fact, it took place in the summer of 1930. This slip in
chronology is very significant: Brecht began the first version of *The Measures Taken* in February of 1930 before—not after, as Arendt claims—the
beginning of the liquidation of the old guard. Even though Arendt incor-
rectly reads the play as a supportive response to Stalin's policies, she argues
that it is not a bad play. On the contrary, in *The Measure Taken*, Brecht "had
done what poets will always do if they are left alone: He had announced
the truth to the extent that this truth had become visible."[85] Notwithstand-
ing the intentions that Arendt imputes to Brecht here, the party hated the
play for speaking the truth, and so Brecht's "poetic luck" did not leave him
just then. Arendt describes watching *The Life of Galileo* twice, first in New

York and later in East Berlin, where "every line rang out like an open declaration of war against the regime and was understood as such." Like *The
Measures Taken*, *Galileo* spoke the truth against the party, even if that was
not Brecht's original intention.[86]

Although Brecht was able to speak the truth about the party, Arendt
writes that his allegiance to the party prevented him from understanding
the situation in Germany—that the Nazis were not persecuting workers, but
Jews, "that it was race, not class, that counted." Here the sin of following
the party and promoting it in his verse resulted in the "wooden prose
dialogue in *Fear and Misery in the Third Reich*" and a selection of "so-
called poems, which are journalese divided into verse lines." But even
after this, while in exile, Brecht was able to write some of his greatest
works. The punishment caught up to him once he returned to East Berlin: "His poetic faculty dried up from one day to the next."[87] It was not
when he himself sinned, but when he experienced life under Communism that he lost his gift.

Arendt is not entirely fair to Brecht here. She knew Benjamin's "Conversations with Brecht" and even cites one passage from it in the essay. She
knew very well, therefore, that Brecht criticized the official party literature
of the period and was disturbed by the purges and repressions in the Soviet
Union, at least in private. Her reading of *Fear and Misery in the Third Reich*
also ignores one of the most powerful vignettes within the play, "The Jewish Wife," built around long monologues by a Jewish woman preparing to
flee from Germany. Arendt's claim that Brecht wrote "odes to Stalin" was
also challenged after the essay's publication.[88]

Arendt's turn to divine intervention in "What Is Permitted to Jove" is
puzzling. She seems to abdicate judgment (when it comes to poets, who are
we mortals to judge?) even while at the same time she insists how important it is, for politics as for literature, that we judge poets. It is hard to tell
how serious Arendt is in her appeal to Apollo. Brecht parodied the convention of deus ex machina in many of his plays, as when a messenger arrives
to pardon Mack the Knife as he stands on the gallows or gods descend to
find a good person in Szechuan. In these happy endings, Brecht satirizes
the way that Aristotelian theater teaches audiences to wait for divine intervention. By estranging the convention of deus ex machina in his plays,
Brecht reveals that people can change the world themselves; they need not
wait for the gods to do it for them. One way of reading Arendt's appeal, then,

is in the spirit of Brecht's own deployments of deus ex machina, a dialectical argument that forces the audience (the essay was initially delivered as a lecture) to take a critical stance toward the reliance on divine explanation. We are supposed to find the argument about Apollo uncomfortable; it prepares us for Arendt's turn—at the end of the essay—to human judgment and forgiveness.

While most of Arendt's essay is dedicated to Apollo's punishment of Brecht, the conclusion is about human judgment. She responds to Brecht's plea for forgiveness in "To Those Born After":

> You who will emerge from the flood
> In which we sunk
> Remember
> When you speak of our weaknesses
> Also the dark times
> That you escaped
>
> . . . .
> Remember us
> With clemency.[89]

The final word of the poem asks for a particular type of clemency: *Nachsicht*, literally "after-sight." It is the type of forgiveness that is only possible for those who come after and who are able to tell the full story. A storyteller of dark times offers illumination by telling of people who came before, but she also does more; she grants the forgiveness that allows for the possibility of future action. The only way to bring something new into the world, to step out of the processes that past actions have begun is through promising and forgiving.[90] Whenever we judge, we also open the possibility of forgiveness. Judging and forgiving, though,

follow different rules. The majesty of the law demands that we be equal—that only our acts count, and not the person who committed them. The act of forgiving, on the contrary, takes the person into account; no pardon pardons murder or theft but only the murderer or the thief. We always forgive some*body*, never some*thing*. . . . [W]e forgive for the sake of the person, and while justice demands that all be equal, mercy insists on inequality—an inequality implying that every man is, or should be, more than whatever he did or achieved.[91]

While judgment relies on the rational application of given precepts, forgiveness is about a person. Forgiveness, then, is a bit like both kadi justice and aesthetic judgment: it is about particulars, and cannot be subordinated to a universal law. Forgiveness requires a relationship between people—you forgive *somebody* not something—just as aesthetic judgment depends on an "enlarged mentality" in which spectators take other people into account.

By turning to the theatrical convention of deus ex machina, Arendt resolves a paradox central to her conception of action: that the public realm depends on constant mutual forgiving and promising, which would seem to require the preexistence of agents who forgive and promise. Yet those agents are only created through action.[92] Apollo resolves this paradox, not because he swoops down from Olympus to punish people, but because we can all judge like Apollo, that is, based on virtuosity rather than morality (as Arendt does in the opening sections of her essay); it is the performance of judging that creates the judge. After all, the "Jove" of the title to whom so much should be permitted is not in fact a god but a human who writes poetry divinely and can therefore be judged as more than a mere mortal.

In one fundamental respect, Arendt is wrong about Brecht: he did not fall silent. He did not publish any major works after settling in East Berlin, but instead he became a director. He wrote less, perhaps, but talked more. Although Brecht never joined the SED and pushed against the GDR's cultural policy, he believed in the East German regime in principle.[93] He sought to help the regime even at its most oppressive moment. For Brecht, this meant setting down the pen and turning to the stage in order to show that justice does not depend merely on laws but on groups of people practicing judgment together. If the 1953 uprising registered dissatisfaction with the party-controlled judiciary, Brecht positioned theater as an institution that could provide another outlet for thinking and judging that would quell dissatisfaction with the regime. Perhaps Arendt missed this aspect of Brecht's work after the war because he showed something quite uncomfortable: Brecht revealed how plurality and democracy are not necessarily aligned. As the visiting journalist tells us, everyone is entitled to his or her own opinion, but ultimately, it is done just how the Boss likes it.

Chapter Three

ERWIN PISCATOR
Theater After Auschwitz

The last time Hannah Arendt saw Walter Benjamin was in September 1940 in Marseilles. Unable to secure a French exit visa, Benjamin gave Arendt a collection of manuscripts. One of these manuscripts was hardly a manuscript at all; it was a series of fragments scribbled on the paper bindings of a Swiss newspaper, his "Theses on the Philosophy of History." Arendt and her husband, Heinrich Blücher, carried Benjamin's manuscripts with them as they escaped France. In Lisbon, while waiting for a ship to America, Arendt and Blücher read Benjamin's theses out loud to one another and to other refugees who gathered to listen and discuss Benjamin's words.[1] Looking back at the Continent as they set sail for America, Arendt and Blücher may well have felt like Benjamin's famous angel of history, based on Paul Klee's painting *Angelus Novus*: "His face is turned toward the past. Where we perceive a chain of events, he sees one single catastrophe which keeps piling wreckage upon wreckage and hurls it in front of his feet. The angel would like to stay, awaken the dead, and make whole what has been smashed."[2] But the angel cannot stay. He is caught in a storm that "propels him into the future to which his back is turned." This storm, Benjamin tells us, "is what we call progress."[3]

Benjamin's theses warn against narrating the past as a triumphalist march of history. This march is the march of the victors; it treads over the bodies of the oppressed. Arendt, too, saw this sort of historical writing as "always a supreme justification of what has happened."[4] In place of linear narratives based on the idea of progress, Benjamin and Arendt employ historical methods that bring the past into the present. Both Arendt and Benjamin use spatial metaphors to describe the relationship between the past and the present—Benjamin reaches toward the sky, Arendt into the ocean—to select moments to draw into the present. The past, Benjamin writes, "can be seized only as an image which flashes up at the instant."[5] Benjamin uses the metaphor of a constellation to describe the copresence of moments from the past with the *Jetztzeit* (now-time). To describe her own historical method, Arendt uses the term "pearl fishing."[6] This conception of the past—at once temporal and spatial, infused with our lived time—is fundamentally theatrical.[7]

The past makes its own entrances on the world stage. In courtrooms, past events are narrated, reconstructed, and sometimes even restaged with the idea that by drawing the events into the present, it will become possible to understand the past. At the International Military Tribunal (IMT) in Nuremberg, prosecutors did not present one single event. Rather, history itself was called before the court. Shoshana Felman argues that the IMT inaugurated a conceptual revolution in the relationship between history and justice. In the time since Nuremberg, "not only has it become thinkable to put history on trial, it has become judicially necessary to do so. . . . In the second half of the twentieth century, it has become part of the function of trials to repair judicially not only private but also collective historical injustices."[8] Trial plays, in turn, can put both history and historiography on trial by revealing and reflecting on the theatrical and narrative devices through which lawyers and judges present history.

Starting with his production of *The Burning Bush* in New York in 1949, Erwin Piscator led the development of documentary, trial-based theater in the United States and Germany. Like Arendt and Benjamin, Piscator was deeply concerned that staging history as a linear narrative would justify, or at least naturalize, atrocities. Piscator reached this conclusion in different ways than Arendt, Benjamin, and Brecht, though the biggest influence on them all was the dark times in which they lived. Piscator had a close relationship with Brecht, who began his theater career working in Piscator's theater and who tried to secure directing engagements for Piscator in Germany after the war. This relationship, though, was not quite a friendship; it was mired in both professional competitiveness and personal disapproval, and Piscator waited until after Brecht's death to direct any of his plays. Piscator did not share Brecht's philosophical interests, and he did not engage with either Marxist theory or the Frankfurt school as Brecht did. But he nevertheless developed a critique of teleological history in and through his directing practice, creating a form of theater that stages spatial constellations of historical moments instead of narrating history temporally over the course of a performance. In doing so, Piscator posed theater as a space for presenting and judging both historical events and competing interpretations of history.

STAGING HISTORY IN *THE BURNING BUSH* AND *THE CRUCIBLE*

Up to now, I have told a story about the development of epic theater through Bertolt Brecht. While such an account is an important one, it is only a partial one. It is also possible to tell a rather different story of epic theater, a story in which Erwin Piscator is the protagonist.[9] As Piscator tells it, his engagement with political theater began in 1914. Piscator's budding career as an actor was interrupted by a call to military service. He arrived to the front lines just before the second battle of Ypres, the first military encounter in which the Germans used poison gas on a large scale. Piscator's company was sent to clamber over decaying bodies and fill out the trenches. As grenades fell around the men, their commanding officer shouted to spread out and burrow into the ground. Piscator scrambled to dig, but found that he was unable to bury himself like the other men. The officer crawled over to him and screamed, "Forward, damn it!" Piscator frantically responded, "I can't." The officer demanded to know what Piscator's profession was. Aware of how trivial it would sound in the midst of corpses and heavy artillery, Piscator admitted that he was an actor. In Piscator's account, at this moment, his shame of his profession exceeded even his fear of the incoming grenades. For the rest of his life, Piscator would strive to create art capable of fighting on the front lines.[10]

Throughout the 1920s, Piscator's ideas about political theater developed out of collaborative practice. Unlike Brecht, Piscator was quick to emphasize the role of his collaborators in the development of his theories of theater, going so far as to describe the birth of epic theater as emerging out of collective improvisation. For Piscator, epic theater was born when his "Proletarian Theater" was performing at meeting halls in working-class neighborhoods in Berlin.[11] In their production of a play called *The Cripple*, Piscator played the title role. At one performance, John Heartfield, who had designed the backdrop for the production, was late arriving. Heartfield burst into the hall with the backdrop under his arm in the middle of the first act and shouted, "Stop, Erwin, stop! I'm here!" As the audience turned to look at Heartfield, Piscator set aside his role for a moment, stood up, and yelled, "Where were you? We waited for almost half an hour (*murmurs of agreement from the audience*) and then started without your backdrop." With the audience watching, Heartfield and Piscator began to argue. Heartfield blamed Piscator for not sending a car and became increasingly agitated as he described how he'd had to run through the streets and coax his way into a tram because nobody was willing to transport him with the large curtain. Piscator interrupted him with a little improv, "Be quiet, Johnny, we have to play on!" referencing Ernst Krenek's recent opera *Johnny spielt auf.* But Heartfield insisted that they hang his backdrop before continuing the performance. What Piscator did next is remarkable and provides insight into what he meant by calling epic theater "collective improvisation": he put the matter to a vote among the audience members. An overwhelming majority voted for hanging the backdrop, which they did before starting the play again from the beginning.

In his account of the incident in *The Political Theater*, Piscator jokes, "Today, I view John Heartfield as the founder of epic theater."[12] In this founding story, we see a number of elements that cohere to the notion of epic theater that we have received from Brecht: Piscator's decision to step out of character, the breaking of the fourth wall, and self-reflexivity about the theatricality of the event. But there are also elements that indicate important differences between Piscator's and Brecht's conceptions of epic theater. Brecht never opened up his plays to a vote. In his epic plays, Brecht wanted the audience to react critically, to judge the characters, and to learn how to critique social and political circumstances. But this was primarily a retrospective practice of critique, a working through for the audience that happened not during the action of the play but during interruptions of the action within the play and after the play was over. In his learning plays, Brecht was more interested in communal learning through performance; but those plays did not have audiences, they only had actors who were learning through studying a script rather than discussing what they had seen impromptu.

Piscator sought to transform the theater into a meeting hall and to turn audiences that had not been prepared beforehand into actors in his performances. These performances took a variety of forms. In his production of Carl Credé's play *§218* (1929), which advocated the legalization of abortion, Piscator planted actors in the audience to speak about abortion from different professional perspectives. He then opened the discussion Künste to the audience in general, leading one reviewer to call the performance the first time "the ending of a play corresponded to a public meeting."[13] An image from a Berlin production of *§218* shows the "prominent jurists" invited to observe and take part in the discussion of abortion law. In this and other plays, Piscator experimented freely with different ideas of audience reception and participation.

Piscator's notion of epic theater is far more loosely defined than Brecht's. For Piscator, epic theater is "a broadening of the plot and the illumination of its background, in other words, an expansion of the play beyond the frame of the merely dramatic."[14] Unlike Brecht, Piscator does not set epic theater in opposition to dramatic theater but rather sees epic theater as an

FIGURE 3.1. Trial scene in *§218*, directed by Erwin Piscator (1929). Courtesy of the Akademie der Künste Archive, Berlin.

FIGURE 3.2. Photograph of the audience at *§218* with a handwritten caption on the back: "Berlin lawyers and prominent jurists follow the dramatic discussion with interest from the orchestra seats." Courtesy of the Akademie der Künste Archive, Berlin.

expansion beyond the dramatic core of a play. The two most important aspects of epic theater for Piscator are, first, providing historical depth through the introduction of documentary material and, second, incorporating the audience into the action.[15] For Piscator, unlike Brecht, epic theater is necessarily documentary theater; adequately revealing the "truth" about the historical moment requires material evidence. Piscator's onstage documents included print documents and posters, films taken from newsreels, projections of photographs of historical figures, and even a parade of actual mutilated war veterans. When the former Kaiser Wilhelm II sued Piscator for libel because of his portrayal in *Hoppla, We're Alive!*, Piscator had the actor who was supposed to play the role of Wilhelm read the court order forbidding the performance in place of his lines.[16]

Piscator was tremendously successful during the Weimar Republic and moved from producing agitprop shows at beer halls to producing spectacular (and spectacularly expensive) performances that were among the first to incorporate film, projections, and stage technologies such as massive conveyor belts and rotating sets. He used these new stage technologies to push his theater away from literary drama and toward mass rallies, breaking down boundaries between theater and political life. *Trotz alledem!* (In Spite of It All!), which premiered at the Berlin Großes Schauspielhaus (Great Theater) in 1925 as part of a Communist Party convention, was Piscator's first entirely documentary production. The production was created through a montage of speeches, essays, newspaper clippings, pamphlets, photographs, and films portraying World War I, the October Revolution, and historical figures. Piscator described the production's fusion of art and life in terms emblematic of the historical avant-garde: "The masses took over the stage direction. . . . The theatre had become reality for them and very quickly it was no longer the stage versus the audience, but one larger meeting hall, a single large battle field, a single large demonstration."[17] By blurring the distinction between actors and spectators, Piscator sought to turn the theater into a public forum, breaking down any separation between the theater and reality.

Trotz alledem! is a version of epic theater that is in many ways diametrically opposed Brecht's ideal of a distanced audience. Piscator writes, "For the first time we were confronted with the absolute truth, that we ourselves had experienced. And it had moments of suspense and dramatic climaxes just like lyrical drama, and they caused just as strong a shock."[18] Piscator celebrates the effect of the performance on the audience members in the very same terms—"suspense," "dramatic climax," "shock"—that Brecht uses to criticize dramatic theater. In his repeated emphasis on how "we" experience the production, Piscator imagines that there is no difference in the way that the director, actors, or audience experience the event. They all experience the event as a collective forged by the performance itself: "An audience (*Publikum*) was always a collective. A thousand people who fill a theater are no longer just a sum of individuals, but a new being, gifted with special emotions, impulses, and nerves." This collective consciousness is achieved by pulling the audience into the stage: "The lifting (*Aufhebung*) of the boundary between the stage and the audience, the pulling of each individual spectator into the action fuses the audience completely into a mass, for whom collectivism does not remain a learned concept, but an experienced truth."[19] Such a performance sounds like Brecht's nightmare. While Brecht's epic theater distances the spectators from the stage, Piscator draws them into the staged action; while Brecht wants to show the world as contingent on individual choices, Piscator shows the irresistible rise of the proletariat; while Brecht maintains a deep skepticism about theatrical politics, Piscator collapses the difference between the theater and the meeting hall.

Piscator also differs from Brecht in that he freely used anachronisms within his productions. When hired to direct plays set in the past, Piscator incorporated contemporary elements. In his production of Schiller's *Robbers*, he costumed the character Spiegelberg as Trotsky and played the "Internationale" during his death scene; in his production of Ehm Welk's play *Thunder Over Gotland*, set in 1400, Piscator had his main character wear a mask of Lenin while film footage of Moscow and Shanghai appeared over the set. Despite being, at that time, a member of the Communist Party, Piscator made no effort to offer a teleological narrative of the growth of workers' movements throughout history or to represent the particular socioeconomic structures of specific historical periods in his plays as Brecht did. He would not let the past reside in the past but infused it with contemporary references.

Throughout most of the 1920s, Piscator focused on the politics of class struggle and economic inequality, but from the late 1920s on, he became increasingly concerned with anti-Semitism. Piscator was not himself Jewish. In fact, he came from a long line of Lutheran clergy (he was descended from a prominent Calvinist theologian whose seventeenth-century translation of the Bible was also known as the "God-punish-me Bible"). Nevertheless, he was the subject of anti-Semitic smears, including a rumor that his actual name was Samuel Fischer, and that he was an Eastern European Jewish immigrant.[20] In response to these rumors, Piscator wrote a letter to *Die Welt am Montag* that was published in the paper on March 1, 1927, which explains that despite rumors that he was a Jewish immigrant, "unfortunately it is not the case." In New York, too, Piscator was mistakenly assumed to be Jewish, not because of his politics (as in the Weimar Republic), but because of his being an exile from Germany.[21] Piscator's concern with anti-Semitism in the 1920s marked the beginning of his turn away from the Communist Party. Piscator saw early on that anti-Semitism was central to the Third Reich in a way that could not be fully explained by political economy. The failure of Communist ideology to account for anti-Semitism shook Piscator's faith in the party even before the Stalinist purges of the 1930s. Piscator's concern with anti-Semitism in particular, and bigotry in general, strongly informed his later work in New York and postwar West Germany.[22]

Piscator left Germany in 1931 and, after many nomadic years, arrived in New York in 1939 to lead the New School's Dramatic Workshop. The spectacles of Fascism and Stalinism unsettled Piscator's faith in the transformative power of theater and the creation of mass audiences. His turn against the ideal of a unified mass audience was linked to his growing concern with anti-Semitism both in Europe and in the United States.[23] In Berlin, Piscator had created *performances* in which the text was secondary, in some cases angering playwrights who saw his events as distortions of their work.[24] In New York, Piscator directed *plays*, many of them canonical, and provided students with a curriculum that included ballet lessons and lectures on Renaissance painting.[25]

There are a number of possible reasons for these changes—practical, political, and artistic. Piscator had pragmatic reasons for not staging spectacular agitational theater in New York: as his FBI file reveals, Piscator had been under continual surveillance since 1943.[26] He also had far more limited financial resources than he had enjoyed in interwar Berlin. It may seem that Piscator's decisions to incorporate psychological realism and to stage canonical works were a turn away from political theater, and indeed, this is how many biographical accounts describe Piscator's time in New York.[27]

There is also another way of reading these shifts in Piscator's work: as an interest in the capacity of theater *as* theater to engage politically. The changes in Piscator's interests in his wartime and postwar work are closely connected to his role as a teacher and the same sorts of collaborative practices that shaped epic theater in the first place. He spent his exile in New York collaborating closely with teachers who were committed to psychological realism and the Stanislavski Method, such as Stella Adler and Raiken Ben-Ari. Feminist performance artist Rachel Rosenthal, who studied with Piscator, described the workshop as "a multifarious affair, from the ultra realistic Actors Studio to the ultra Epic political."[28] Piscator, along with his many students and collaborators, began to develop a new sort of documentary theater, whose political impact would rely not primarily on the content of the documents or the collective effervescence of a mass rally but rather on the conventions of theater itself.

The Burning Bush was the first documentary play that Piscator directed at the Dramatic Workshop and is among the earliest postwar plays about the persecution of Jews in Europe. The stage adaptation of *The Diary of Anne Frank*, for example, would not premiere for another six years. *The Burning Bush* is based on the transcripts of an 1884 court case in a remote village in what is now Northern Hungary. A young Christian girl disappeared—it turned out she had committed suicide—and most of the town's Jewish men were charged with ritual murder. They spent over a year in prison before being cleared. The trial was covered in newspapers around Europe and led to widespread anti-Semitic agitation. Heinz Herald and Geza Herczeg (the first a Hungarian, the second a German refugee) began to investigate the case following Kristallnacht and determined that it was a "direct predecessor to the Dreyfus case, to Lueger in Austria, to Hitler in Germany."[29] Herald and Herczeg had recently coauthored the screenplay of *The Life of Emile Zola* (1937), a film about the Dreyfus affair. *The Life of Emile Zola* was both a box-office hit and a critical success, winning Academy Awards for best picture, best supporting actor, and best screenplay.

Despite the success of *The Life of Emile Zola*, it took Herald and Herczeg ten years to find a producer for *The Burning Bush*. Herald and Herczeg were trying to produce a play indicting anti-Semitism at a time when anti-Semitism was on the rise in the United States. In 1942, 15 percent of Americans believed that "the Jew" was the greatest threat to the United States; by 1944, that had risen to 24 percent (by comparison, only 9 percent named Japan and 6 percent named Germany as America's greatest threat).[30] There were several false starts for productions in New York between 1942 and 1944, but according to Herczeg, "fear of misunderstanding, refusal of concessions by the author[s] to water down the material, postponed every planned production."[31] Finally, in 1948, the play was produced at the New Lindsey Theatre in London and in the same year was adapted as a Hollywood film. The film version was directed by W. Lee Wilder (Billy Wilder's older brother, himself a Jewish refugee from Galicia), with music by Paul Dessau (a German Jewish refugee and Brecht's longtime collaborator who wrote the music for *The Caucasian Chalk Circle*). In the film, the issue of anti-Semitism is watered down if not erased altogether. A wealthy landowner frames Jewish farmers in order to buy their land cheaply; he is driven primarily by profit, not anti-Semitism, and the villagers he manipulates have no anti-Semitic prejudices at the outset of the film. The film received poor reviews and was recut and rereleased in the following year under the name *The Woman in Brown*. In this new version, the farmers were no longer identified as Jewish.

In 1949, one year after the release of the film adaptation, Piscator directed the play at the New York Dramatic Workshop; a year after that, it received its Los Angeles premiere. In contrast to the film, Piscator's production emphasized the role of anti-Semitism in the historical trial and was designed to alert audiences to the dangers of American prejudice. Publicity materials for *The Burning Bush* presented the play as a lesson in history, "highlighting prejudice, which played a major role in the fomentation of World

War II."[32] At the same time, audiences were instructed to apply the lessons of the play to the present. The program urged audiences to consider the nineteenth-century trial in relation to both the Holocaust and contemporary anti-Semitism in the United States: "The lessons learned in *The Burning Bush* are not dead, antiquated nor unnecessary. The time of the play is not only Hungary in 1882, but the United States, or any other country at any time."[33] In his program notes, Piscator bemoans the failure of Eisenhower's revelations about genocide to change anti-Semitic attitudes in the United States and warns, "One of the reasons anti-Semitism made such headway in Germany was because the majority never realized its danger and did not oppose its growth until it was too late."[34] He also suggests that the play is about both anti-Semitism in particular and also racism and bigotry more generally: "Reaction and intolerance are working hand in hand, no matter which minority is selected as its victim."[35]

While directing his audience to use the past to recognize and fight contemporary injustice, Piscator also sought to understand the specifics of the Hungarian trial. Archival materials from the production include extensive notes on the history of anti-Semitism in Austro-Hungary.[36] Piscator sought to incorporate this history into the staging and to draw connections between nineteenth-century anti-Semitism and the Holocaust. But at the same time, he did not want to portray the Holocaust as the inevitable outcome of this history. In directing *The Burning Bush*, Piscator faced a similar challenge to the one Arendt faced in writing *Rahel Varnhagen*, *The Origins of Totalitarianism*, and *Eichmann in Jerusalem*: how to account for the history of anti-Semitism in Europe without presenting the Holocaust as its inevitable culmination. *The Burning Bush* shows how theater—by allowing for multiple simultaneous representations of history—respects seemingly contradictory ethical and political imperatives: first, to heed the historical specificity of Jewish persecution in Europe and, second, paradoxically, to forestall the repetition of the unique event of the Holocaust (Never Again).

While the printed play takes place entirely in the courtroom over the course of the proceedings, Piscator added an additional prologue. The Dramatic Workshop production opened with an empty courtroom and two poster boards onstage. One reproduced an authors' note printed in the program, stating that the play is "based on the actual courtroom records of the trial. No pertinent fact is altered, the drama of the situation being so real that no fiction was necessary."[37] The other board presented a list of the

"Trials of History": Socrates, Jesus, the witch hunts, Danton, Nyíregyháza, Dreyfus, the Haymarket case in Chicago, Sacco and Vanzetti, and the burning of the Reichstag, each with its respective date. According to Piscator's notes, the new prologue began with a Bailiff (a character Piscator added) walking up the middle aisle of the theater, through the audience. He held an old oil lamp that illuminated only a streak of the board at a time. He whispered the names, "like crying far away, out of the mist of history." After each case, a chorus of actors among the audience repeated the name of the case, alternately whispering and yelling, "like night-mare-dreams of humanity." When his lamp illuminated Nyíregyháza (the city where the trial of *The Burning Bush* was held), the Bailiff rang a bell and called out, "Case number 8. Nyíregyháza 1882. The case against Joseph Scharf and his codefendants."[38] The lights then went up on a courtroom, revealing a set designed by students at the Dramatic Workshop under the guidance of Heinz Condell. Condell, the head of the design department, was himself a refugee who had designed the *Nathan the Wise* production with the Cultural Association of German Jews (*Kulturbund deutscher Juden*) before fleeing Berlin.[39] According to Piscator's handwritten notes, the set featured posters in Hungarian, English, French, and other languages about the trial, including caricatures of the supposed ritual murder. Echoing the poster in the prologue, the set also included murals of the Crucifixion, the Sacco and Vanzetti trial, and the Haymarket case. These murals both contextualized the Hungarian trial and also challenged how the audience might understand the cases depicted in the murals. By linking the persecution of Jesus with the persecution of European Jews and anarchists, Piscator offered both a moral, religiously inflected condemnation of the recent trials and a revisionist account of the Crucifixion.[40]

Five years later, Piscator would present a similar mural in his production of another documentary trial play: *The Crucible* by Arthur Miller, who had briefly studied at the Dramatic Workshop.[41] Piscator directed *The Crucible* in Mannheim in 1954 (its German premiere) and subsequently revived his production in Göteborg, Tübingen, Essen, and Marburg. The actors played in historical dress, but the set, designed by Paul Walter, was far from a re-creation of seventeenth-century Salem. It featured a number of metal platforms with grated floors, wooden crates, and a series of murals along the wall. Each depicted a historical event with a brief description: "Christ is crucified"; "Persecution of the Jews"; "July 20th" (the date of the failed

FIGURE 3.3. *The Crucible*, directed by Erwin Piscator in Mannheim (1954). Courtesy of the Akademie der Künste Archive, Berlin.

assassination of Hitler, which resulted in mass executions); "Spanish Inquisition"; "Counterrevolutionaries Executed by the Red Army"; and "Dragging of Mark the Evangelist."[42]

The program book for the Essen production of *The Crucible* includes a far longer chronicle of events, including colonial history, slavery, and segregation. The list begins in 399 BCE with the death of Socrates and ends in 1958 with the Notting Hill race riots. It includes the Crucifixion, the Inquisition, the slave trade, the Jacobin Reign of Terror, show trials in the Third Reich and Soviet Union, pogroms in Europe, and lynchings in the United States.[43]

In both *The Burning Bush* and *The Crucible*, the murals and lists place the particular event that is restaged in the play within an expansive history of persecutions. There is certainly no narrative of historical progress in the chronology of the Essen program. The events include Christian religious history alongside secular history and crimes committed by the Catholic Church. It includes religious intolerance, colonialism, genocide, violence

FIGURE 3.4. Chronology of atrocities in the Essen program for *The Crucible* (1958). Courtesy of the Akademie der Künste Archive, Berlin.

perpetrated by dictatorships of both the right and left, and violence perpetrated or condoned by democracies. These murals and lists offer a history of the oppressed, a history that, to return to Benjamin, "teaches us that the 'state of emergency' in which we live is not the exception but the rule."[44]

Judith Butler argues that Benjamin's philosophy of history offers a particular form of remembrance, a remembrance that "may be nothing more than struggling against amnesia in order to find those forms of coexistence opened up by convergent and resonant histories."[45] Piscator's program notes

Das Verhör

1692
Der Hexenprozeß von Salem

1944
Volksgerichtshof

399 v. Chr.
Sokrates wird wegen angeblicher Irrlehren durch den Giftbecher hingerichtet.

33 n. Chr.
Jesus von Nazareth gekreuzigt.

71 n. Chr.
Spartacus. 6000 Sklaven getötet. 4 n. Chr. wurde Gesetz erlassen, das zu Folterungen der Sklaven ermächtigte.

1. bis 3. Jahrh.
Christenverfolgungen.

1252
Inquisition beginnt Anwendung der Folter.

1290
Nach 100jähriger Verfolgung Ausweisung der Juden aus England.

1306
100 000 Juden enteignet und aus Frankreich vertrieben.

1415
Johannes Hus wegen reformatorischer Lehren verbrannt.

1431
Jeanne d' Arc als Hexe verbrannt.

1440
Gefangennahme von Negern für den Sklavenhandel

1481
Einführung der Inquisition in Spanien.

1484
Beginn der Hexenverfolgungen.

1492
Vertreibung glaubenstreuer Juden aus Spanien.

1498
Der Bußprediger Savonarola wird verbrannt.

1509
Beginn des Negersklavenhandels nach Amerika

1521
Montezuma und das Aztekenreich in Mexiko werden aus Glaubensgründen und ihrer Schätze wegen vernichtet.

1572
Bartholomäusnacht. Katharina v. Medici läßt 2000 protestantische Hugenotten ermorden.

FIGURE 3.4. (continued)

for *The Crucible* present the resonance between contemporary forms of violence and historical events, encouraging audiences to feel solidarity with those with whom they may not immediately identify. In both *The Crucible* and *The Burning Bush*, Piscator does this by placing the audience within three different temporal frames: in the historical event unfolding according to the conventions of realist theater, in the images of disparate moments of oppression in the backdrop imagery, and in the present time of the audience in which racism and bigotry threaten a resurgence. These triple frames offer a liminal experience of time in which, as Benjamin writes in the *Arcades Project*, "it is not that what is past casts its light on what is present, or what is present its light on what is past," but rather "what has been comes together in a flash with the now to form a constellation."[46] It is easy to imagine stagings of *The Burning Bush* and *The Crucible* that present historical analogies (this persecution was like that persecution). But Piscator did something else, making audiences vacillate between multiple temporal and spatial frames. This vacillation relies on theatricality and aims to open aesthetic experience, in addition to rational understanding, for the audience.[47]

In *The Burning Bush* and *The Crucible*, Piscator responded to the particular challenge of narrating history after the Holocaust. In *The Burning Bush*, he staged the epistemological break that Michael Rothberg in *Traumatic Realism* has called the crisis of historiography "after Auschwitz." Rothberg reads Adorno's famous dictum (no poetry after Auschwitz) as a chronotope—Mikhail Bakhtin's term for the fused time-space ("after" is a time; "Auschwitz" is a place)—that makes it impossible to continue to conceive of time as linear. Auschwitz challenges linear temporality because the time-space of Auschwitz threatens to recur. The dictum Never Again underscores the perpetual threat that time may loop back. Rothberg argues that, for Adorno, "'After Auschwitz,' . . . philosophical categories must themselves become chronotopes—'time-places' that serve as imperfect embodiments of historical events and tendencies."[48] Adorno's chronotope, like Benjamin's constellation, links the spatial and the temporal and in doing so becomes theatrical. Adorno's philosophy is, in Rothberg's analysis, a "'restaging' of Auschwitz."[49] *The Burning Bush* offers a sense of what it looks like to move from this philosophical restaging to an actual theater production. When the Bailiff illuminates the list of events and pauses on Nyíregyháza, the set becomes a chronotope; time "thickens, takes on flesh, becomes artistically visible, likewise; space becomes charged and responsive to the movements of time, plot and history."[50] The linear temporality into which the event seems to be archived is set aside as the event becomes present to audience members.

In *The Burning Bush*, Piscator kept dim houselights on and had actors enter through the aisles of the theater. According to the reviewer for the *New York World Telegram*, "The theatre is turned into a courtroom and the audience treated like spectators. The stage terraces down to the auditorium floor, and the aisles are part of the acting space. This approach is tremendously effective, once one accepts the fact that this is all true, and is being depicted as such."[51] Audiences were immersed into the play and became part of a late nineteenth-century courtroom. Yet the very elements that transformed the theater into a courtroom (the lights on, the entrances and exits through the audience) also broke the fourth wall of realistic illusion. According to the experience of the *Telegram* reviewer, this conjunction worked because the events portrayed were true. Audiences did not vacillate between the fiction of the play and the reality of the auditorium but rather between two realities: the historical case and the present. Rebecca Schneider has recently termed this sort of vacillation the "syncopated time of reenactment, where *then* and *now* punctuate each other."[52] At issue here is not only the ability to draw the historical past into the present but also the aim of creating an archive through performance itself. The play presents the struggle "not only to 'get it right' as it *was* but to get it right as *it will be* in the future of the archive."[53]

At the same time, the production encouraged audiences to reflect on the relationship between historiography and the conventions of dramatic form. The dramatic actions of *The Burning Bush* and *The Crucible* follow storylines with beginnings, middles, and ends. They follow recognizable plots, and indeed, these plots are themselves doubled: the historical tragedy of a persecuted community is paired with family melodrama (a son's betrayal of his father, a husband's betrayal of his wife). Although they are both documentary plays, neither *The Burning Bush* nor *The Crucible* makes any attempt to underplay or disavow its theatrical construction. History is represented as tragedy, and individual biographical narratives parallel a historical narrative. But in Piscator's staging, the lists of events (trials, atrocities, etc.) and murals that framed the plays presented a chronology devoid of a dramatic arc. Though the lists of events are related thematically—instances of persecution, violence, murder, or oppression, almost all at the hands of state authority—they do not tell a story in any conventional sense. They resist the conventions of historical narrative as described by Hayden White; they have "no central subject, no well-marked beginning, middle, and end, no peripeteia, and no identifiable narrative voice."[54] Without the murals and prologue in *The Burning Bush* (or murals and program notes in *The Crucible*), an audience could be caught up in the dramatic aspects of the tragedy and understand the events as the natural outcome of forces beyond the characters' control. But, to use Brecht's terms, the murals estrange these personal stories and historical narratives. Theater can have it both ways: making the audiences identify with the victims while simultaneously pushing for remembrance and solidarity with multiple histories of oppression. For Piscator, theater could allow for feeling with and for others without forgetting the crucial differences and gaps between historical and personal experience. I do not want to claim here that Piscator's lists are comprehensive or representative of all global injustices throughout history. But they attempt to open the way for what Rothberg has called "multidirectional memory," a way of remembering and reflecting on atrocity that is "subject to ongoing negotiation, cross-referencing, and borrowing."[55]

Piscator's productions of *The Burning Bush* and *The Crucible* use stage design to layer multiple historical moments and to spatially link different histories of oppression. In doing so, Piscator reveals how theatrical conventions (projections, backdrops, acting, even the stage itself) are able to represent multilayered histories of atrocity in ways that neither other art forms nor indeed courtrooms themselves can. Piscator created both of these productions before the start of philosophical and artistic debates about the representation of the Holocaust. *The Burning Bush* premiered two years before Adorno first published his famous claim that "to write lyric poetry after Auschwitz is barbaric."[56] Even when *The Crucible* premiered in West Germany in 1954, there was not yet a public discourse about the Holocaust much less about theatrical representation of the Holocaust. But by Piscator's late work in postwar West Berlin, this had changed. After years of freelancing at provincial West German theaters, Piscator was named artistic director at West Berlin's Freie Volksbühne in 1962. In each of the following three years, he produced and directed the world premieres of the most important works of postwar documentary theater in Germany: Rolf Hochhuth's *The Deputy* (1963), Heinar Kipphardt's *In the Matter of J. Robert Oppenheimer* (1964), and Peter Weiss's *The Investigation* (1965). *The Deputy* and *The Investigation*—both about genocide in Auschwitz—stirred widespread debate and controversy in East and West Germany and the United States regarding the representation of the Holocaust. In *The Investigation*, his final production before his death in 1966, Piscator engages these debates directly, claiming the importance of theater—and theatricality—in judging Germany's past.

REPRESENTING ATROCITY IN *THE INVESTIGATION*

Between 1963 and 1965, approximately twenty thousand spectators traveled to a Frankfurt courthouse to watch proceedings against a group of mid- and low-level guards, doctors, and functionaries from Auschwitz. The year that the trial concluded, thousands more in both East and West Germany attended performances of Peter Weiss's documentary play *The Investigation*, based on testimony from the trials. Questions regarding the ethics and politics of theater about the Holocaust surrounded the production and were central to a larger public debate in West Germany concerning how the country could best achieve a *Vergangenheitsbewältigung* (coming to terms with the past). Unlike Piscator's productions at the New York Dramatic Workshop or provincial West German theaters, the premiere of *The Investigation* was a hugely debated and discussed public event: Piscator had returned to his old role as Berlin's controversial impresario. Piscator issued a call for theaters across both East and West Germany to join in the play's premiere. It opened simultaneously in fifteen German cities (Peter Brook also held a staged reading in London), the first multicity theater premiere since *The Diary of Anne Frank*, which had premiered simultaneously in seven German cities in 1956. In the weeks preceding the premiere alone, more than one thousand articles about the play appeared in East and West Germany.[57] The sheer magnitude of this debate about a documentary play reveals how intertwined aesthetic debates about theater were with political debates about Germany's responsibility for legally addressing its past.

Beginning two years after the Eichmann trial, the Frankfurt Auschwitz trial was the largest and most publicized West German trial to charge individuals for their roles in genocide. Most of the accused had spent the previous two decades living prosperously in West Germany, in some cases building up successful businesses with start-up capital carried out of Auschwitz.[58] Because West Germany did not prosecute war crimes or crimes against humanity, a court had to show that the defendants had personally murdered individuals against or without explicit orders in order to convict them.[59] The trial proceeded amid debates about whether to extend the statute of limitations for murder; if it were not extended, the perpetrators of genocide would be immune from prosecution starting in 1965.[60] The Frankfurt Auschwitz trial also began the same year as the premiere of Hochhuth's *The Deputy*, which includes an act set in Auschwitz and which led to public controversy over the role of the Catholic Church in the Holocaust. In the same year as the trial's conclusion, the Second Vatican Council's *Nostra Aetate* declaration and other statements issued by the Catholic and Protestant clergy garnered anger from the radical right by decrying anti-Semitism.

Debates about the trial were interwoven with political debates connected not only to Germany's past but also to the contemporary context of the Cold War. From across the border, East Germany condemned the lenient sentencing of German "denazification" trials, arguing that this leniency showed the direct ideological consistency between Fascism and West Germany's capitalist expansion. East Germany's propaganda campaigns denounced West Germany for allowing former Nazi leaders to remain in high government positions (an accurate though certainly hypocritical claim). To prove these accusations, the East German supreme court staged trials in absentia of Theodor Oberländer (1960) and Hans Globke (1963). Oberländer, who had helped to shape policies of ethnic cleansing in Poland and the Final Solution, was appointed the minister for displaced persons, refugees, and victims of war from 1953 through 1960. Globke, a lawyer who had helped write the 1933 Enabling Act giving Hitler dictatorial powers as well as the Nuremberg race laws, served as Konrad Adenauer's chief of staff from 1953 through 1963. While Oberländer stepped down following the East German trial, Globke remained in office—despite tremendous controversy—until the end of the Adenauer administration.[61]

In West Germany, right-wing politicians and voters rejected the Frankfurt Auschwitz trial, arguing that it was time to move forward and that the trials were a distraction from the crimes of the Soviet regime. During the trial, defense attorneys led a campaign to dismiss the testimonies of the witnesses (most of whom traveled from Eastern Bloc countries), arguing that the accusations betrayed foreign influence—explicitly charging that the testimony was coaxed by Communist regimes and implicitly hinting at an international Jewish conspiracy. The defense team also argued that because many of the witnesses were foreign (most of the victims of Auschwitz were from Eastern Europe), their testimonies could not be trusted at the same level as those of the German witnesses (witnesses for the defense), because foreign witnesses were not accountable to perjury charges. After the trial, one witness reflected, "If I had guessed . . . that I would be interrogated by the attorney of my tormentor as though I myself were the defendant, I would not have come."[62] Of the twenty-two defendants, five were released, ten received sentences of less than ten years, one received a fourteen-year sentence, and six were given life sentences. The judgment was condemned from the right and the left. Conservatives found it monstrous to imprison guards and soldiers who had only been following orders, especially after so many years. Leftists found the light sentences and the treatment of survivors during the proceedings a travesty.

Peter Weiss, whose father was a Hungarian Jew and mother a German Christian, was born in Germany but spent most of his life in Sweden, where his family settled after fleeing Germany, and then Czechoslovakia. Weiss attended the Frankfurt trial and even traveled with the court to visit Auschwitz. *The Investigation* is based entirely on dialogue recorded in his own notes and in other contemporary reports, in particular Bernd Naumann's articles for the *Frankfurter Allgemeine Zeitung*.[63] The play was conceived of as a criticism of the trial, demonstrating how the survivors of Auschwitz are not only denied justice but, during the day of judgment, are forced to relive the distain and disrespect visited upon them in the camp.

Although *The Investigation* is a documentary play, Weiss stressed its literary construction. *The Investigation* is part of a trilogy of plays based on Dante's *Divine Comedy*. Weiss intended the trilogy to give "a comprehensive world picture" of the contemporary world.[64] In this trilogy, *The Investigation* was to be a bitterly ironic *Paradiso* because Auschwitz was the final destination of the innocent. *The Investigation* is subtitled "An Oratorio in Eleven Cantos (*Gesänge*)," and each of the cantos is further divided into three parts. These cantos are modeled on the structure of the *Divine Comedy* in that each canto draws the audience into a deeper ring of the camp. Some of these cantos are about places: the oratorio begins with the "Canto of the [Train] Platform" and ends with the "Canto of the Ovens." Other cantos are about methods of killing, including the "Cantos of Phenol" (the lethal chemical injected into the hearts of inmates), the "Canto of Zyklon B" (the chemical used in the gas chambers), and the "Canto of the Swing" (a torture device). Several cantos have broader themes: the "Canto of the Possibility of Survival" and the "Canto of the Camp." At the center of *The Investigation* is the "Canto of Lili Toffler" (Weiss's Beatrice), which recounts the story of a woman who was discovered smuggling a letter to another inmate in the camp and was subsequently executed.[65]

The Investigation was debated in mainstream as well as fringe newspapers, daily tabloids, and weekend feuilletons. Debates about the play were heightened just over a month before the premiere, when Peter Weiss published an op-ed expressing his solidarity with Socialist countries and nations engaged in anticolonial struggles. Weiss's op-ed qualified his support for real existing Socialism but nevertheless was widely condemned by right-wing politicians and journalists. Attacks on Weiss from the far right saw the play as a Jewish-Communist conspiracy. In a three-part exposé in the *Deutsche Wochenzeitung* and the *Deutsche Nachrichten* called "Communist Auschwitz-Theater: Show Trial or Trial Show? Spartacist Piscator and SED-Friend Weiss," Heinrich Härtle presented *The Investigation* as part of a plot by Jewish refugees and survivors (like Weiss) as well as Jews in the East German government to use the "demonization of German anti-Semitism" to "distract from the terrors and crimes of the Communist world revolution."[66] Both Weiss and Piscator received extensive anti-Semitic hate mail and threats around the time of the premiere.[67]

While many of the articles about Weiss from right-wing publications attacked his politics, articles in centrist papers tended to focus on the limits of aesthetic judgment and theatrical representation. Joachim Kaiser's "Plea Against the Theatre-Auschwitz," published in the centrist *Süddeutsche Zeitung*, was perhaps the most widely cited op-ed about the presentation of Holocaust testimony onstage. Although Kaiser's op-ed argued against aesthetic representation of Auschwitz, his concern was very different from Adorno's. The victims and survivors of Auschwitz were absent from Kaiser's argument; his concern was about the play's effect on its spectators and on the theater stage itself. Kaiser argued that Weiss's subject matter made aesthetic judgment impossible. Auschwitz, Kaiser wrote, "explodes the boundaries of theatre, is clearly not consumable under the aesthetic conditions of the stage." Audience members could not leave at intermission, criticize the acting or set design, or say, "They should have cut that part about the bunker," because "such criticism would be pure shamelessness." Representing Auschwitz onstage, Kaiser claimed, was tantamount to an act of violence against both the theater and the audience members who had to "cower under the violence of the facts."[68] Kaiser's article relied on extended metaphors of impotence and sexual violence: the stage would be "raped" (*vergewaltigt*) by the play; attending the performance would be like watching "a difficult abdominal operation"; the opening night would be a "premiere-orgy" (*Uraufführungsorgie*).[69] Many other publications took up Kaiser's argument and condemned Weiss for writing a play that, by allegedly prohibiting criticism, robbed audience members of their freedom. Opinion pieces in the West Berlin tabloid *B. Z.* called the play "terrorism of opinion,"[70] while *Die Welt* complained that "catharsis, insight into guilt and atonement require freedom. *The Investigation*, however, and the mode of its presentation aim to rob us of our freedom of thought."[71]

Few theaters, directors, and critics dissented based on the idea that *The Investigation* had to be presented outside the usual theater season and without the usual theatrical machinery. Of the sixteen premiere performances in East and West Germany and London, only nine were fully staged; seven were presented as staged readings. Although *The Investigation* is an oratorio, productions including those in East Berlin and Stuttgart also left out the soundscape that Luigi Nono had composed for the play in collaboration with Weiss. During a podium discussion after a performance at the Munich Kammerspiele, only one discussant, theater critic Reinhard Baumgart, questioned the distancing of *The Investigation* from the usual conventions of a night at the theater. Baumgart argued,

It has been said that there shouldn't be an intermission during this play because it would be awkward if people drank beer during it. To me, that's an example of received wisdom that is completely unproductive and perhaps even somewhat hypocritical. We all encountered Auschwitz before Peter Weiss, we have read books by Hannah Arendt, or Reitlinger, or, twenty years ago, Kogon's *SS-State*—and we drank beer after that as well.[72]

Baumgart points to the hypocrisy of theaters whose proclaimed sensitivity about Auschwitz stemmed more from their concern with the feelings of conservative theater patrons than from a concern with the Holocaust. In response to op-eds like Kaiser's and concerns that people unprepared for the material in the play would accidentally attend, a number of theaters decided to exclude *The Investigation* from season subscriptions.[73] Within the context of West Germany, protecting people who were unprepared or unwilling to confront the content of the play meant, as a reviewer for the *Abendzeitung* suggested after the premiere, that perhaps none of the people who really needed to see *The Investigation* went.[74]

Within the East German context, distancing *The Investigation* from the usual theater apparatus was a way to shape the play to suit the governing party, the SED. The East Berlin production was not held in a theater but rather in the plenary room of the Volkskammer (the People's Chamber, the unicameral legislature of the GDR). This staged reading was directed by Karl von Appen, Lothar Bellag, Erich Engel, Manfred Wekwerth, and Konrad Wolf. Coming only a few weeks after Weiss's public declaration of solidarity with Socialism, the East Berlin reading was a self-congratulatory state event.[75] All the roles were played by the political and artistic elite of East Berlin, many of whom had been political exiles or concentration camp inmates during the Third Reich. Among the performers were Helene Weigel and Ernst Busch (both in exile during World War II; the former had played the governor's wife and the latter had played Azdak and the singer in the 1954 *Caucasian Chalk Circle*), journalist Peter Edel (an Auschwitz survivor and Globke trial witness), writer Bruno Apitz (a Buchenwald survivor), and Alexander Abusch (a Resistance fighter, journalist, and deputy chairman of the GDR Ministry of Culture), along with other painters, sculptors, writers, and actors.[76] The emphasis of the evening was not on the testimony or the figures within the play but on the political and cultural elite themselves and their Western enemies. Abusch told the East German *BZ am Abend*, "Here we are proceeding against men, who today are again in high positions, and who are planning new harm against our nation. Our participation in the reading proves that in the GDR there are no difficulties in spreading the truth."[77]

In fact, significant cuts were required to bring Weiss's play into line with the "truth" of the SED. While Piscator's production lasted about three hours, the televised version of the Volkskammer production was only one and a half hours. Lothar Orzechowski, a West German journalist who attended several East German productions, wrote that while parts of the play (such as an emphasis on the role of West German corporations in the Holocaust) cohered well with official GDR ideology, other parts did not. Orzechowski cited a passage about the bonus given to guards who shot prisoners attempting to escape and asked, "Does the audience associate such sections with their own situation?" (that is, with the *Schießbefehl* whereby East German guards were required to shoot East Germans attempting to cross to West Germany).[78] This passage was cut from the East Berlin production. Indeed, all descriptions of barbed wire fences and walls surrounding Auschwitz (a

FIGURE 3.5. Holocaust survivor Peter Edel testifies at the Globke trial (1963). Wikipedia Commons.

FIGURE 3.6. Peter Edel as a witness in *The Investigation* in East Berlin (1965). Courtesy of the Akademie der Künste Archive, Berlin.

familiar sight to the Berlin audiences) and references to escape attempts were cut from the production. The East Berlin reading also cut lines referencing mass complicity with genocide, such as the declaration of Witness 3:

> I only ask
> to be allowed to point out
> how crowded the sidewalks were with audiences
> as they drove us from our apartments
> and loaded us into cattle wagons.[79]

Both these cuts and the anti-Fascist credentials of the cast members (those playing the accused as well as the witnesses) effaced the play's theme of widespread complicity, instead focusing on the most prominent West German perpetrators.

Although the casting of the East Berlin performance emphasized the anti-Fascist resistance of GDR politicians and artists, some of the most significant cuts within the play were of the sections that explicitly discuss the treatment of political prisoners. The cantos that deal with the political department at Auschwitz—"Canto of the Swing" and "Canto of the Black Wall"—were almost entirely cut and with them the references to denunciation, false charges of sabotage, torture, and forced confessions. Cut, too, from the East Berlin telecast were the two references to show trials held at the camps (in "Canto of Junior Squad Leader Stark" and "Canto of the Ovens"). Presumably, the discussion of political repression would hit too close to home. While the GDR wanted to remember the war as a fight between the Nazis and the anti-Fascists, any specific discussion of political repression ran the risk of becoming fodder for critique of the GDR itself. This had the paradoxical consequence that while the casting of the East Berlin production suggested that the victims of the camps were first and foremost anti-Fascist, the stories that the witnesses told were not about the experience of political repression but of ethnic genocide.

Outside the GDR's capital city (and off national television), theaters had more freedom to diverge from the party line. According to Orzechowski's account, the Dresden production included reference to rewards given to guards at Auschwitz for shooting escapees. In Rostock, director Hans Anselm Perten used a stage design (by Falk von Wangelins) that invoked both the camp and the fortified borders of the GDR. Wangelins's set was

FIGURE 3.7. Ernst Busch reading at *The Investigation* in East Berlin. Courtesy of the Akademie der Künste Archive, Berlin.

composed of three levels of scaffolding. Defendants sat on each level, each of them dressed in a black suit and with a machine gun and iron helmet close at hand. Though on trial, they maintained their instruments of power and violence, looking down at the witnesses and audience. At the top of the scaffolding sat two policemen, each controlling two spotlights. The entire scaffolding was backlit, de-emphasizing the defendants as individuals and turning them into part of the architectural edifice. Witnesses for the prosecution appeared dressed in striped inmate clothing and would stand in front of the scaffolding, facing the audience, to present their testimony. While the defendants maintained their power, the witnesses continued to live as prisoners. Of course, officially, the set was supposed to invoke Auschwitz for the audience and show the continuities between the Third Reich and West Germany, but in reality, it visually connected the walls of Auschwitz to the fortifications dividing East and West Germany.

Perten worked with Weiss to add a passage about the resistance of Soviet prisoners of war in the camp.[80] While the East Berlin production had taken

FIGURE 3.8. *The Investigation* at the Rostock Volkstheater, directed by Anselm Perten (1965). Copyright © Deutsches Theatermuseum München, Heinrich Fürtinger Archive.

the paradoxical position of trying to tell a story about anti-Fascists without any reference to resistance, the Rostock production added an extra scene of sabotage as a heroic act against authoritarian power. Perten also added a short epilogue. After the final speech, a chorus of witnesses stood up and named those who did not survive: "Over six million dead Jews and Roma, of those, three million in Auschwitz alone. Over three million Soviet prisoners of war and over ten million civilians senselessly and brutally murdered in the occupied territories." The epilogue listed Jews and Roma first, and while mentioning Soviet prisoners of war, made no mention of German anti-Fascists.[81]

In West Germany, the Essen and West Berlin productions relied most heavily on theatrical machinery and techniques. In different ways, each of these productions developed an argument for how theater—as an institution—could support public discussions about the Third Reich. The artistic director of the Essen theater, Erich Schumacher, decided to produce *The Investigation* as *Gemeinschaftsarbeit* (communal work).

Staged by the company as a whole through a process of discussion about the material, the rehearsals were intended to be a democratic process of deliberation and "coming to terms with the past." At the same time, though, the performance was presented as a theater piece rather than as a reading or town-hall-style discussion. In Essen, the witnesses were made up to appear unnaturally pale and sat at a low table that took up almost the whole stage. When they presented their testimonies, they would stand on top of the table and speak to the judge and prosecutor. The defendants sat on benches upholstered with red velvet in the orchestra pit with their backs to the audience. As the witnesses gave their testimonies, they would gesture simultaneously to the accused in the front of the auditorium and to the audience itself. The accused wore black suits and presumably appeared like a first row of audience members for as long as they were seated. Yet, when called forward, they turned to face the audience, revealing glass half masks that gave their faces an unnatural shimmer. The makeup and masks stylized the witnesses and the accused into two opposing choruses. The masks introduced a tension between distance and identification: while the masks distanced the actors from the audience and emphasized the theatricality of the performance, the masks also anonymized the fig- ures and thus made their actions generalizable.[82] The Essen production earned some of the best reviews, and critics argued that the production was particularly effective in transferring a sense of accountability to the audience through its use of masks, costuming, and stage and sound design.

It will come as no surprise, perhaps, that of all the premiere directors, Piscator was the most adamant about presenting *The Investigation* as the- ater. According to a profile on the rehearsals published in *Christ und Welt* (a conservative Protestant weekly), there was debate about the theatrical nature of the play during a rehearsal at the Freie Volksbühne, where Pisca- tor was artistic director as well as the director of *The Investigation*. Pisca- tor told his actors, "There is background there. And one must act it out. Scenes must develop out of scenes. Theater must be played here." The actor playing the prosecutor broke in and objected, insisting that the play was not really theater. "But it is!" Piscator insisted and prevailed.[83] Not only did he emphasize the theatrical nature of the performance, he even used the premiere as a celebration of the Freie Volksbühne. As the program reveals, the production's premiere marked the theater's seventy-fifth anniversary. A program insert offers excerpts from speeches given for the occasion. The chairman of the Freie Volksbühne, Social Democratic Party politician Günther Abendroth, spoke about the seeming disjuncture between the anniversary celebration and the theme of the play: "Genocide in Auschwitz was something incomparable, something that cannot be understood with received concepts. And now we are simultaneously commemorating the founding of our organization and some may ask: is it still possible, after Auschwitz, to have celebrations in Germany?"[84] Theater, Abendroth declared, had become more essential than ever, teaching people the humanity that they had lost.

Piscator pushed his conviction that *The Investigation* legitimized the mission of the Freie Volksbühne to a questionable extreme by using an image of witness testimony from the play for the theater's annual Christmas and New Year's card. Piscator's use of this image for a greeting card shows how quickly a theater's deep concern with political events can tip into tasteless self-promotion. Despite this overreach, though, Piscator did offer a compelling argument for presenting the trial as theater. In his own program essay, Piscator discusses Kaiser's op-ed and rejects his argument that *The Investigation* robs spectators of their freedom of opinion. Instead, he insists that the play itself is about the importance of dissent and demonstrates that the defendants, "in spite of all of the talk about 'superior orders,' had the freedom to make moral decisions."[85] By showing that the defendants had a responsibility to judge and reject their genocidal orders, the production encouraged the audience to judge for themselves: "The freedom of the

FIGURE 3.9. Martin Berliner testifies, on the Freie Volksbühne holiday card. Courtesy of the Akademie der Künste Archive, Berlin.

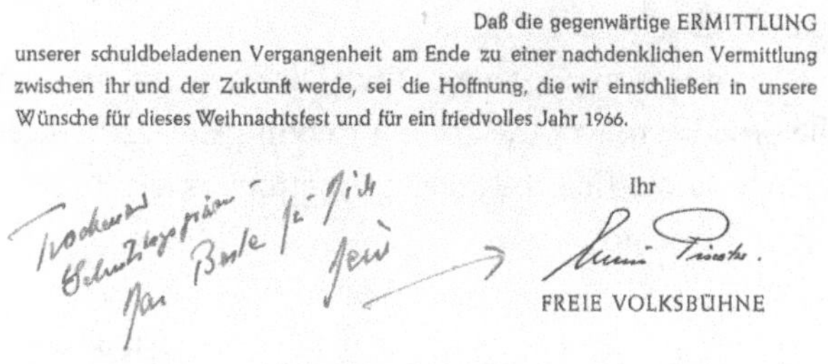
Daß die gegenwärtige ERMITTLUNG unserer schuldbeladenen Vergangenheit am Ende zu einer nachdenklichen Vermittlung zwischen ihr und der Zukunft werde, sei die Hoffnung, die wir einschließen in unsere Wünsche für dieses Weihnachtsfest und für ein friedvolles Jahr 1966.

Ihr

FREIE VOLKSBÜHNE

FIGURE 3.10. Inside of the Freie Volksbühne holiday card, a holiday message from Erwin Piscator.

spectator with respect to the facts is not restricted: he can define his own moral responsibility unhindered; he can make himself a witness or even a defendant; he can become a juror, who wants to reach *his* judgment."[86] Piscator argues that contemporary drama has become increasingly successful and political by emphasizing the individual's responsibility to judge.

Piscator does not, however, disagree with Kaiser about the impossibility of "consuming" *The Investigation*. For Piscator, the play's resistance to easy consumption was its strength. The program includes a section with the names, biographies, and sentences of the defendants, most of whom were either released or sentenced to less than ten years in prison despite their direct roles in genocide. In this section, Piscator includes a note stating his desire to leave audiences unsatisfied:

> Why is the outcome of the Frankfurt trial and of the play *The Investigation* unsatisfying?
>
> Because the catharsis is missing: the sublimation, cleansing, and lifting of the soul through regret and sympathy.
>
> And it is missing because the remorse of the perpetrators is missing.
>
> But it is regret that spurs transformation, change, that changes bad to good deeds and forecloses repetition—becomes a measure of future actions—whether they now take place in Vietnam, in the Congo, or in India.[87]

Like Arendt, Piscator believed that neither postwar trials nor theater about the trials should or could offer catharsis. Piscator hung signs asking the audience not to applaud.[88] By forestalling applause, Piscator prevented the audience from distancing themselves from the action onstage; in keeping with the absence of catharsis, they were implicated in the trial and meant to feel a distinct lack of resolution.

Immersed as it was in ongoing political debates, the production sought to stress the broader role of theater in providing an aesthetic education to its audiences. Insisting that the theater functions as a "moral institution in Schiller's sense," Piscator writes,

As long as we have not completely accounted for our past, as long as we try to bracket our past from our present and future . . . the task of political theater will be to recapitulate the unresolved. . . . [T]heater must not remain neutral and distanced, even at the risk of certain artistic inadequacies. And what our teachers always told us is true here as well: *non scholae sed vitae discimus.* We learn not for school but for life.[89]

Piscator's celebration of theater as a moral institution is a far cry from his Weimar-era hopes for a theater that would break the boundaries between art and revolutionary action. He is no longer preoccupied with political agitation but with aesthetic education. Piscator's turn to the tradition of German aesthetics is, like Arendt's turn to Kant and Lessing, a response to anti-Semitism and genocide. But Piscator, unlike Arendt, maintains faith in the humanist tradition.

From the beginning of his exile, Piscator had sought to stage *Nathan the Wise* in every country he passed through. In its second season, the Dramatic Workshop's presentation of *Nathan the Wise* was that theater's biggest success; it was picked up by the Belasco Theatre on Broadway for twenty-eight performances in 1942 and remounted at the Dramatic Workshop in 1943 and 1944.[90] Piscator had produced *Nathan the Wise* at the same time that the Nazis were perpetrating genocide but also at a time when he saw anti-Semitism growing in America. In connection to the Dramatic Workshop production of *Nathan the Wise*, he organized a public symposium and series of talks calling for freedom, humanity, and tolerance "because these occurrences in this land, at this time, are an uncanny reminder of the beginnings of Nazism in Germany."[91] Piscator drew from Schiller's "Stage as a Moral Institution" the conviction that theater was uniquely capable of teaching tolerance. If his Weimar Republic–era productions had aimed to fuse together a mass audience with collective consciousness, Piscator's later works emphasized respect for difference and solidarity across ethnic, racial, and religious lines. With *The Investigation*, Piscator sought to tread a delicate balance. On the one hand, he was concerned with self-representation onstage, having Jewish characters speak for themselves and seeking to cast Jewish actors in plays about the persecution of Jews. On the other hand, he also wanted to avoid essentializing ethnic, religious, or racial identities. The final section of this chapter is about how theater may be capable of this paradoxical task.

THE POLITICS OF CASTING

In 1943, Piscator directed a pageant called *The Golden Doors* at Madison Square Garden. Written by Walter Mehring and narrated by Stella Adler, the pageant featured one thousand Jewish schoolchildren. It was composed of a series of vignettes ("Children of Europe in Wartime," "Children from Czechoslovakia," "Children in the Train," "The Goose-Steppers," "Ballad of the Battlefields," and "Song of the Sea") that told the story of children driven by the Nazis from one country to another until they found loving homes in Palestine.[92] The pageant was presented as part of a *Rally of Hope* that had been organized to bring attention to atrocities against the Jews in Europe and to promote Zionism. The program emphasized that the participants were asking not for pity but rather an acknowledgement of their rights: "Our youth is appearing before the world not in the role of beggars with a plea for mercy. They come to declare to foe and friend their implicit faith in the eternity of the Jewish people and in its God-given right to a life of independence and freedom."[93]

Though not himself Jewish, Piscator incorporated ideals of Jewish self-representation and self-determination into his work. We can see this conviction in his changes to the script of *The Burning Bush*. In the printed edition of the play, the title appears in lines spoken by the anti-Semitic politician Baron Onady. He claims to be well versed in the Torah and, conflating the stories of Abraham and Moses, asserts that the Jewish God "told Abraham to slit the throat of his *OWN* son—his *own*, mark you!—and only stopped him in the nick of time, by appearing as *a burning bush!*"[94] Piscator added a speech here for one of the defendants, Rabbi Taub, who rises and quotes from Exodus 12:

RABBI TAUB: I have surely seen the affliction of my people . . . and have heard
their cry . . . by reason of their taskmasters; for I know their pain and I came
down to deliver them out of the hands of the Egyptians, and bring them up out
of that land unto a good land and a—[95]

The stage manager's script indicates that the Rabbi speaks these lines with
a rising cadence of optimism, only to be interrupted by the judge who
demands that Onady be allowed to continue. But Rabbi Taub will not be
silenced and continues, "*This* is our Burning Bush, Baron. *This* is our Bible
and yours. . . . You commit blasphemy upon your own God when you
do not tell the *truth* about our Lord. For there is only *one* God for all
Mankind . . . and only *one* love."[96] In Piscator's version, it is Rabbi Taub,
not Baron Onady, who names the play.

Piscator's additions to the published script have the Jewish defendants
speak for themselves and their community. But at the same time, this new
dialogue points to a certain fluidity between religions. Taub tells Onady that,
much to the latter's dismay, they have the same God, and thus to condemn
the Jewish God is to blaspheme against the Christian one. Emphasizing that

FIGURE 3.11. *The Burning Bush* at the Dramatic Workshop (1949). Courtesy of Marianne Simon.

Jews and Christians have one shared God, one burning bush, Taub challenges the boundaries of identity that Onady is so eager to demarcate. Through his revisions, Piscator made what might seem to be contradictory claims about the importance of self-representation and the fluidity of identity. To testify about crimes committed against them, Jews had to be able to speak for themselves, to tell their own stories. But at the same time, Piscator pushed his audiences toward modes of identification across religious and ethnic boundaries. Piscator's simultaneous commitment to self-representation and to solidarity across religious and ethnic lines parallels his commitment to focus on historical particularity while also placing single events within a multidirectional history of oppression. In *The Burning Bush*, the physical space of the theater and the relationship of the audience to the live performers enacted a proto-identity-politics while also blurring the boundaries of ethnic and religious identities.

In the hundreds of pages of reviews and opinion pieces about *The Investigation*, there is one topic that is conspicuously absent: the question of casting. Who should play the survivors of Auschwitz? The absence of almost any public discussion on the topic suggests that it was taken for granted that Auschwitz survivors would be played by German actors who were not Jewish. This casting could make audiences identify more closely with the survivors by minimizing their ethnic difference (as the productions of *The Diary of Anne Frank* had), but it would do so at the expense of effacing the ethnic and religious difference of the victims and survivors of Auschwitz, most of whom were Jews from Eastern Europe. This problem of representation was a problem within the trial as well as the play. Although the vast majority of people who died at Auschwitz were Jews from Eastern Europe, most of the survivors called to testify at the Frankfurt Auschwitz trial were not Jewish. Because the prosecution needed to prove that the defendants had killed against or in excess of their genocidal orders, their witnesses were people who worked closely with the defendants, mostly non-Jewish Polish or Ukrainian political prisoners or German criminals.[97] There were, however, exceptions, including a number of Jewish women who worked as secretaries in the political department.[98] Their testimonies, as well as the testimony of Austrian Jewish doctor Otto Wolken, were central to the prosecution's case.[99]

In *The Investigation*, the testimony of one of the secretaries, Dounia Wasserstrom, became the basis for the testimony of Witness 5, and Otto

Wolken's testimony was the basis for Witness 3.[100] The Jewish identities of these two witnesses are not made explicit in the text of the play, however, which omits all proper nouns (including the words "Jew," "German," and "Auschwitz") except for the names of the defendants. Weiss's decision not to use proper nouns, and specifically not to use the word "Jew," spurred decades of scholarly condemnation.[101] James E. Young calls the play "as *Judenrein* as most of post-Holocaust Europe," equating Weiss's play with literary genocide.[102] For Young, Weiss's omission of the word "Jew" was a direct result of Weiss's ideological preoccupations; his Marxism led him to portray the persecuted as "victims not of anti-Semitic terror but of monopoly capitalism gone mad."[103] Certainly, Weiss wanted to reveal the participation of German industry in the Holocaust. But he also saw anti-Semitism as central to Nazi ideology. Weiss drew connections between anti-Semitism and other (contemporary) forms of racism.[104] In his notebooks from the time of the Auschwitz trial, Weiss writes that anti-Semitism "always runs parallel to hatred of Negroes, hatred of yellow-skinned people, and other racial hatred."[105]

While the play does not contain the words "Germans," "Jews," or "Auschwitz," it does give the names of the defendants at the trial (a choice that emphasizes individual culpability over collective guilt). The testimony within the play also contains Jewish names. One of the defendants tries to argue that he had no personal animosity against the inmates, and states,

> Before they were taken
> I always told my family
> go ahead and shop from the Krämers
> they are people too.[106]

The play makes multiple references to a Jewish inmate called Bunker Jakob in the camp (his actual name was Jakob Kozelczuk). Robert Cohen points out that critics who emphasize the absence of the word "Jew" also neglect a crucial scene in which one of the inmates is referred to as Sarah, which was the generic name given to all Jewish women by the Third Reich.[107] The use of the name Sarah signals the effacement of the individuals within the camps, a deprivation that Weiss wants to show continues to the present. According to Weiss, he did not give the witnesses names in the play because "they had none in the camp, they were only numbers."[108] Witness 5 expresses this loss in the second canto ("Canto of the Camp"):

Family home occupation and property
those were concepts
that were extinguished
as the number was cut in.[109]

Weiss left out the proper names of witnesses because he wanted to demonstrate continuity between the treatment of witnesses in the camps and their treatment during the trial.

Of course, the text of *The Investigation* is only half the story. The text alone does not indicate who the actors should be or how their own personal biographies and bodies should appear to the audiences. Weiss not only omits mention of Auschwitz, Jews, and Germans by name, he also omits all punctuation and all stage directions, with the exception of noting when the defendants laugh and clap together. There are elements of a play that can only be completed in the staging; one of them is the decision of what bodies occupy which roles. As the premiere productions showed, these decisions are always political and can radically change the meaning of the play.[110]

The premiere productions in Stuttgart and East Berlin both minimized the Jewish identities of witnesses and victims in order to tell a collective national story. In Stuttgart, this story was "we were all both victims and perpetrators"; in East Berlin, this story was "we were all always anti-Fascists." In the Stuttgart production, the set featured large photos of the defendants from the trial, hanging above a series of chairs. These photos on the set seemed to highlight the guilt of the individual defendants. But the staging and textual edits told a different story. The director Peter Palitzsch removed the names of the defendants from the play and double cast all the witnesses as defendants. Between each canto, actors playing the witnesses and defendants would switch positions. One positive review of the Stuttgart production asserted that its strength was in portraying Auschwitz as the place of "anonymous mass murder, in which everything is exchangeable: the murderers and the murdered, the guards and the prisoners, they are all the same for the 'system.'"[111] The claim that there was no difference between the SS guards and the inmates of the camp is absurd. By portraying a system in which the defendants as well as the survivors were mere victims, the Stuttgart production (perhaps unintentionally) upheld the defense of Nazi defendants from Nuremberg to Jerusalem to Frankfurt: that they were not personally responsible, that they were merely following superiors' orders and doing their duty, that anyone else would have done the same. Despite the images of the defendants, the staging undermined any strong sense of their particular individual culpability. This narrative of collective guilt, as Arendt writes, ultimately protects perpetrators: "Where all are guilty, no one is; confessions of collective guilt are the best possible safeguard against the discovery of culprits, and the very magnitude of the crime is the best excuse for doing nothing."[112] Moreover, by double casting the victims and perpetrators, the staging presented a story of shared victimhood as well as shared culpability, erasing the crime of genocide by erasing difference.

While the Stuttgart production echoed justifications within West Germany for ceasing the prosecution of people who carried out genocide, the East Berlin production reflected the GDR's own national myth about the Nazi regime: that East Germans were always all anti-Fascists. In the service of opposing political messages, these West and East German productions offered skewed perspectives of the victims of Auschwitz: in Stuttgart the victims were German Nazis as much as Jews; in East Berlin the

FIGURE 3.12. *The Investigation* at the Stuttgart Staatstheater (1965). Copyright © Deutsches Theatermuseum München, Madeleine Winkler-Betzendahl Archive.

victims were the anti-Fascists who went on to found the GDR. There is little room in these productions for considering the central role of race in the mass murder of Jews, as well as Poles and Roma, in Auschwitz. Strikingly, though, the East Berlin reading featured more people with Jewish heritage in the cast and production team than any other German production (including Peter Edel, Wolfgang Heinz, Helene Weigel, Alexander Abusch, Wieland Herzfelde, Stephan Hermlin, Peter Sturm, Paul Dessau, and Konrad Wolf). None of the short supertitles that gave their names and brief biographies in the television broadcast mentioned that they were Jewish or had Jewish ancestry but instead emphasized their anti-Fascist politics.[113]

Piscator was the only director—as far as I could tell from reviews and archival materials—to explicitly seek to cast Jewish actors in his production. As Witness 8, Piscator cast Martin Berliner, a Jewish Austrian actor who had escaped to the United States during the war. Another key witness (Witness 4) was played by Angelika Hurwicz (who had played Grusha in the 1954 *Caucasian Chalk Circle*), who was of Jewish Russian descent. According to an article in *Aufbau* (a Jewish German journal started by and for refugees), Piscator had hoped to cast more Jewish actors, but many who were approached did not think they could bear the physical and psychological strain of performing the piece.[114] The decision to emphasize the Jewish victims in this production is particularly significant because *The Investigation* was produced at a time of public debate over whether Jews should be allowed to pass judgments on or even testify against former Nazis. Critics of the Eichmann trial complained that Jews could not be impartial judges—neglecting, as Hannah Arendt points out, that Polish and Czech judges had judged crimes against their people as well.[115] During the Frankfurt Auschwitz trial, the defense insisted that Jewish survivors could not be trusted as witnesses. Among Piscator's directing materials is a memo written by Henry Ormond, a lawyer who represented the families of victims. Ormond, a Jewish survivor who had spent five months in the Dachau concentration camp before fleeing to England, describes and condemns the anti-Semitism he saw in the trial.[116]

Piscator's production foregrounded not only the genocidal policies of the Nazis but also a persistent anti-Semitism in postwar West Germany. Early in the rehearsal process, he planned to costume each of the survivors in a generic gray pant or skirt suit, with a yellow number on the left hand side of his or her jacket.[117] Such costumes would visually signal that, though the war was over, the court had treated the survivors who testified as legally inferior to German defense witnesses. Furthermore, because the Jewishness of Jewish actors like Berliner and Hurwicz might not immediately read to an audience and because Piscator could not cast as many Jewish actors as he sought, this costuming made the Jewish identity of the survivors unambiguous. According to the *Christ und Welt* profile, not everyone at the theater agreed with Piscator's casting choices. The profile's author, Wolfgang Ignée, begins by describing a Jewish actor who, "despite contractual obligations to the Freie Volksbühne," could not bring himself to act in *The Investigation*.[118] Later in the article, Ignée quotes Berliner as telling him, "No one knows if it's a good thing that I am taking part."[119] This ambivalence suggests a fear that casting Jewish actors might undermine the veracity of the production's political message or allow it to seem biased. After the premiere, Michael Stone, another reviewer for *Christ und Welt*, singles out the two Jewish actors (Berliner and Hurwicz), accusing them of overacting and bias. According to Stone, Berliner and Hurwicz had been too biased to even play the *roles* of witnesses as well as non-Jewish actors could: "Martin Berliner, and who would blame him, showed too strong an investment as a witness, and also Angelika Hurwicz could not completely suppress her bias [*Befangenheit*] during the narration of pseudo-medical experiments on young women."[120] (One wonders what this reviewer would see as an unbiased attitude toward experiments on young women in Auschwitz.) Tellingly, the same article from *Christ und Welt* that criticizes Berliner's "invested" performance at the Freie Volksbühne praises the Stuttgart production, arguing that the decision to mix the perpetrators and the victims was a good one.[121]

Part of the audience's reception of Piscator's *Investigation* seems to have relied on how audience members perceived the testimonies of Jewish survivors. Heinz Elsberg, the reviewer for *Aufbau*, has the opposite reaction to Berliner's and Hurwicz's performances and emphasizes the difficulty rather than the bias of Jewish actors cast in the roles of witnesses. He notes,

Some Jewish artists turned down roles because they thought they could not bear the physical strain. It was all the more astounding, then, to experience what was doubtlessly the most striking performance of the evening by Martin Berliner, himself among those persecuted by the Nazis. He lived in the text and actually only found comparable achievements in the two female roles.[122]

FIGURE 3.13. Berliner testifying in *The Investigation* at the Freie Volksbühne. Copyright © Deutsches Theatermuseum München, Ilse Buhs Archive.

Although Piscator emphasized Jewish identity in his production, he did not want to mark the witnesses in a way that would marginalize their testimony. The set, designed by Hans-Ulrich Schmückle, positioned the defendants in a shallow orchestra pit, facing the stage, while the accused sat on risers on the stage, looking out into the audience. The judge and attorneys sat stage left. When witnesses were called to testify, they walked up a short flight of stairs to a triangular playing area so that they appeared to be rising from the first row of the audience. One reviewer for the *Frankfurter Allgemeine Zeitung* described the set design: "The witnesses . . . crouch in front of the auditorium, in the first row, as though it [*sic*] were people like you and I."[123] In an essay in the program, Angelika Hurwicz writes that theater is a crucial place for reflecting on the Holocaust because, "on the stage, a person steps immediately before other people. There's no topic for which this [immediacy] is more necessary than the debasement of people by other people."[124]

Hurwicz's claim about the immediacy of theater can be interpreted in two different ways, each with different implications for thinking about casting and identification. On the one hand, we can understand this immediacy through Arendt's conception of theater and the public realm. For Arendt, immediacy—the copresence of people in their plurality—is what makes the theater a synecdoche, standing in for the public realm while also affording a particular space for judgment that creates political ways of being together. On the other hand, we might understand Hurwicz's concept of immediacy through humanist ethics: theater creates forms of identification between the audience and actors onstage that cultivate empathy and tolerance. Piscator's work draws together both of these ideas about immediacy. He was not a philosopher and was little concerned with the distinction between ethics and politics (for him, they were equivalent) or the possible friction between universal humanism and attention to plurality. Instead, he was an eminently political director, savvy to how the politics of identity played differently in different contexts.

In *The Burning Bush*, Piscator had worked closely with his Dramatic Workshop colleagues Stella Adler and Raiken Ben-Ari, the latter a Jewish Russian actor who was closely involved in the development of Hebrew-language theater in Moscow and New York. Ben-Ari's Method approach to acting in *The Burning Bush* encouraged both the audience and the other actors to identify with the Jewish characters in the play. The production was staged in a context in which it could be assumed that audiences would include Jews and non-Jews alike, and further, that a number of the Jewish actors and audience members would have personal experience of anti-Semitism in either the United States or Germany. In this New York context, the Method approach to empathy and identification had a greater chance of stirring an empathy that did not rely on presenting the sympathetic Jews as exceptional or on downplaying their Jewishness.[125]

The West German context for the premiere of *The Investigation* was very different than the New York context of *The Burning Bush*. At a time when it was still common to draw equivalences between German and Jewish suffering during the Second World War, Piscator wanted to prevent the audience from identifying themselves as victims of the Third Reich. This meant including Jewish actors whose presence would remind the audience that— contra the Stuttgart production—it was not mere chance who was a guard and who an inmate at Auschwitz. But foregrounding the suffering of Jews also came with its own dangers. One was the danger that Arendt warns of in her discussion of the early reception of *Nathan the Wise*: that making

Jews out to be "exceptional specimens of humanity" can feed into anti-Semitism.[126] Another was the danger of turning suffering into spectacle or even aesthetic pleasure (the danger that Benjamin and Adorno both warn against). In a sense, it was an impossible bind. A theater without a plural audience cannot become a public site in the sense that Piscator and Arendt would have it be, and the National Socialists had seen to it that Berlin was no longer a city with a sizeable community of Jewish theatergoers and artists. But at the same time, Piscator was determined that the theater must be a place to address the crimes of the Third Reich, even if that reckoning had to be staged for and by an ethnically cleansed public.

Piscator's production grew out of multiple imperatives, many in tension with each other: the need to emphasize the centrality of Jewish suffering without making Jews out to be "exceptional specimens"; the need to stir the audience toward solidarity with the survivors without making the audience identify as victims themselves; and finally, the need to present the trial as theater without turning the spectacle of suffering into aesthetic pleasure. Despite practical difficulties, Piscator cast Jewish actors (and would have liked to cast more), creating some measure of plurality within the theater and also belying the idea in Method acting that anyone could fully identify with and act as anyone else. In this sense, the play pushed against a universalism that would emphasize—as *Nathan the Wise* did— that we are all just human and—as the Stuttgart production did—that it was mere chance that made some victims and some perpetrators. At the same time, Piscator decided against emphasizing the historical specificity of the Holocaust through any visual representation of the camps. Although Piscator had planned to incorporate several images of Auschwitz in the early stages of the project (including projected photographs of the trains leading to Auschwitz and the yellow numbers on the witnesses' clothing), he later decided against these.[127]

Piscator instead relied on Luigi Nono's recorded soundscape—created using adult and child choruses, acoustic instruments, and electronics—to give a quasi-mimetic representation of Auschwitz and to evoke discomfort, even physical pain, in the audiences. While Weiss's text mediates descriptions of Auschwitz through the testimony of witnesses, the recording offers the audience a representation of the camp itself. In the recording, one hears gunshots and shrill whirring and whistling that sound like gas. Distorted human voices sound like gasps, sobs, coughs, moans, and the gurgles of infants. Critics, whether they praised or rejected the play, all seemed to agree that the music was the most penetrating element of the staging. A reviewer for the *Heidelberger Tagesblatt* wrote,

The strongest emotional effect came from the composer Luigi Nono. . . . [The music] portrayed the atmosphere of the camp with unrelenting severity. That which the predominantly matter-of-fact and sometimes also ideologically digressing tenor of the testimony perhaps did not allow for, was expanded through this electronic sound-image to a tragedy of classical severity. It bears witness to peoples' fear of other people, and attained for the play an efficacy on stage that would certainly not have been reached by the documentary report alone.[128]

The review in *Christ und Welt* similarly commented that the audience seemed reflective but not ill at ease or emotionally stirred by the text: "Only under Nono's shrill flagellations did they now and then cringe, or cover their ears."[129] Through this soundscape, rather than through psychological identification, Piscator created a sense of immediacy that prompted an affective response among audience members. For some audience members, the music may have conjured not just a sense of the camps but also personal memories of aerial bombardment. According to Elsberg in *Aufbau*, Nono's music, with "its bloodcurdling chords, . . . intensifies the atmosphere to rupture."[130]

Essen and Rostock both used Nono's music as well, whereas in East Berlin, the Volkskammer production opted instead for music by Paul Dessau (Brecht's long-term collaborator who also composed music for the film version of *The Burning Bush*). Dessau's music linked *The Investigation* to the leftist musical theater of the interwar period, emphasizing again the role of East Berlin's artists in resisting Hitler. In Stuttgart, Palitzsch played sentimental Nazi-era songs like *Lili Marleen* and *Es geht alles vorüber* (everything comes to an end) in between scenes. While the Nazi songs were included to make the audience reflect on how they themselves experienced the Third Reich, one critic noted that far from unsettling the audience, these melodies were taken as an invitation to relax between the scenes.[131] The music in Stuttgart and East Berlin allowed the audience to distance themselves from the atrocity being described onstage. But Nono's music forced the audience to respond viscerally. Just as *The Burning Bush* and *The Crucible* had overlaid multiple modes of historical representation, *The Investigation* used multiple modes of theatrical representation: the diegetic theater of the courtroom proceedings as well as a mimetic soundscape that sought to impact spectators on a physiological level.

The same reviewer who praised the Stuttgart production for making the defendants and survivors interchangeable also praised it for "radically de-theatricalizing" *The Investigation*.[132] He contrasts the Stuttgart production to Piscator's overtly theatrical one, which uses "shrill electronic noises" paired with "mimetic naturalism" to appeal to "the so-called human capacity for sympathy."[133] It is impossible to tell whether the "de-theatricalized" Stuttgart production or Piscator's theatrical production had a deeper effect on audience members. We can say with certainty that at least one audience member in Stuttgart was unmoved by the staging of survivor testimony. Erwald Bucher, the federal minister of justice at the time of the premiere as well as a former Nazi Party and SA member, sat through the entire performance and, after leaving, maintained his support for preserving the statute of limitations.[134]

At the Freie Volksbühne, though, audience members walked out of the performance. The theater had anticipated this and distributed a survey to audiences as they entered the theater:

Please do not leave the performance; try to push through—like the actors have through a long rehearsal process, like they do every night. What's the length of one such evening compared to the unending depth of suffering that came to the victims of Hitler's regime? If you do want to leave, however, we ask you to please give us the reason or reasons.

You are leaving,

Because you are opposed to dealing with Jewish problems on the stage? Yes—No

Because you are opposed to putting the Auschwitz trial on the stage? Yes—No

Because you already know the things you are told in *The Investigation*? Yes—No

Because you could no longer bear the testimony? Yes—No

Because you are bored? Yes—No

Or are there other reasons? If so, what?[135]

To an extent, we can take the purpose of this survey at face value. Its aims were to discourage audience members from walking out of the performance, to encourage them to think about their reasons for wanting to leave, and to collect information about those who did leave. But distributing this survey at the beginning of the performance also issued a challenge to audiences. In distributing the survey, the Freie Volksbühne signaled that the performance would make some audience members want to leave, that this was part of its goal. The survey addressed the audience members as people who were not themselves victims of Hitler's regime, who had an ethical obligation to disregard their own discomfort in order to bear witness to the suffering of the victims testifying in the play. The theater was no place for audience members who did not want to see "Jewish problems" or the Auschwitz trial onstage, who were bored by the proceedings, or who thought that there was no further need to address the crimes of the past.

In *Eichmann in Jerusalem*, Arendt condemns Eichmann to death while at the same time banishing him from the public realm. Eichmann and his superiors enacted a policy of mass murder in order to not share the world with others; likewise, "no one, that is, no member of the human race, can be expected to want to share the world with you."[136] Piscator's production issued a similar challenge within the framework of the theater: those who refused to share the theater with the testimony of survivors would have to leave the theater. Enacting this challenge was a matter not only of the subject matter of the play and the documentary text of the testimony but also of theatrical representation. According to Piscator, many people who responded to the survey wrote that they left because they could not take Nono's music, bearing out the observation of critics that it was the music rather than the text that most deeply seemed to affect the audience.[137] By linking the documentary with the theatrical, *The Investigation* became the sort of theater that Piscator had first imagined while lying in the trenches of Ypres: "activist, combative, political."[138]

Chapter Four

TRIALS IN NUREMBERG

In the early spring of 1969, the former head of the Reichsbank, Hjalmar Schacht, traveled from Munich to see a play at Vienna's Burgtheater, perhaps the most prestigious stage in all of Europe.[1] He sat in the very first row of the theater, face to face with a younger version of himself. The play was *Trial in Nuremberg*, and Schacht sat both onstage and in the audience. Schacht had been one of the few acquitted defendants at the International Military Tribunal in Nuremberg (IMT), but the play did not unequivocally exonerate him.[2] When the curtain fell, Schacht lost no time in passing judgment on the play. He told reporters that the actor playing him was wonderful, mimicking him very effectively in both gesture and expression.[3] And he was particularly honored that his character was played by Paul Hoffmann, the artistic director of the Burgtheater as well as a successful film and television actor. Schacht also had high praise for the stage director of the play: "Outstanding, simply outstanding, the man knows what it's about!"[4] But Schacht condemned the playwright:

It is a miserable work. The Nuremberg trials should have been fantastic material for a dramatist. The author (who actually wrote all this? A young German, born in 1932? Hmph!) unfortunately couldn't make anything of it. With a little skill he could have used the material to prepare a wonderful indictment [*Anklage*] of the absurdity of the accusations [*Anklage*] against my person![5]

As a crowd gathered around him in the coat-check area, Schacht decided to make up for the author's lost opportunity to exonerate him:

The author shows me in the wrong light. He wants to make the audience believe that I joined the Hitler government because of rearmament. That's nonsense! ... I wanted to tame unemployment, that's why I joined the government. You have to keep in mind that at that time there were 6.5 million people out of work. And furthermore, in the thirties we had to rescue Germany from the Communists. There were 230 National Socialist deputies against 100 Communists. And so I ask you: Who tamed unemployment? I was the only person in all of Europe who did it.[6]

At the end of his speech, one woman shyly approached Schacht and asked him to sign her program. Schacht leered: "Aren't you afraid of me? But I'm a 'war criminal'? Finally! Someone who's not afraid."[7] At the end of the impromptu performance, Schacht got one last moment in the spotlight, which he used to claim the legacy he thought he deserved. When a reporter asked him who he thought was the greatest economist of the century, he replied, "Well, if you ask me like that: me, of course!"[8]

Schacht used the Vienna premiere of *Trial in Nuremberg* to try to rewrite history. There is no reason to doubt that Schacht genuinely believed that he was the greatest economist of the century, that supporting National Socialism was the best way to defeat Communism, and that the charges brought against him at Nuremberg were a gross miscarriage of justice. But his version of history clashed with the history that the play *Trial in Nuremberg* presented, a history that emphasized Jewish persecution and the Holocaust, linked genocide with capitalism and imperialism, and drew connections between Germany's war crimes and the United States' War in Vietnam. These divergent histories were narrated and contested in the theater, both on the stage and in the lobby, and the theater provided a public institutional space in which people could judge the evidence of such contesting historical narratives.

THE NUREMBERG PRECEDENT, TWENTY YEARS LATER

It is no coincidence that debates about the history and meaning of the Third Reich in West Germany reached their height at the same time when documentary theater's popularity peaked in German-speaking countries. In plays like *Trial in Nuremberg*, the play's meaning and narrative arc are derived not from the transformation of a human protagonist but from the transformation of artifacts and documents into evidence for a particular interpretation of history. In a documentary trial play, the audience watches the lawyers construct accounts of the past and judges which of these stories is more convincing. Documentary trial plays emphasize the importance of documentary evidence for making claims about history at the same time that they present multiple possible interpretations of that evidence. In doing so, this mode of theater can offer a middle ground between seeing history as a matter of subjective interpretation or of objective truth. In this sense, *Trial in Nuremberg* treads the same line that Arendt does in her theory of judgment, rejecting the dangerous trend to regard all evaluative judgments as mere subjective opinions, while also dismissing the idea that objective truth can be accessed by one individual and exists outside the world of human interactions. What documentary theater at its best might create and sustain is a sense of objectivity that is generated through the collaboration of artists as well as the shared experiences of the audience.[9] In the case of *Trial in Nuremberg*, this meant challenging East Germany's ideological misrepresentation of the Third Reich by creating a subversive public through which this challenge could be articulated and discussed.

Midcentury documentary theater shows that some interpretations of history are more accurate than others without relying on claims to pure objectivity. In the 1990s, postmodern common sense about the impossibility of objective history made its way from the academy to the courts. In 1996, David Irving brought a libel suit against Deborah Lipstadt for condemning him as a "falsifier of history" in her book *Denying the Holocaust*. Irving claimed that his views of the Holocaust—that there were no gas chambers at Auschwitz, that Hitler did not know about the Final Solution, etc.—were equally as valid as any historian's. The claim that history is merely a matter of interpretation has since become central to the anti-elite, postfactual politics of the far right in the United States and United Kingdom. A film based on the Irving trial, *Denial*, was released in the fall of 2016. Falling between the Brexit vote and Donald Trump's election, the film could not have been timelier. At a key moment in the trial (and the film *Denial*), the judge asks, "If somebody is anti-Semitic . . . and extremist, [is] he perfectly capable of being, as it were, *honestly* anti-Semitic and *honestly* extremist in the sense that he is holding those views and expressing those views because they are, indeed, his view?"[10] This logic suggests that Irving, like all of us, is just expressing his own personal truth. What the judge proposes here is generally agreed upon—that ideology shapes how we write history—but this does not mean that any interpretation of history is equally valid.

In postwar Germany and Austria (as well as in the United States' 2016 presidential election), it was the radical right that had the most to gain from so-called alternative facts and histories, especially when it came to the history of Fascism and white supremacy. Today, as in 1960s East and West Germany and Austria, it has become essential to defend the notion of proof, facts, and historical evidence without disavowing the power of interpretation, staging, or narration. Documentary theater combines rhetoric with proof, fortifying literary narrative and staging with pieces of evidence, showing that far from being incompatible, rhetoric and proof are intertwined. Documentary theater, like a courtroom trial, relies both on pieces of evidence and on a convincing narrative of events. But documentary theater has the freedom to cast a broader net than the courts. While judges are bound to focus exclusively on the events connected to individual culpability and to pronounce a sentence, historians and stage directors are not.[11]

Trial in Nuremberg and Schacht's cloakroom performance following the play's premiere were two small parts of a much larger public discourse about the legacy of the Third Reich and the legitimacy of post–World War II trials. The 1960s debates in West Germany about what it meant to come to terms with the nation's past had as much to do with contemporary politics as with historical events. Theater artists and politicians alike mobilized the legacy of the Nuremberg trials to engage in Cold War politics. It is no big surprise that Schacht disliked *Trial in Nuremberg*; the play came from the far side of the Iron Curtain, where Schacht's acquittal—not his indictment—was seen as unjust.[12] But the play, as originally conceived and produced in East Berlin in 1967, was not primarily about Schacht or the other Nuremberg defendants at all but rather about the precedent of the Nuremberg trials and the development of international law in the era of the Cold War. The East Berlin production encouraged audiences to use the proceedings of the International Military Tribunal to judge and condemn current events of the time: the rearmament of West Germany, the Vietnam War, the Six-Day War, and though it could not be explicitly mentioned in the program because of East Germany's GDR censorship, Stalin's Great Terror and the crushing of the 1956 Hungarian Revolution.

While the immediate postwar period saw denazification trials and trials of collaborators on a large scale across Europe, this project of postwar justice was soon subordinated to Cold War realpolitik and reconstruction.[13] Within West Germany, popular opinion turned increasingly against prosecutions in the late 1940s. Between 1946 and 1950, the percentage of Germans in the American zone who viewed the Nuremberg trials as "fair" dropped from 78 to 38 percent.[14] West Germany stopped prosecuting former Nazis and stressed amnesty and reintegration up until the end of the 1950s. In East Germany, summary judgments against alleged former National Socialists took place, but without any attempt to publicly demonstrate the guilt of the accused or the legality of the proceedings.[15]

Around 1960, the bracketing of Nazi war crimes in West Germany again began to change. In 1957, East Germany launched a public relations campaign revealing how many former Nazi judges retained their positions in the government of the Federal Republic of Germany (FRG, West Germany).[16] The following year, the trial of Einsatzgruppen members in Ulm showed how comfortably perpetrators of Nazi atrocities lived in the FRG. With the Ulm trial, West Germany slowly began prosecutions again, pushed by a growing left in the 1960s and the Eichmann trial in Jerusalem.[17] As discussed in the previous chapter, the 1963 Frankfurt Auschwitz trial was the first trial to charge lower-level camp functionaries for their roles in genocide, while at the same time, a massive public debate took place over whether to extend the statute of limitations for crimes committed during the Third Reich in order to enable prosecutions after 1965.[18]

While the early 1960s revealed how reticent the Adenauer administration was about prosecuting wartime perpetrators, the 1960s also showed how selectively the Nuremberg precedent would be applied internationally. At Nuremberg, the chief American prosecutor, Robert Jackson, had declared in his opening statement, "We must never forget that the record on which we judge these defendants today is the record on which history will judge us tomorrow."[19] By the late 1960s, however, it was clear that the United States and Allied powers would not be judged by the same measures as the Nuremberg defendants. At the time that Rolf Schneider wrote *Trial in Nuremberg*, there was outrage both within the United States and internationally that the United States would not be held to the Nuremberg precedent for its war in Vietnam.

In 1965, draft resister David Mitchell sought to use the Nuremberg precedent in a Connecticut court, arguing that the United States was committing war crimes and crimes against humanity in Vietnam and that his serving in the army would thus violate the Geneva Conventions, the United Nations Charter, the Kellogg-Briand Pact, and the Nuremberg Charter of London. The court ruled against Mitchell, sentencing him to the maximum of five years' incarceration and a $5,000 fine for failing to report for induction into the armed forces.[20] The trial garnered public attention from both sides of the political spectrum; Bertrand Russell led a petition campaign in support of Mitchell, and William F. Buckley supported the conviction while nevertheless conceding "the not uninteresting points of law" that the case raised.[21] The Nuremberg tribunal had ruled that superior orders could not be used as an excuse to participate in a war of aggression. Could American soldiers therefore be held accountable in the same way that German soldiers had been? Following Mitchell's case, army medic Dr. Howard Levy and three privates, known as the Fort Hood Three, refused orders and likewise charged the United States with crimes enumerated in the Nuremberg Charter.[22] The courts rejected these challenges to the legality of the Vietnam War by ruling that the war was a political question for the legislative and executive branches and thus outside the purview of the courts.[23]

Even before citizens used the Nuremberg precedent in legal courts, artists, activists, and intellectuals had staged extralegal trials based on the Nuremberg proceedings in theaters, in cinemas, and in public tribunals. Stanley Kramer and Abby Mann's film *Judgment at Nuremberg* was released in 1961 in West Germany and the United States and in 1963 in East Germany. Also in 1961, director and producer Paul Shyre optioned G. M. Gilbert's *Nuremberg Diary*—an account of the trial by the court-appointed prison psychologist—for a planned Broadway production in the 1962–63 season, though the production never panned out.[24] Other internationally successful plays, including *The Investigation* and Saul Levitt's *The Andersonville Trial* (1959), staged the transcripts of other postwar trials as a way to judge US actions in Vietnam (as well as other contemporary events).[25]

Outside theater and cinema, Bertrand Russell and Jean-Paul Sartre developed a new form of extralegal tribunal to interrogate US crimes in Vietnam for an international audience. The International War Crimes Tribunal on Vietnam (also called the Russell Tribunal) used the Nuremberg Charter to legitimate its work. The first Russell Tribunal included lawyers, activists, and politicians as well as artists and writers, among them Tariq Ali, Stokely Carmichael, Simone de Beauvoir, Alice Walker, and James Baldwin. After a second Russell Tribunal on Latin America, activists created a Permanent Peoples' Tribunal that has since held almost forty sessions on a variety of topics. These tribunals replicate the structure of legal trials to judge cases that are not tried in legal courts. Many of these tribunals pass their findings on to the United Nations and the International Criminal Court.[26]

The program book for the East German production of *Trial in Nuremberg* argues that theater and extralegal activist tribunals like the Russell Tribunal keep Nuremberg's legacy alive. By positing that theater and extralegal tribunals are Nuremberg's legacy, the premiere performance of *Trial in Nuremberg* highlighted the tensions between law, evidence, and justice. The East Berlin and Vienna productions of *Trial in Nuremberg* revealed how dependent the meaning of the play (and thus the public legacy of the trial) is on staging choices and local context. Indeed, the meaning of any genre of theater performance is always contingent on the audience and local circumstances. But this contingency creates a particular paradox for documentary trial plays, especially those like *Trial in Nuremberg* that support the mission and findings of the court. Such performances emphasize the performative character of justice: that justice, to be done, must be seen to be done. And, moreover, that the context in which the showing occurs (who is doing the showing, who is doing the seeing, and where it all takes place) changes what it means for justice to be done. At the same time, though, *Trial in Nuremberg* appeals to human rights and to the authority of international law. This appeal to authority and rights suggests that there must be an objective standard of law; whether or not the public sees justice as having been done is irrelevant. The divergence between what it means for the law to be followed and for justice to be seen to be done is not only a legal but also a political issue. Take, for example, the change in West German public opinion about the Nuremberg trials between 1946 and 1950. What does it mean that there was a 50 percent drop in the number of people who saw the proceedings as fair? We might say this difference in perception changes nothing about the legitimacy of the trial, which can only be measured according to law, not public opinion polls. Or we could say this drop shows that the meaning of the trials had changed for people. Even if the legal precedent of Nuremberg still held, political work was required to make the public recognize the criminal policies of the Nazi regime as criminal.

Restaging the Nuremberg trials in the theater does three things at once. First, it does the political work of showing audiences that murder and genocide are criminal, even when they are ordered or sanctioned by the state. Second, it stages the possible disjuncture between justice being done and justice being seen to be done. Third, it historicizes the trial and reframes the arguments of the trial to address contemporary questions: What did it mean for justice to be done *then*, and what does it mean for justice to be done today?

TRIAL IN NUREMBERG IN EAST BERLIN

The Deutsches Theater commissioned Rolf Schneider to write *Trial in Nuremberg* as part of a series of three plays by East German authors that would be performed for the Berliner Festtage (Berlin Festival) in 1967. The play developed out of an intense collaboration between Schneider and dramaturges, actors, and directors at the Deutsches Theater.[27] Meeting and rehearsal notes about the development of the script and staging show how Schneider and his collaborators grappled with the narrative framing of the play and debated how documentary evidence should be presented onstage.[28] These conversations, along with the final script and premiere staging of *Trial in Nuremberg*, exemplify how theater can present history as well as reflect on how history is presented. The context of East Germany meant that this historical work was also political in the sense that it confronted—in some ways propagating and in some ways challenging—the interpretation of the Third Reich and Nazism that was accepted by the governing party, the SED.

When *Trial in Nuremberg* premiered in East Berlin, Schneider was a young, up-and-coming writer in East Germany known for his radio plays. *Trial in Nuremberg* was Schneider's second trial play, and it was he who proposed the topic to the Deutsches Theater. His first trial play, *The Trial of Richard Waverly*, had been a radio play based on the life of Claude Robert Eatherly, who had served as a pilot supporting the nuclear bombing of Hiroshima. After the war, he was tormented by guilt over his participation. Unable to hold a steady job, he was charged with a series of petty crimes, deemed mentally ill, and committed to a Veterans Administration hospital in

Texas. There, he began to correspond with Günther Anders. Anders went on to publish this correspondence, which Schneider used as material for his play along with reports of Eatherly's trial from a local Texas reporter.[29] In an interview, Schneider spoke of *The Trial of Richard Waverly* (1963) and *Trial in Nuremberg* (1967) as bookends to the height of documentary theater's popularity in German-speaking countries: Rolf Hochhuth's *The Deputy* (1963), Heinar Kipphardt's *In the Matter of J. Robert Oppenheimer* (1964), and Peter Weiss's *The Investigation* (1965) were all produced within those years.[30] While the mid-1960s were particularly strong years for documentary trial theater in East and West Germany, the relationship between theater and trials was already, as Schneider puts it, "old and venerable. A courtroom trial is also performance: with fixed roles, with a dramaturgy, with an often-unknown outcome, which naturally creates suspense."[31]

Nevertheless, it took considerable work by Schneider and his collaborators to stage the International Military Tribunal in a dramaturgically compelling way. Despite the novelty of the international tribunal and the unprecedented scale of the crimes, the IMT was, in words of journalist Rebecca West, "a citadel of boredom."[32] The structure of the trial was responsible for some of this boredom. The proceedings were structured according to charges, with each Allied power presenting one charge. The Americans prosecuted the crime of conspiracy to wage aggressive war; the British, the crimes against the peace; and the French and Soviets, war crimes and crimes against humanity (in the West and East, respectively). Because the conspiracy charge included the other charges within it, the American team preempted the material of the other teams, who nevertheless went on to present the same material for a second or even third time. The judges ruled that all documents submitted as evidence had to be read out loud in full to the court. Given the overlaps in the prosecution, this meant that lengthy documents were sometimes read multiple times by different prosecution teams.[33] These documents, rather than witness testimony, were the core of the prosecution's case at the IMT.[34] The trial lasted a full year, far longer than the organizers had anticipated. For the trial's organizers, boredom was not a primary concern. In fact, the very elements of the trial that were the most boring—the level of detail, the lack of rhetorical flourish in the prosecution's presentation, the use of documents over testimony— bolstered the court's legitimacy. As Lawrence Douglas has argued, the organizers of the IMT and subsequent postwar trials faced the challenge of demonstrating two different things simultaneously: they had to show the guilt of the accused, but they also had to legitimate the court itself.[35] Proving the legitimacy of the court in this case meant minimizing the "show" of the prosecution.

In the theater, however, boredom is usually seen as an existential threat. On the most pragmatic level, creating a play based on the proceedings of the IMT meant contending with the forty-two-volume transcript of the trial.[36] Schneider radically condensed the trial in order to convey the scope of the full trial within a single evening's performance.[37] In place of the written documents and affidavits that were read out loud during the trial, in the dramatization, the prosecution plays audio recordings of the defendants' public speeches and wiretapped phone conversations. These recordings were not authentic (they were made for the play), but they were based on the evidence used during the trial. By adapting written affidavits into audio recordings, Schneider combatted the monotony of having prosecutors read from long documents. This presentation also gives a sense that the audience is experiencing the evidence more directly: hearing the evidence *itself* rather than hearing the prosecutor read the evidence for them.[38] Schneider's biggest intervention was changing the structure of the charges. Instead of following the IMT's division of the proceedings by prosecuting nation, Schneider reorganized the transcripts into five thematic acts: "The Technique of Legality" (about the rise of the Nazi Party and internal purges); "The Technique of Aggression" (on rearmament after World War I and military aggression); "Demands of the Market 1" (on German industry and slave labor); "Demands of the Market 2" (on economic policy and banking; this act was cut in both the East Berlin and Vienna productions); and "Opinion Shaping" (on anti-Semitism, the Final Solution, and concentration camps). These acts are framed by a prologue and epilogue that were also taken from trial transcripts and which focus on the legality of the IMT.

The bulk of the prologue is devoted to a discussion about whether the industrialist Gustav Krupp von Bohlen (who was known as Gustav Krupp) could stand trial because of his health. During the IMT, the question of whether Krupp should be indicted was essential for how the court understood and claimed its legitimacy. At the time of the trial, Gustav Krupp was seriously ill, and his counsel filed a motion to suspend proceedings against him.[39] Additionally, Gustav Krupp was likely indicted accidentally in the first place, for he had retired from his firm in 1940, and it was his son,

Alfried, who had overseen the manufacture of armaments and the use of slave labor in the Krupp factories.[40] The prosecution realized their mistake and proposed that Alfried take Gustav's place in the defendants' box. This proposal shocked all the judges and, seeing the idea of substituting one defendant for another as antithetical to the principles of criminal law, they rejected the motion to add Alfried to the defendants.[41]

Beginning *Trial in Nuremberg* with the arguments about whether to release Gustav Krupp legitimizes the proceedings by showing that the court was both rigorous in its demand for evidence and willing to offer clemency. At the same time, though, the play presents convincing arguments by the British, French, and American prosecutors about the importance of having a representative of German industry on the docket even if it meant substituting one defendant for another. This prologue shows the tension between focusing on individual culpability (which is legally necessary) and understanding genocide and war crimes in relation to historical and structural forces (which is politically necessary).

Schneider's prologue and his restructuring of the charges had both a dramaturgical and a political function. Dramaturgically, the alteration allowed him to cut down on repetition and to create acts that feature more than one nation's prosecutor. Politically, this restructuring moved the emphasis of the proceedings from the question of individual culpability toward a historical and structural analysis of the Nazi regime. As a trial, the IMT was structured around charges: *what* the defendants did. The titled acts of the play, however, all offer an interrogation of *how* and *why* the defendants did what they did; the titles emphasize the causes of the war and the strategies and ideology of the Nazi Party. The play shifts emphasis from the completed criminal acts of the defendants to the question of how they were able to commit those crimes.

Schneider's restructuring reveals a paradox within the IMT and subsequent postwar trials. The IMT was oriented toward both the past and the future: it judged the criminal culpability of the defendants and set a precedent that would not only provide a legal framework for addressing future war crimes but would, indeed, *prevent* future war crimes.[42] The paradox here is that a focus on the individual culpability of each defendant can come at the expense of structural change that may prevent future atrocities. Mahmood Mamdani argues that Nuremberg's legacy is a human rights paradigm in which mass violence is understood and judged in terms of individual criminality. Responsibility for violence has come to be seen as "ethical, not political."[43] Mamdani argues that this form of justice cannot sustain peace in countries where victims and perpetrators must continue to live together because it does not offer a pathway for structural reform. Schneider's adaptation of the IMT shifts the focus from the individual criminal charges to the politics of the Third Reich or, as Mamdani puts it, from the ethical to the political. By organizing the play around the techniques that National Socialists used to gain and maintain control, Schneider engages both history and politics. He offers a historical account in which the rise of National Socialism was not inevitable but rather the result of particular tactics that could have been more effectively resisted. This historiographical intervention rejects several influential ways of understanding the Third Reich: the theory of a German *Sonderweg* (exceptionalism) that cast Nazism as the logical result of a particularly German character and history; a Marxist understanding of Nazism and Fascism as the final stage of capitalism (the position of the SED); and finally, the understanding of the Holocaust as the inevitable result of centuries of European anti-Semitism (the position of the prosecution in the Eichmann trial). This historiographical intervention is connected to a political intervention. By understanding how the Fascists consolidated power in the 1930s, audiences would become better prepared to recognize those techniques and resist the rise of Fascism in the present and future.

The historical and political aims of *Trial in Nuremberg*, and documentary trial plays more generally, can be mutually reinforcing. But they can also introduce tension between a commitment to the details of the historical record on one hand and, on the other, a desire to distance the play from those particularities enough for audiences to understand their contemporary relevance. In *Trial in Nuremberg*, only the defendants and witnesses are referred to with their proper names; the large prosecution and defense teams are condensed into four prosecutors (the American prosecutor, the French prosecutor, etc.) and two defense attorneys. The four chief and four alternate judges are condensed into one figure. Condensing the court officials lowers the number of participants down to a manageable number for the audience to follow. Giving these court officials generic titles also suggests that the tribunal itself could be replicated to try other defendants. Although the judges, prosecutors, and defense attorneys are all unnamed roles, the defendants and their witnesses retain their proper names.[44] By

using the actual names of the defendants while naming the court officials only by function, the play is able to mediate between the demands
of historical specificity and contemporary applicability. Giving the names
of the defendants also legitimizes the trial as an interrogation of individuals' culpability. As Arendt puts it in *Eichmann in Jerusalem*, this is a
matter of countering the defense that "where all, or almost all, are guilty,
nobody is."[45]

Schneider's decision to name only the defendants and witnesses was
echoed by Wolfgang Heinz's stage direction of the play for the Deutsches
Theater. In rehearsals, Heinz focused most of his attention on developing
the roles of the defendants and witnesses rather than those of the lawyers
and judges.[46] For the production team, the need to create a theatrically compelling production also meant, at times, focusing on individual psychology over more politically significant structural questions. In his rehearsal
notes, Ulrich Engelmann, a staff director at the Deutsches Theater who sat
in on rehearsals, describes a "contradiction between the political value of
information and theatrical effect." If the goal was to focus on information
about the Nazi regime on a systemic level, then the individual psychology
of the accused was irrelevant, and what happened on the stage itself was
secondary, meaning "the theatrical effect is almost absent."[47] According to
the rehearsal notes, Heinz provided the actors with material about the psychological states of the defendants, recommending in particular the
Nuremberg Diary by American court psychologist G. M. Gilbert.[48] His
directing style was often closer to Stanislavski than Brecht; he asked actors
to identify with the thoughts and motives of their characters, using improvisation exercises to encourage the actors to think like the characters they
were playing and discover the subtexts of their actions.[49] Heinz moved
closer to a Brechtian approach when it came to portraying the trial's theatricality. Heinz encouraged the lawyers to adopt a "Gestus of showing" (*Gestus des Zeigens*) in their presentation of evidence, telling them that, within
the trial, what needed to be shown was "not just argumentation, but the
demonstration of argumentation."[50] He asked the actors to emphasize the
theatricality of the defendants and defense attorneys, particularly Hermann
Göring. Heinz directed the actor playing Göring to perform his testimony
as a speech, for which the defense lawyer acted like a prompter, whispering
key words.[51] The defense attorney himself, meanwhile, built his case "like
a bad actor."[52]

During the rehearsals, the collaborators began to worry that the defendants came across as too sympathetic and that an evening-length performance would not offer enough time to adequately demonstrate the guilt of all the defendants.[53] Schacht was the most difficult case. In the play (and in the trial), Schacht defends himself by claiming that he was secretly working with the Resistance, and that all the public support he gave Hitler that is used as evidence was necessary to hide this Resistance work. These arguments persuaded most of the judges at Nuremberg, who acquitted him. The Deutsches Theater ensemble, however, agreed with the Soviet judge's dissenting opinion and sought to demonstrate Schacht's guilt. During one rehearsal, Heinz expressed concern that "Schacht's arguments are actually very convincing," and Engelmann noted down the ensuing conversation:

DRINDA [actor playing the US prosecutor]: It would have been conceivable, that a real Resistance fighter would have behaved like Schacht. . . .
HEINZ: So how can we take away the persuasiveness of his arguments?
MEVES [Heinz's assistant]: By showing that Schacht knows the persuasiveness of his arguments and deploys it as a tool.
DRINDA: He must put on a "show."[54]

Heinz agreed, saying that the actor playing Schacht "must not play honesty, but 'honesty.' "[55] His solution was to make the characters bad actors, whose excessive theatricality and mendacity is immediately apparent, thereby forestalling the audience's sympathy for Schacht and Göring. He used the performance of theatricality to differentiate between the testimony of these defendants and the testimony of Abraham Sutzkever, a Yiddish poet and partisan fighter who testified at Nuremberg about the murder of the Jews of Vilna. Heinz told the actor playing Sutzkever that when Sutzkever "swears to tell the truth and nothing but the truth, he is not reciting a formula, rather he promises. Here, already, the first victim in the courtroom will be differentiated from the others." Sutzkever's promise is performative rather than theatrical. His testimony must come across as immediate and unrehearsed: "The questioning of Sutzkever is not arranged in advance. That was not necessary. Sutzkever did not learn his text."[56]

In this production, theatricality and show are used multiple ways. First, theatricality is cast in a negative light in the "show" that Göring and Schacht put on, which demonstrates to the audience their falseness. Sutzkever's testimony contrasts to theirs in its lack of theatricality by seeming unrehearsed and authentic. Second, along Brechtian lines, the prosecutors in the play performed the "Gestus of showing," offering not only an argument but a "demonstration of argumentation." In this sense, "showing" is a positive thing.

By restaging the trial in a theater, the play draws attention to the tensions between these negative and positive elements of "show" at the IMT. In doing so, the play also underscores the political importance of theater itself. The metatheatrical quality of the trial play (the defendants as bad actors) lays bare the theatrical techniques of the trial. Lawrence Douglas argues that we should understand Nuremberg and subsequent Holocaust trials as "dramas of didactic legality" in which theatricality is an essential part of teaching.[57] If incorporating theater into the courtroom enables the court's didactic function, bringing the courtroom into the theater engages politics and histories that expand beyond the question of culpability. The restaging of such trials in the theater opens the possibility of making explicit the connections between the trials and other contemporary events. While an excess of extralegal context and framing could undermine the legitimacy of the court, these plays offer a way to present the proceedings to audiences while offering a wider framework for understanding the proceedings.

PERFORMING DOCUMENTS, WRITING HISTORY

The proceedings at Nuremberg were designed to teach history as well as pass judgment. As Robert M. W. Klemper, a member of the prosecution team, put it, the trial was to be "the greatest history seminar ever held in the history of the world."[58] The IMT inaugurated a new way of conceptualizing the relationship between history and justice: history itself was put on trial.[59] In the 1960s, the IMT continued to serve as a model for teaching history to an international public. As radically opposed as Schacht and Sartre were in every other respect, they both saw the Nuremberg trials as a place where history was written. They also saw public performances modeled on the proceedings at Nuremberg—whether onstage or before a tribunal—as a way to challenge existing historical narratives, to engage contemporary politics, and to show people what justice and injustice look like.

The question of how to stage and frame documents and transcripts was the central question for the production team in East Berlin. The collaborators on the production team understood that using the documents and transcripts of the trial selectively would allow them to offer a historical narrative with contemporary political implications. While creating the East German production of *Trial in Nuremberg*, the collaborators were constrained as to the history they were able to tell. In the GDR, censors would read plays and attend final rehearsals in order to approve of or demand changes to the production. The GDR never acknowledged the existence of this censorship, and the rehearsal notes make no mention of censorship by name, but Engelmann describes how the final textual changes for *Trial in Nuremberg* "were inspired by" guests invited to the final rehearsals. The changes that these guests "inspired" included "corrections of expressions and maxims that could be politically misunderstood"; "strategic cuts to enhance the accusations against the defendants"; and "an elevation of the role of the Soviet prosecutor."[60] According to Schneider, these changes were mostly a matter of staging and casting rather than textual edits.[61]

The Deutsches Theater's difficulties with censorship led to two public scandals in the years surrounding the premiere of *Trial in Nuremberg*. In the 1962–63 season, Peter Hacks, a staff director and author at the Deutsches Theater, fell afoul of the authorities for a play about factory workers, *Worries and Power*. The scandal over this play (which was applauded by audiences but condemned by the authorities) forced Hacks to leave the Deutsches Theater. Nevertheless, Hacks was one of the three playwrights commissioned (along with Schneider) for the Berliner Festtage. The year after directing *Trial in Nuremberg*, Heinz codirected a highly controversial staging of *Faust I* that government officials walked out of in protest.[62] Schneider himself took increasingly critical positions toward the government over the next decades and was expelled from the GDR Writers Union in 1979. Nevertheless, the relationship between the SED and Deutsches Theater was not purely adversarial, as Schneider put it in our email correspondence: "The SED as the State Party was omnipresent, even inside [our] heads. Both the dramaturges and the director were party members."[63]

In the rehearsals of *Trial in Nuremberg*, we can see a dialectical relationship emerge between censorship and transgression: some of the very aspects of the performance that might seem to adhere most closely to the demands of the SED actually become the most subversive. This dynamic is apparent both in how the collaborators decided to frame the trial historically and in the play's focus on anti-Semitism and the Holocaust (a choice which challenged the SED's emphasis on Resistance fighters and the Soviet Union as the main victims of the Nazis).

Schneider and his collaborators considered framing the trial in several different ways. The first idea was to begin with a speaker who would address the audience directly, introducing the time and place of the trial and then inviting the spectators to step into the roles of judges. The collaborators worried, though, that by telling the audiences that they were judges, they would collapse the critical distance between the judge onstage and the audience members, making it more difficult for the audience to differentiate between their own judgment and the judgments of the judge character onstage.[64] The problem here is one that Brecht articulates in his criticism of realist theater. Brecht argues that by emphasizing the reality of the world onstage, realist theater reifies existing social reality, convincing audiences that the world onstage is natural and unalterable. This problem of realist theater is even more pronounced in a documentary play like *Trial in Nuremberg* in which the proceedings onstage are part of the recent past. This can make it even more difficult to think critically about the actions onstage and to imagine how they could have gone differently. For Brecht, teaching audiences to consider how the events onstage could have gone differently is a crucial step toward teaching them to approach current events critically. While the collaborators wanted audiences to support the mission of the IMT, they also wanted the audiences to reach that conclusion by judging the trial for themselves (only then could they begin to apply the lessons of Nuremberg to the present).

The collaborators developed a couple of Brechtian solutions to the problem of establishing a critical distance between the audience and the events onstage. Their second plan included a speaker who would introduce the trial and then step in and out of the role of the judge, questioning defendants, informing the audience of historical events taking place outside the courtroom, initiating jumps in the proceedings, organizing the documentary material, and encouraging the audience to make associations between the trial and contemporary politics. This speaker/judge figure would "constantly alienate the actions onstage" in classic Brechtian style.[65] A third proposal radically expanded the fictional framing of the play. In this version, the play would begin with a group of actors trying to adapt Shakespeare's *Richard III* in order to turn it into a parable about the fall of Hitler. As the actors discuss *Richard III*, they are struck by how Richmond pardons the soldiers who fought for Richard III. They decide to improvise a trial against Buckingham based on the Nuremberg proceedings.[66] Here again, Brecht's influence is unmistakable. The play that these actors are trying to stage closely resembles Brecht's *The Resistible Rise of Arturo Ui*, a loose adaptation of *Richard III* that offers a parable of the rise of Hitler.

The discussion about which of these frames to use was in part a discussion about how the staging should present the role of the author and production team in shaping the documentary materials into a history of the trial. The collaborators discussed two possible approaches to documentary materials. The first approach was to emphasize to the audiences that the documents were chosen to present a particular interpretation of the trial. The second was to appear to make only minor "editorial changes" to the documents. Engelmann writes that this first approach would allow the theater greater "ideological-aesthetic freedoms" in shaping the documentary material into a play, while the second approach would remain closer to the specifics of the IMT.[67] Schneider ultimately opted for the second approach, dispensing with a contemporary frame in the text of the play altogether. In the context of the GDR, taking greater "ideological-aesthetic freedoms" with the documentary materials could actually mean giving the audiences less freedom to interpret those materials for themselves. If a speaker within the play were to inform the audience of how the evidence at the trial should be interpreted, this interpretation would have to fall in line with the SED. By creating a play in which the playwright's intervention was presented as minimal, however, the collaborators could claim that the play was simply adhering to historical fact. Here, documentary materials served as an alibi. Claiming the play was a direct presentation of the trial transcript, with little artistic license, provided cover for the quite significant—and often transgressive—ways that Schneider adapted the transcript for the stage. After all, censors were unlikely to check through forty-two volumes of court proceedings to monitor how the author had edited and assembled the documents.

After Schneider decided not to include a fictional contemporary frame in the text of the play, the Deutsches Theater ensemble still considered whether the staging should add an additional frame through projections or design. During the initial read though, the ensemble discussed beginning with projections of war crimes in Vietnam so that the play would be presented as a sort of flashback. At the end of the play, the Nuremberg set would disappear, and projections on the stage would show photos from the Russell Tribunal.[68] The ensemble also returned to the idea of a prologue that staged a "Gestus" of selecting and ordering photographs and documents into themes, which would then become the "chapters" or acts of the performance. After the epilogue, there would be a projection of the empty defendants' box, suggesting that it should be filled.[69] Nevertheless, just as the collaborators had decided for minimal textual framing, they also ultimately decided for minimal framing in the staging. Projections announced the titles of the individual sections ("The Technique of Aggression," etc.), and the play concluded with a projection: "The judgment was legally binding; there was no appeal; it was carried out. The proceedings are repeatable!"[70]

Instead of taking place onstage, the bulk of the historical framing took place in the program book. Of the Deutsches Theater's twenty-two-page program, only the first four pages give information about the Nuremberg trials themselves. The rest is about what happened afterward. The program features a two-page spread celebrating how the Russell Tribunal was continuing the work of the IMT and stresses in page after page the importance

FIGURE 4.1. Schacht on the stand in *Trial in Nuremberg* at the Deutsches Theater (1967). Courtesy of Gisela Langner.

of the Nuremberg precedent. It describes how the United States and Britain rebuilt the same industries that had encouraged Hitler's rise and how the companies that profited from slave labor were expanding in West Germany. It tells of how the Nazi generals were let off easy and of rearmament in West Germany. The program points to similarities between West Germany, the United States, and Nazi Germany and argues that the inevitable consequence of anti-Communism is Fascism. The crimes referred to are not genocide, of which there is no mention in the program, but rather the persecution of Communists, the mistreatment of prisoners of war, and the arbitrary killing of civilians. The program book also draws analogies between the Nazis and the Israelis. A section titled "Subdue the Aggressors!" suggests that Israeli general Moshe Dayan may have trained with the German army because his tactics are "pure German" (*rein deutsche*, a claim that uses the Nazi language of racial purity to describe the Israeli general).[71]

The program book frames the production as propaganda for SED policy. But at the same time, the program allowed Schneider and his collaborators to get away with producing a play about the abuses of state power within a dictatorship. Because the program stuck to party-line dogma, the performance was free to evoke very different associations, associations that would challenge the exercise of state power in the GDR and the Soviet Union. Schneider described his motivation for the play, saying,

For me, from the beginning, it was about the principle of international law at the foundation of the Nuremberg trial: war crimes, committed in the name of the State, must be judicially punished. . . . I accepted the one-sided focusing [in the program] on the US because of the Vietnam War [but did so] with a heavy sigh, in the justified hope that attentive spectators would in equal measure think about the crimes of Stalin and the events in Hungary in 1956.[72]

In addition to alluding to the crimes of the Soviet Union, Schneider also challenged the peripheral place of the Holocaust in East German accounts of the Third Reich.

By 1967, the Eichmann trial (1961) and the Frankfurt Auschwitz trial (1963–65) had brought the genocide of European Jews to the center of how Nazi criminality was understood in the United States and West Germany. In the GDR, however, official historical accounts minimized the role of racial politics, promoting instead an interpretation of National Socialism in economic terms as the final stage of capitalism. As a university student, Schneider had studied with Jewish scholar and survivor Victor Klemperer, whose experiences under Hitler made a deep impression on Schneider. In 1957, Schneider visited Auschwitz. His autobiography describes the horrors of the camp at length as well as his sense of responsibility as he visited: "Difficult, to walk around here, and one knows, one has a German name."[73] Schneider was concerned about anti-Semitism not only in Nazi Germany but also in the Soviet Union and the GDR. He saw in Stalinism and in East German politics an anti-Semitism that he "always tried, not just in this play, to put to rights."[74]

Trial in Nuremberg devotes a larger proportion of the proceedings to anti-Semitism and genocide than the IMT did. At the time of the Nuremberg trials, the Holocaust was not yet a part of the discourse surrounding Nazi crimes in the United States or Europe. Unlike some persecuted groups (such as homosexuals and gender-nonconforming people), crimes against Jews were addressed at the IMT, but they were not the central focus of the trial, as they would become at the Eichmann trial. For *Trial in Nuremberg*, Schneider adapted the transcript so that crimes against Jews became a more important topic than it had been in the original trial. A long final act titled "Opinion Building"—almost a quarter of the total play—focuses on the Holocaust and anti-Semitism. Schneider also expands the role of the Soviet attorney in prosecuting crimes against Jews by attributing lines spoken by other prosecutors in the trial to the Soviet prosecutor in the play.

What Schneider presents in this play is, in a sense, a bad history of the trial: it misrepresents the importance of crimes against Jews during the Nuremberg trials, making it seem as though the prosecution were more focused on genocide than it actually was. The play also exaggerates the role of the Soviet prosecution in prosecuting the crimes of the Holocaust. But in this case, an inaccurate representation of the trial offered audiences a better history of the Third Reich than the histories propagated by the SED. And the play is shrewd in that it gratified the SED's sense of Soviet importance while opening a space for survivor testimony. In the act "Opinion Building," the Soviet prosecutor demonstrates how it was not only structural economic forces but also ideologues like Julius Streicher who shaped how the SS ran the camps. The play presents this as a coup against the defendant Streicher, demonstrating the skill of the Soviet prosecutor. The prosecutor shows that, contrary to Streicher's claims, his anti-Semitic magazine, *Der Stürmer*, had a direct hand in genocide. While this act may seem to curry favor with the SED by showing the Soviet prosecutor in a good light, it simultaneously undermines the SED position that capitalism, rather than anti-Semitism, was at the heart of Nazi ideology.

In the play, the Soviet prosecutor elicits testimony about the Jewish victims of the Third Reich. In addition to Abraham Sutzkever, he questions Marie Claude Vaillant-Couturier. Vaillant-Couturier was a political prisoner at Ravensbruck and Auschwitz who, at the time of the IMT, was a deputy of the French Communist Party in the Constituent Assembly. In the play, the Soviet prosecutor asks her whether the "majority" of inmates in her transport to Auschwitz were Resistance fighters, and Vaillant answers no, that "the majority were Jews from every country in Europe."[75] In the actual trial, Vaillant-Couturier was questioned by the French, not Soviet, prosecution. Although her testimony made many references to the Jewish inmates at Auschwitz, the exchange about whether Resistance fighters or Jews made up the majority of the inmates never took place. By creating this (fictional) exchange and putting it in the mouths of the Soviet prosecutor and a French Communist Party member, Schneider gave his history the appearance of party orthodoxy. In East Berlin, the veneer of historical authenticity allowed Schneider to subvert party history.

The Vienna premiere offered a very different story. A review for the Vienna production praised Schneider's emphasis on anti-Semitism in the play, assessing it as a challenge to East German ideology. It was therefore puzzling, the review continued, that the Burgtheater did not follow the structure of the printed version and instead chose to swap the two final acts before the epilogue. Instead of ending with the Holocaust, the Vienna premiere ended on a "lighter" note with Hjalmar Schacht's testimony.[76] Another reviewer wrote that Hoffmann's performance gave Schacht "so much intellectual superiority and witty repartee that he, very much against the will of the author, becomes the actual hero of the evening."[77] The audio recording of the premiere of *Trial at Nuremberg* at the Burgtheater bears this out, capturing eleven significant rounds of laughter from the audience at Schacht's jokes.[78] The real Schacht liked the way the play portrayed him for good reason. His character's dry dismissals of the prosecution's case and his mockery of Hitler during this scene played well with the audience (at least on the night he attended, which was also the night of the recording). When the real Schacht began his monologue in the cloakroom after the show, the audience was already primed to listen. By reorganizing the order of the acts, the lighthearted final act before the epilogue could have been perceived as one of exoneration: it not only exonerates Schacht but all the Germans and Austrians who may have made a career out of collusion with the Nazis while nevertheless dismissing Hitler, as Schacht does in the play, as a "fanatical, half-educated," petty bourgeois.[79]

The experience of theater transforms the individuals in the audience into publics. The German word for audience, *Publikum*, already carries this meaning, from the Latin *publicum* (of the people, state, or community).[80] In Vienna and in East Berlin, *Trial in Nuremberg* constituted multiple publics simultaneously. Within the group of people who attended the performance in Vienna, there were those who laughed with the staged version of Schacht and asked for the real Schacht's autograph after the show. But there were also those who applauded Sutzkever's testimony about the Holocaust. In East Berlin, the program engaged one type of public, a public that would embrace official GDR history and politics. But at the same time, that performance sought to create another sort of public consisting of people who, if they were paying attention, could see parallels between the purges and violence of the Nazi regime and Stalinism and Soviet aggression. *Trial in Nuremberg*'s documentary character allowed Schneider a particular freedom to create among his audience members a dissident public who could see beyond the party line of the program and understand the play as an indictment of Stalinism and a challenge to GDR anti-Semitism at the same time that it condemned the war in Vietnam, West German rearmament, and Israel's Six-Day War.

JUDGMENT AT NUREMBERG ON THE SCREEN

In the 1960s, theater may already have seemed an outdated medium for addressing current political affairs and an unlikely site for creating publics. This was, after all, the age of film, radio, and television. Film had been used at the IMT in two unprecedented ways: films were submitted as evidence, and the proceedings were filmed.[81] A documentary film crew, led by John Ford, produced a short documentary about the IMT before the trial began, titled *That Justice Be Done*. Soon enough, a Russian film crew joined the American crew in Nuremberg. Various US attempts at a documentary of the trial itself were delayed for both logistical and political reasons. Pare

Lorentz, a New Deal filmmaker who was leading the project, resigned in protest after being targeted for making potentially "subversive" films under the Roosevelt administration. In the meantime, French producers created a two-reel news montage of the trials, and the Soviet Union sponsored a documentary film called *Nuremberg: The Trial*. This Soviet film premiered in New York in 1947 before its premiere in Moscow. The following year, the American film *Nuremberg: Its Lesson for Today* was released in Germany but not in the United States. In 1959, another documentary, *Der Nürnberger Prozess* by Felix von Pomanitzky, came out in West Germany.[82] In addition to these documentaries, a number of feature films, including André de Toth's *None Shall Escape* (1944), Orson Welles's *The Stranger* (1946), and Samuel Fuller's *Verboten!* (1959), presented fictionalized versions of postwar justice. Before deciding to adapt the IMT for the stage, Schneider had discussed creating a film based on the trial with an East German movie director. His decision to create a stage adaptation instead was based in part on the existence of a recent film about the Nuremberg trials, Abby Mann and Stanley Kramer's *Judgment at Nuremberg*, which had premiered in West Berlin in 1961 and East Berlin in 1963.

The courtroom drama flourished as a film genre in the 1950s and '60s. Of the twenty-five greatest courtroom films, as voted on by members of the American Bar Association in 2008, eight were made between 1952 and 1966. All but one of these eight films are based to some extent on actual historical or contemporary trials.[83] In the late 1950s and '60s, courtroom dramas also become a staple of television programming, starting with *Perry Mason*'s first season in 1957. *The Defenders*, which ran on CBS from 1961 through 1965, turned the courtroom serial into a way of addressing hot-button topics such as civil rights, McCarthyism, and abortion. Episodes of *The Defenders* presented fictionalized versions of actual cases or fictional cases that engaged current events and debates in a manner similar to more recent courtroom serials such as *Law and Order*, *LA Law*, and *The Good Wife* but with a more consistently progressive slant.

One of the most striking aspects of the proliferation of transcript-based trial plays in the postwar period is that it occurred at the precise moment when mass communication first made it possible for large audiences to listen to the trials on the radio and watch clips in newsreels and on television. Transcript-based plays were not primarily about disseminating information or conveying the reality of the trial as it really was—this was the purview of newsreels, radio, and television. As this chapter has argued, plays like *Trial in Nuremberg* are more concerned with adapting the trial to speak to contemporary circumstances rather than providing a mimetic reproduction of the trial itself. But this ambition to make the trial contemporary raises another question as well: Why produce this work in and for the theater instead of for a medium (film or television) to which contemporary viewing publics were more attuned? How does a play like *Trial in Nuremberg* relate to its audience differently than a film like *Judgment in Nuremberg*, which also restages a postwar trial in order to intervene in contemporary politics?

Judgment at Nuremberg is based on the Judges' Trial at Nuremberg, one of the Nuremberg Military Tribunal (NMT) trials led by American prosecutors and judges that took place after the IMT. Abby Mann first adapted the Judges' Trial into a television drama for CBS's *Playhouse 90*. Mann based the screenplay on trial transcripts as well as interviews with Hjalmar Schacht and Leni Riefenstahl among others.[84] Mann took a freer approach to the material than Schneider had, fictionalizing the defendants and defense attorney and changing some of the historical dates and facts in the case. The television version of *Judgment at Nuremberg* caught the attention of actor Spencer Tracy and director Stanley Kramer. Kramer and Tracy had recently collaborated on another courtroom drama, *Inherit the Wind* (1960) about the 1925 trial of a Tennessee teacher for teaching evolution.[85] Kramer and United Artists recruited a cast of stars for *Judgment at Nuremberg*—among them Judy Garland, Burt Lancaster, Montgomery Clift, and Marlene Dietrich as well as Spencer Tracy. The film was a popular and critical success, winning Abby Mann an Academy Award for best screenplay.

Like *Trial in Nuremberg*, *Judgment at Nuremberg* adapts transcripts of the proceedings at Nuremberg in order to intervene in contemporary politics. The film criticizes the willingness of both the Adenauer and Eisenhower administrations to brush aside Nazi crimes in order to promote Cold War unity against the Soviet Union.[86] It concludes with a voiceover stating solemnly that none of the defendants sentenced at Nuremberg served out their full term. In East Germany, where the film premiered in 1963, critics focused on this aspect of the film and emphasized the continued presence of former-Nazi judges in the Adenauer administration.[87] *Judgment at*

Nuremberg also draws connections between the crimes of the Nazi regime and domestic politics within the Unites States, in particular McCarthyism and violence against African Americans.

Judgment at Nuremberg focuses on two cases in which the former judges on trial used the law to enact violence against political dissenters and racial minorities. The first was the forced sterilization of a Communist, and the second was a death sentence for a Jewish man accused of sexual relations with a Christian woman. Of the many injustices of the Nazi judiciary, Mann chose two that the United States itself sanctioned. Within the film, the defense attorney points out that forced sterilization is an accepted practice in the United States and reads a 1927 ruling supporting the practice by Justice Oliver Wendell Holmes (a ruling that still stood in 1961 and indeed still stands today).[88] Like forced sterilization, antimiscegenation laws were still enforced in the United States at the time of *Judgment at Nuremberg*'s premiere. The death sentence for the Jewish man (and prison time for a German woman, played by Judy Garland) for interracial sexual relations links the racial laws of Nazi Germany to state laws in the United States. When *Judgment at Nuremberg* was released, the murder of Emmett Till was still a recent memory, and the novel *To Kill a Mockingbird* had just been published. The American prosecutor in *Judgment at Nuremberg* describes atrocities at Buchenwald, including the hanging of children. As he describes children being hanged, the camera pans over to an African American soldier, linking the concentration camp hangings to lynchings and the brutal, legally sanctioned murder of children like Till.

Like *Trial in Nuremberg*, *Judgment at Nuremberg* faced censorship. The Eisenhower administration unsuccessfully sought to block the broadcast of the first television version of *Judgment at Nuremberg* out of concern that it might turn American public opinion against America's West German allies in the Cold War.[89] Mann and the director, George Roy Hill, in turn threatened to take out a full-page ad in the *New York Times*, making the controversy public, if CBS submitted to pressure from the White House to drop the show. CBS refused the White House, but it did submit to censorship by one of the network's commercial sponsors. At the insistence of American Gas, the network edited out every mention of gas in postproduction, including the judge's verdict that he could not "forgive sending millions of people to the gas ovens."[90]

The censorship of the CBS broadcast underscores a key difference between the play *Trial in Nuremberg* and the film *Judgment at Nuremberg*: the play is written to be performed and experienced live. Unlike film, theater is an open form; a "work" of theater is only completed at the moment of performance. This means that censorship works differently across these two art forms. The postproduction editing of the film would have been impossible in the theater. Even though authorities in the GDR were able to prevent productions from premiering or could cancel the run of a production once it began, they could not remove words from a performance after they had been spoken or know with absolute certainty that an actor would not (purposely or accidentally) speak words that were banned.

Theater shares the space of its audiences in different ways than film. Theater is created through what Erika Fischer-Lichte has termed an "autopoietic feedback loop" in which the way that the actors perform is linked to the way that the audience behaves, with energy circulating between actors and audiences.[91] In his study of theatrical representations of the Holocaust and the French Revolution, Freddie Rokem argues that it is through the energy of live performance, rather than the mimetic representation of testimony, that an actor connects audiences to the past. Through these energies, the actor draws history into the present and "can be perceived as a hyper-historian, a witness presenting testimony for the spectators."[92] Both the energy of live performance and the possibility of failure on the part of such actor-witnesses link theater more closely to courtrooms than film.

The producers of *Judgment at Nuremberg* understood the importance of "liveness" for presenting witness testimony and constituting new postwar communities. In fact, they made the premiere of the film as close to theater as possible. The premiere was staged as an event that stressed both its own liveness and its physical embeddedness in a particular place (West Berlin rather than Hollywood). It was a gala event attended by German and American celebrities and dignitaries as well as three hundred reporters. East Germany had just erected the Berlin Wall, and the film premiered on the very same day that the verdict of the Eichmann trial was announced. The studio spent an estimated one million deutschmarks (one-twelfth of what it had cost to produce the film) on the premiere and surrounding events for journalists, including an open bar at the hotel and a photo op of Judy Garland in tears in front of the Berlin Wall. West Berlin's mayor, Willy

Brandt, welcomed the guests to the screening, calling the premiere "an important political event."[93] The film's premiere had a quality similar to the premiere performances of *Trial in Nuremberg*: the audiences experienced the premiere of the film as an event, and the meaning of this event was partly determined by the other audience members in the room.[94] Although it was a film, the premiere was staged as a live event.

Live testimony and presentation are essential to legal procedure. Philip Auslander demonstrates that courtrooms have, in fact, resisted the incursion of media technology to an even greater extent than theater itself has.[95] Despite some experiments in using recorded testimony, the legal system greatly prefers live testimony—"a live performance of memory-retrieval."[96] Courts generally prefer live testimony to edited prerecorded testimony even though live testimony means that witnesses or lawyers may make objectionable statements that jurors are not supposed to hear. Like theater, law—and especially Anglo-American court procedure—demands that evidence is shown and testimony is given live.

When the organizers of the IMT first gathered in London to discuss its structure, Robert Jackson insisted that the tribunal follow Anglo-American procedure, arguing that the American public would not believe Nuremberg was a real trial if the evidence was not presented in court.[97] The live demonstration of evidence and presentation of testimony was so important for Jackson because it proved the fairness of the trial by allowing for the possibility of failure: an unexpected answer during witness testimony, a document debunked in the courtroom. Indeed, the possibility of failure—on the part of lawyers as well as witnesses and defendants—is how we differentiate between a show trial (in the negative sense) and a fair trial. Weeks before being appointed as the chief prosecutor at Nuremberg, Jackson had declared, "You must put no man on trial under forms of a judicial proceeding if you are not willing to see him freed if not proved guilty, . . . [T]he world yields no respect for courts that are organized merely to convict."[98] Indeed, the IMT and NMT did fail to convict a number of defendants.[99] Because some defendants at the IMT were freed (and many others sentenced to jail time rather than death), and because radio broadcasts of the trial aired twice daily and films of the trial were distributed, many Germans who initially rejected the trial as "victor's justice" changed their minds.[100]

In courtroom theater, actors step into the roles of witnesses, performing not only their own lines but also the fallibility of live recollection and testimony. Just as with courtroom trials, the possibility of failure is what gives theater its power.[101] Even when the theater does not seek to replicate a trial mimetically, it still opens an energy that is closer to a courtroom than a movie theater. This is in part due to the liveness of theater as an art form, but it is also connected to the theater as an institutional space. This space exists before and after the particular night's performance and frames the performance within a series of other performances, a theatrical tradition, and a public building.

COMPLICITY, APPROPRIATION, AND RESISTANCE

Schacht was not the only participant from Nuremberg to visit the Vienna Burgtheater in the spring of 1969. Witness Abraham Sutzkever was there, too. He was working as a producer with Tel Aviv's Habima Theatre ensemble, which was on tour, performing a play about Jewish Resistance fighter Hannah Szenes at the Burgtheater at the same time that *Trial in Nuremberg* was playing.[102] Although Sutzkever did not see *Trial in Nuremberg*, he knew that his testimony was part of the play, and Schneider mailed him a copy of the script.[103] The Burgtheater hosted a dinner for the Habima ensemble at which Sutzkever sat in between Schneider and the actor who played him in *Trial in Nuremberg*, Paul Hörbiger. Meeting Sutzkever was a deeply moving experience for Schneider, who recounts that he had, "a melancholy aura of homelessness" about him.[104] When the conversation turned to the Israel-Palestine conflict, the younger actors took a hard nationalist line, but Sutzkever "gently, but authoritatively" contradicted them.[105] As it became warm in the room, he removed his jacket, revealing the concentration camp tattoo on his arm.

While Schneider participated in the conversation, Hörbiger remained silent. This may have been because he could not follow the conversation in English, or he may have felt out of place even though he was sitting next to the person he played onstage. Despite being cast as Sutzkever, Hörbiger's life history was closer to Schacht's. Hörbiger had grown up in Austro-Hungary but gained fame in Berlin in the 1920s as an actor in Max Reinhardt's productions at the Deutsches Theater (the same theater that premiered *Trial in Nuremberg*). When the Nazis came to power, Hörbiger was already a successful theater and film actor. He rubbed shoulders with the party elite, and his autobiography recounts attending a dinner hosted by Hitler and dining with Goebbels on multiple occasions. According to his autobiography, Hörbiger was always privately opposed to the Nazis, valued his Jewish friends and mentors, and rejected the anti-Semitism of the party, on one occasion defending Reinhardt to Goebbels.[106] Nevertheless, Hörbiger continued to act in films produced by the Nazi-controlled UFA film studio (*Universum Film-Aktien Gesellschaft*). He pushed in some small ways against the occupation, for example, saying the word "Austria" onstage in public. At the same time, his autobiography acknowledges that the Third Reich used the nostalgic popular films that he acted in to distract people from reality (though he rejects labeling them as propaganda).[107]

Like Schacht, Hörbiger became involved in the Resistance at the end of the war. After learning that he was on a list of celebrities who could only be arrested with the explicit consent of Goebbels, Hörbiger was emboldened to contribute money to the Resistance and to recruit other actors to join. He was caught and imprisoned during the final three months of the war. Although Hörbiger recounts a couple of crises of conscience, his autobiography ultimately justifies his actions during the war, emphasizing the dangers of even slight acts of resistance and the fact that he was always privately opposed to the Nazi regime. After the war, his role (albeit small) in the Resistance increased his popularity among Austrians and gave him privileged standing with the Allies. He used this popularity to secure the release of friends who had been detained by the Allies for being former Nazi Party members and testified at several denazification trials, at one point telling an American soldier, "I have met party members who were highly respectable, and others without party insignia who behaved like rascals."[108]

Hörbiger's casting as Sutzkever raises a number of ethical and political questions. These questions are intimately connected to how theater works as an institution that selects who gets to step into which roles onstage. What did it mean for Hörbiger to play Sutzkever? We can read this casting and performance in multiple ways. The first is that this casting erased the Jewish voice that Schneider had sought to emphasize in the play. By casting an Austrian actor who had been primarily a beneficiary but also victim of the Nazi regime, the production invited audiences to identify themselves with the victim, supporting the questionable (and popular) narrative of Austria's victimhood during the war. In the parallels between Schacht's and Hörbiger's relationships with the Nazi leadership (publicly supporting but claiming to privately resist, early elite treatment but ultimate imprisonment), this casting implicitly exonerates Schacht as well. Even someone who had acted similarly to Schacht during the war, the casting suggests, understands and sympathizes enough with the experience of Jewish survivors to embody one onstage. We might also see this casting as a way to emphasize the importance of the Jewish witness in the play. By casting Sutzkever with the most famous actor in the production, this staging drew the audience's focus to Sutzkever. The casting of a beloved actor in this role ensured the audience's investment and sympathy toward his testimony. All the same, it can be said that transforming Sutzkever into an ethnic German onstage in order make him sympathetic to audiences catered to and affirmed the anti-Semitism of those in the audience who would not feel sympathy for a Jewish man recounting the murder of his family.

On the audio recording of the premiere performance, the audience applauds immediately following Hörbiger's performance of Sutzkever's testimony. It is the only time during the performance that they applaud in the middle of a scene. Were they applauding Sutzkever or Hörbiger? The Jewish survivor or the "good" Austrian? Were they clapping at Sutzkever's indictment of the regime or because Hörbiger exonerated them all? We can never know for sure, though it seems safe to say that there were probably people clapping for both reasons. We also do not know why Hörbiger remained silent during that dinner. As he sat among those Israeli actors, did he feel proud of his own work in the Resistance? Did he feel remorseful for acting in Nazi propaganda films? Was he simply bored because he could not follow the conversation?

All we know for certain is that thirty years after his Jewish colleagues had been expelled from theater and film, Jewish theater artists were once again at the table. By inviting these actors and artists to sit together at the meal, the Burgtheater opened a conversation that the Nazis had sought to destroy. It was not an easy conversation; certainly, Schneider and the younger Israeli actors had strong disagreements about Israeli politics. And a gesture as simple as Sutzkever removing his coat was an indictment of those like Hörbiger who were, if not perpetrators, then certainly beneficiaries of a murderous regime. This dinner achieved on a small scale what the Burgtheater intended on a larger, public scale by simultaneously producing a play about Nuremberg written by an East German author and featuring a guest performance about Jewish resistance by an Israeli theater company. This sort of programming does not, of course, make the theater a utopian or even a politically progressive space. Arendt argues that such coexistence is merely the minimal requirement for the emergence of a public realm. Respect for human plurality is not progressive; it is just not genocidal. The Burgtheater was certainly a conservative institution, one that had not fully addressed its own history of support for the National Socialist regime. As this chapter has argued, the production of *Trial at Nuremberg* absolved both Schacht and the Austrian audience of any strong sense of responsibility. The Burgtheater's representation of the victims and perpetrators of Nazi war crimes was regressive. Yet, at the level of the institution, the Burgtheater nevertheless offered a space in which people from both sides of the Iron Curtain could eat together and where survivors, refugees, and their children had a seat at the table. The politics of a particular production or director might be questionable without undermining the importance of the theater institution itself. As Bonnie Honig argues in her book *Public Things*, public things are rarely all good or all bad. Rather, "at their best, in their public thingness, they may bring people together to act in concert. And even when they are divisive, they provide a basis around which to organize, contest, mobilize, defend, or reimagine various modes of collective being together in a democracy."[109]

At first glance, this meal may appear to have been much like the social outreach programs discussed in this book's introduction, such as the Munich Kammerspiele's Welcome Café or the Berlin Staatsoper's Welcome Classes, which offer lectures, workshops, and free meals to refugees. One key difference, though, is that the Habima ensemble shared the main stage and partook of the meal as visiting artists, equal participants in telling the story of the Third Reich. The visiting artists were not only invited to share food and drink at social events but also to stage public performances that challenged how Austrian visitors to the theater understood their own history. To put this difference in Arendt's terms, the Israeli actors did not remain in the private spaces of sustenance and charity but acted in public, and in emerging before the public, they also changed the constitution of the public itself.

ARCHIVES, LAW, AND THEATER TODAY

Plays like *The Burning Bush*, *The Crucible*, *The Investigation*, and *Trial in Nuremberg* are based on official documents such as court transcripts, legal records, and evidence presented at court. This documentary theater brings together two seemingly opposing forces: the state archive and theater performance. The tensions between archives, law, and performance have been a central focus for the field of Performance Studies since its inception.[1] Diana Taylor influentially distinguishes between the archive (documents and artifacts that sustain state power) and the repertoire (ephemeral performances of embodied memory).[2] Seen in this way, states use the archive to write history over and against the lived experience of marginalized people. Rebecca Schneider in *Performing Remains* argues that the story of the archive begins with the house of the Greek archon, the head of state, and eventually becomes the "arm of [colonial] empire" that uses documents to disable local knowledge and to support "a mode of governance against memory."[3] The documents of civilization contained in the archive are, in Benjamin's famous formulation, also documents of barbarism.[4]

Yet archives can also be used against those who assemble them. At the Nuremberg and Frankfurt Auschwitz trials, much of the evidence was taken from the archives of the Third Reich. As Marianne Hirsch shows, archival documents collected by perpetrators can become part of a repertoire of materials that are used by contemporary artists against the intentions of their original collectors.[5] In such cases, archives themselves can become part of a performed repertoire that preserves the cultural memory of atrocity. How these archives and documents work politically depends on how performances engage and create publics. It is impossible to know exactly how any of the performances looked and what they meant to individual audience members. But it is possible to uncover the ways that artists themselves approached the archives that they used to create their work. The playwrights and directors in this book show what it means to not only read but also perform history against the grain. At the same time, they complicate any easy dichotomies between complicity and resistance, law and performance. Brecht's 1953 *The Caucasian Chalk Circle* at once affirms the East German regime and challenges it; the production is both self-serving and publicly engaged. Within a single night, the multiple premieres of *The Investigation* were incorporated into very different sorts of political projects, some of them antithetical to each other. The effect of plays, as Arendt stresses in her discussions of Lessing and Brecht in *The Origins of Totalitarianism*, is like that of political action: it can never be known in advance by the producers and actors.

The plays in this book were written and produced at a time when documentary evidence meant written texts, photographs, and film reels. Today, the relationship between law and documentary theater has changed, in part because of major shifts in how documentary evidence is collected and disseminated. Over the past two decades, technologies such as cell phones and social media have reshaped how Americans document their experiences. Such technology informs how people understand the criminal justice system and can challenge state control over how evidence is collected, archived, and disseminated. Over the past several years, organizations like Copwatch, the American Civil Liberties Union (ACLU), and Amnesty International have developed phone applications that help users record police misconduct and automatically send the recordings to civil liberties and human rights organizations.[6] When there are no bystanders near, a person's cell phone may become his only witness. Jeffrey Robinson, director of the Center for Justice at the ACLU, told a reporter, "I don't leave my apartment without my cellphone charged. . . . [F]or black Americans, it's a witness: so when you're bleeding to death on the ground, at least your family and friends will believe you didn't cause this."[7] Increasingly, cell phone footage of violent police encounters is live streamed, creating a live (virtual) public that witnesses the event through social media.[8]

Given the discordances between police testimony and bystander and surveillance footage in high-profile cases, police departments have been under increased pressure to use body and dashboard cameras and to make that footage public. The circulation of video recordings depicting police violence is so significant because legal proceedings against officers are often confined to the secrecy of grand jury testimony. And yet such video recordings have not had the legal results that one might hope for. In the cases of Tamir Rice, a twelve-year-old boy shot to death in a playground, and Eric Garner, an unarmed man choked to death on a busy sidewalk, the videos seemed to speak for themselves, showing shocking and unprovoked violence by police. Yet not only were the killers, Timothy Loehmann of the Cleveland Police and Daniel Pantaleo of the New York Police Department, not indicted, they were not even fired. The public accessibility of incriminating evidence against police officers, combined with their seeming impunity, raises the same question that Elizabeth Hauptmann asked in East Berlin in 1954: "Is justice always against the law?"

Hauptmann's question is a question at the center of Anna Deavere Smith's documentary theater, particularly Smith's 2016 play, *Notes from the Field: Doing Time in Education*, a documentary work about the school-to-prison pipeline, mass incarceration, and police brutality. I conclude this book by discussing Smith's work because of her insight into how theater can stage the relationship between justice and law using new forms of documentary materials. Over the past three decades, Smith has been creating one-woman shows based on extensive interviews and research about controversial issues. She performs these interviews verbatim, replicating the dialects, speech patterns, and even the hesitations of the people she has interviewed. Smith's theater gives voice to many different storytellers with diverging perspectives while at the same time crafting a history of particular events through these individual stories. Her work challenges the way that events are narrated and judged in courts and in the media. She writes that since the O. J. Simpson trial, it seems that

the courtroom has become ever more present in our lives. The courtroom and the media stand as places where we resolve our differences—in public. Are the courts, together with the media, a collaborative scaffold building? Isn't there some way other than to immediately head to court that we can work out differences?[9]

Smith's first two major successes, *Fires in the Mirror: Crown Heights, Brooklyn and Other Identities* and *Twilight: Los Angeles*, are about moments of civil unrest in which competing claims for justice led to violence. These were moments of violence in which the legal system was not just ineffectual but also, at times, the root of the problem. As the subtitle of *Fires in the Mirror* indicates, both plays are also about identity—in particular, racial, ethnic, religious, professional, and geographical identity—and how different groups of people relate to the legal system.

Bystander videos have played an important role in Smith's work as a way for people to call for justice outside of—and often against—the law. *Twilight: Los Angeles* features one of the earliest bystander videos of police brutality to go viral: George Holliday's camcorder footage of police officers brutally beating Rodney King. The video galvanized outrage against the criminal justice system, and the officers' acquittal sparked the 1992 Los Angeles riots, which Smith uses as the subject of the play. In her most recent play, *Notes from the Field*, Smith reflects on the proliferation of such videos since 1992 and how they have come to shape how people think about racism and policing.

Notes from the Field premiered at Harvard's American Repertory Theatre in 2016 before beginning its New York run the same year. In this production, Smith weaves her performance of personal testimonies together with documentary footage from news reports and cell phone recordings. Among the people she performs are a Native American salmon fisherman, an elementary school social worker, a deli worker who filmed the police brutalizing Freddie Gray, a middle-aged former prison guard turned high school hall monitor, and a schoolgirl who filmed one of her classmates being assaulted by an officer in a South Carolina school. She offers the audience a wealth of information about the school-to-prison pipeline, mass incarceration, and police brutality. But she also does more than that. She gives a virtuosic performance, one that demands to be judged not only on the basis of what it says but also on how she reveals both herself and her interviewees through her performance.

Like Brecht, Smith finds and distills social *Gestus*, a manner of acting that conveys the historical and social situatedness of each character. But she also presents each character with a voice that asks to be heard in all its particularity, replicating cadences and mannerisms that individualize her characters beyond their social positions. Her method of acting offers a different type of virtuosity than the virtuosity of epic theater; she embodies the characters she plays, offering a precise mimetic replication of their voices rather than maintaining a critical distance from the characters. Smith's acting exemplifies Arendt's understanding of theater as a revelatory art, capable of presenting stories that convey not only the meaning "of the story itself, but of the 'heroes' who reveal themselves in it."[10] Smith's style of acting aims for illumination rather than psychological identification or photographic replication: "I try to present what they did, to take care of what they did, but the creative part of me is trying to illuminate what they did."[11] Her theater, in Arendt's terms, reflects both what and who people are, showing their particular places in society while also giving the unique voice of each of her subjects a place onstage.

Smith's virtuosity is itself politically important. By performing people of varied races, genders, ages, religions, and classes in quick succession, Smith reveals the performative quality of these differences.[12] At the same time, though, these performances reveal how much these differences matter, not only in terms of political power but also in terms of theatrical power and the ability to tell a story. By stepping into a diverse range of roles, Smith challenges a history of theater practice in the United States that sees in white actors a universality that allows them to play people of color while relegating people of color to marginal roles.[13] But Smith's virtuosity goes even further.

Through her performances, Smith offers something that none of the other philosophers, playwrights, and directors in this book do: she gives an account of why the performer's own life and identity matters.[14] Smith's work is a rejoinder to the argument for "color-blind casting," which sometimes serves as theater's version of "all lives matter," a claim to universalism that actually obscures inequality. At the same time, Smith challenges essentialist accounts of identity that claim that artists must *only* create work whose subject matter is part of their own identity. Both universalist and essentialist claims about art and identity tend to rely heavily on moral claims: on the one hand, seeing color-blindness as the basis for inclusivity and empathy, and on the other hand, seeing cross-racial casting as appropriation and even violence. Smith offers us both a more insightful take on identity and a more political way of judging what we see onstage. Smith's work is not good because she is telling her own story or because she is bringing diversity to the stage; it is good because she is a virtuosic performer. That virtuosity is not reducible to her race or gender, but it is also inseparable from it. This is equally true when she is playing an African American woman and when she is playing a Hasidic man.

Smith's performances substantiate W. E. B. Du Bois's claim that African Americans "are gifted with second-sight in this American world." Du Bois argues that a white person in America, because he occupies a dominant cultural position, sees white culture as a universal norm and fails to see himself as others would see him. Living within a dominating white culture, African Americans acquire a double consciousness that comes from "looking at one's self through the eyes of others, of measuring one's soul by the tape of a world that looks on in amused contempt and pity."[15] The experience of continual "two-ness" is oppressive, but it also offers a privileged epistemological perspective for understanding America. Smith describes gaining this second sight as a child, growing up in segregated Baltimore. She writes that during her childhood, everyone on television was white. By watching TV, she learned to identify with the white people in her favorite shows though she did not know many in real life. The problem, she writes, was not so much that black children did not have anyone to identify with on television, "Rather, the problem was that white people only had *themselves* to identify with."[16] Smith connects her ability to perform across a range of cultures with the habit of identifying across racial lines that she acquired as a child. The goal of her theater, in turn, is to teach audiences to identify with the diverse cast of people she portrays.

In the Cambridge production of *Notes from the Field*, Smith was only onstage for about half of the performance. At intermission, the audience was told that they were responsible for creating act 2 themselves. Each audience member was assigned to join a group somewhere in the theater to have a twenty-five-minute conversation about the play's themes. According to the American Reparatory Theatre program, Smith broke off the action of the play in order to "make room for the audience to talk to each other. . . . These reflective conversations are a crucial extension of Smith's and [the ART's] shared mission to expand the boundaries of theatre."[17] The subsequent New York production of the play did not include this group-discussion component.

At the performance I attended, when we were instructed to move into our assigned groups, a young African American lawyer sitting in front of me declined to move, declaring loudly enough for everyone nearby to hear, "I don't want to spend half an hour explaining race to old white people." She had a point, and as it happened, that is exactly how she spent the next half hour. The group that I was in met right next to where she was sitting, and she eventually joined the discussion. She was one of two African Americans in the group of about fifteen; the audience as a whole was overwhelmingly white, and the average age must have been around sixty.

In a sense, what Smith herself was doing during her performance was "explaining race to old white people." Within the play, she performs Bree Newsome, an artist and activist who reflects on the burden put on women of color to claim their place in the public sphere. Newsome scaled a flag-pole outside South Carolina's capitol to remove its Confederate flag. It was a dangerous action, both because of the difficulty of scaling the flagpole and because of the presence of police and armed white-supremacist groups around the capitol. Newsome was in a difficult bind: the history of violence against black women in America makes it unfair that Newsome was the one to put her body at risk for this action, but this very history is what makes it so important that black women lead actions against racist violence.

There is, however, a big difference between Smith's performance on a proscenium stage (or Newsome's flagpole action) and the work that the law-yer in my group was being asked to do. Smith's performance and New-some's action are so powerful because they are staged in such a way that Smith and Newsome become the most important people in the space. They are doing the acting while everyone else is watching. The dynamic within a small group, in which everyone was encouraged to participate equally, was very different. The moderator of each group read a question from one of the interviews that Smith had performed and asked the group members to put themselves in the place of the interviewer and consider what follow-up question we would ask. In my group, the moderator read a line taken from the interview with a man who had filmed police officers brutally arresting Freddie Gray. The interviewed man says the reason the police gave for arresting Gray was that he had made eye contact. An older white man in our group spoke first, suggesting that we can never know the truth of what really happened to Freddie Gray and why. The lawyer, now drawn into the conversation despite her intentions, objected that we do, in fact, know exactly what happened to Gray, and she went on to talk about her legal work and her own experience of racism. The moderator responded by speaking vaguely about how everyone has his or her own personal truth.

By insisting that everyone has his or her own personal truth and that everyone's opinion matters equally, the moderator denied the very possibility of justice for Freddie Gray. If police brutality is just a matter of perspective and opinion, there is no legal ground on which to challenge it. More than that, though, her moderation contradicted the very principle of Smith's work, which is dedicated to revealing the voices of those most impacted by a given controversy. Smith's work does not stop at revealing multiple voices and perspectives. It shows that the truth of an event emerges *through* these multiple perspectives, not *despite* them. In my group, a woman who described both her professional knowledge of the criminal justice system and her personal experience of racism was told that her opinion matters the same as a man who himself declared that he knew very little about the issues at hand. The paradox of *Notes from the Field*—and the reason why it is such an important work for considering the merits of different types of judgment in the theater—is that the part that was structured as a democratic debate was, in fact, less conducive to political judgment and equality than the solo performance from a proscenium stage.

Part of the reason this happened was the attitude of the moderator herself and the people who attended on that particular night. Another part of it was the structure of the questions that all the moderators asked. We were asked to align ourselves with the interviewer and to think about how we would question (perhaps challenge) the testimony of the witness. Immediately, there was a conflict between the (white, male) spectator who identified as "objective" and was inclined to side with the police—"we can never know what really happened"—and a (black, female) spectator who was told that her own life experiences and professional knowledge were a matter of personal subjective opinion.

In this exercise, what went unremarked on was the very fact of our being at a theater performance. We did not discuss Smith's acting or her performance's virtuosity. We also did not discuss what it meant to have this discussion within the frame of a theater production. We did not reflect on who was in the room. Instead, the moderator acted as though we were a random sampling of people who just happened to find ourselves together in a neutral space for discussion. This was very clearly not the case. The demographics of the audience did not even reflect the demographics of the city as a whole, much less proportionally reflect those most impacted by the school-to-prison pipeline. Act 2 not only distracted from the political significance of Smith's virtuosic performance, it also obscured unequal access to the theater. In other words, it advocated for a conversation where all opinions matter equally, but it did so within a space where black voices were underrepresented.

Theater does not have to be a democracy. As long as access to theater is unequal, participatory theater tends to replicate that inequality. But as an aesthetic institution rather than a town hall, theater can play by its own rules. It can decide that some voices are more important to amplify than others because those voices are heard unequally in the public realm at large. At the same time, theater is about more than the actor onstage. It is also a place in which, not only by acting, but also by watching and judging, people create publics. While theater may provide a platform for marginalized voices to sound, it might also create a space where people who cannot or choose not to speak nevertheless shape how others experience and judge the performance. This means that theater—if made accessible in ways that it often is not—can challenge the exclusionary assumption that to act politically requires the ability to walk up to a microphone, to speak loudly in English, to vote. At the theater, the public is constituted both by the action onstage and by the people sitting next to each other in the dark, wondering what everyone else thinks. Theater at its best does not offer justice according to law, or morality according to rules, but a space where people judge in the company of others.

NOTES

Note on citations: I include the full original German for archival materials and newspaper articles that are not widely available. Where there are good and widely available English translations of theoretical writings and secondary literature, I cite the English translations. For plays, I cite the original German. Unless otherwise noted, all translations are my own.

INTRODUCTION: SHOW TRIALS AND POLITICAL THEATER

1. Aeschylus, *The Oresteia*, trans. Richard Lattimore (Chicago: University of Chicago Press, 1953), 159.
2. Erika Fischer-Lichte, *History of European Drama and Theatre*, trans. Jo Riley (London: Routledge, 2002), 11–18.
3. Christopher Balme, *The Theatrical Public Sphere* (Cambridge: Cambridge University Press, 2014), 30.
4. Balme, 30.
5. Some of these plays were fictional, but most were based on historical or contemporary trials. Many of these plays and adaptations cluster around overlapping themes: wartime and postwar trials (Saul Levitt, *The Andersonville Trial*; Abby Mann, *Judgment at Nuremberg*; Rolf Schneider, *Trial in Nuremberg*; Robert Shaw, *The Man in the Glass Booth*; Peter Weiss, *The Investigation*; Hermann Wouk, *The Caine Mutiny Court-Martial*); witchcraft, heresy, and religion (Maxwell Anderson, *Joan of Lorraine*; Bertolt Brecht, *The Life of Galileo* and *The Trial of Joan of Arc*; Leon Feuchtwanger, *Delusion, or the Devil in Massachusetts*; Jerome Lawrence and Robert E. Lee, *Inherit the Wind*; Arthur Miller, *The Crucible*; Anna Seghers, *Joan of Arc*); political, ethnic, or racial persecution in the twentieth century (James Baldwin, *Blues for Mister Charlie*; Eric Bentley, *Are You Now or Have You Ever*

Been?; Bertolt Brecht, *The Measures Taken*; Tankred Dorst, *Toller*; Sidney Kings-
ley's adaptation of *Darkness at Noon*; Heinz Herald and Geza Herczeg, *The Burning
Bush*; Fritz Hochwälder, *Holocaust: A Court for the Dead*; Heinar Kipphardt, *In the
Matter of J. Robert Oppenheimer*; Romain Rolland, *Robespierre*; Edgar White,
Burghers of Calais); and contemporary adaptations of canonical trial plays and
novels like *The Oresteia* and Franz Kafka's *The Trial* (André Gide, *The Trial*; Ger-
hart Hauptmann, *Atridae*; John Matthews, *The Scapegoat*; Jean-Paul Sartre, *The
Flies*; Peter Weiss, *The Trial* and *The New Trial*).

6. For the classic articulation of the history of this antitheatrical prejudice, see Jonas
Barish, *The Antitheatrical Prejudice* (Berkeley: University of California Press, 1981).
Martin Puchner's work has made the question of this antitheatrical prejudice into
a central theme in the growing subfield of "performance philosophy." See Martin
Puchner, *Stage Fright: Modernism, Anti-Theatricality and Drama* (Baltimore:
Johns Hopkins University Press, 2002); Martin Puchner, *The Drama of Ideas: Pla-
tonic Provocations in Theater and Philosophy* (New York: Oxford University
Press, 2010).

7. Elizabeth A. Wood, *Performing Justice: Agitation Trials in Early Soviet Russia*
(Ithaca, NY: Cornell University Press, 2005), 20, 194.

8. Hannah Arendt, *Eichmann in Jerusalem: A Report on the Banality of Evil* (New
York: Penguin, 2006), 277.

9. Hannah Arendt, *The Origins of Totalitarianism* (New York: Harcourt Brace,
1968), 90.

10. On the ethical rather than political focus of postwar trials, see Mahmood Mamdani, "Beyond Nuremberg: The Historical Significance of the Post-Apartheid
Transition in South Africa," *Politics and Society* 43, no. 1 (2015): 61–88.

11. Elisabeth Young-Bruehl, *Hannah Arendt: For Love of the World* (New Haven, CT:
Yale University Press, 2004), 95.

12. Hannah Arendt, preface to *Men in Dark Times* (New York: Harcourt Brace, 1995),
viii.

13. Bertolt Brecht, *Die Dreigroschenoper*, in *Werke: Große kommentierte Berliner und
Frankfurter Ausgabe*, ed. Werner Hecht, Jan Knopf, Werner Mittenzwei, and
Klaus-Detlef Müller (Frankfurt: Suhrkamp, 1988), 2:284. "Erst kommt das Fres-
sen, dann kommt die Moral."

14. In other words, what makes judgment political is not what is being judged but
the plural performance of judgment. As Zerilli puts it, "Judging is political, not
because it is about political objects that are prior and external to it, but because it
proceeds by taking into account the perspectives of others and does not rely on
an algorithmic decision procedure or the mechanical subsumption of particulars
under known rules." Linda M. G. Zerilli, *A Democratic Theory of Judgment*
(Chicago: University of Chicago Press, 2016), 10.

15. John Willett, *The Theatre of Erwin Piscator* (New York: Holmes & Meier, 1979),
173.

16. Arendt, *Men in Dark Times*, ix.

17. Hannah Arendt, "Beyond Personal Frustration: The Poetry of Bertolt Brecht," in
Reflections on Literature and Culture, ed. Susannah Young-Ah Gottlieb (Stanford,
CA: Stanford University Press, 2007), 133.

18. Erwin Piscator, *Das politische Theater* (East Berlin: Henschelverlag, 1968), 20.

19. See Bernd Widdig, "Cultural Dimensions of Inflation in Weimar Germany," *German Politics & Society* 32 (1994) 11.

20. Piscator, *Das politische Theater*, 9.

21. Walter Benjamin, *Illuminations*, ed. Hannah Arendt, trans. Harry Zohn (New York: Harcourt, 1968), 242.

22. Willett, *The Theatre of Erwin Piscator*, 146.

23. Federal Bureau of Investigation file on Erwin Piscator, released under a Freedom of Information Act request filed by Jay Ball.

24. Theodor Adorno, "Cultural Criticism and Society," in *Prisms*, trans. Shierry Weber Nicholsen and Samuel Weber (Cambridge, MA: MIT Press, 1983), 34. Although Adorno himself would go on to revise and qualify this statement, it remains the most widely known and cited quotation about art and the Holocaust.

25. Theodor Adorno, "Commitment," trans. Francis McDonagh, *New Left Review I* 87–88 (September–December 1974): 75–89, accessed June 11, 2017, https://newleft review.org/I/87-88/theodor-adorno-commitment.

26. Brett Ashley Kaplan, *Unwanted Beauty: Aesthetic Pleasure in Holocaust Representation* (Urbana: University of Illinois Press, 2007), 21.

27. Hannah Arendt, *The Human Condition* (Chicago: University of Chicago Press, 1987), 7.

28. Susannah Young-Ah Gottlieb, introduction to Arendt, *Reflections on Literature and Culture*, xiii.

29. The first approach is reflected especially in the popularity of documentary plays in the United States, Great Britain, and Australia. Some prominent documentary plays along these lines include *The Laramie Project* (2000, about the murder of Matthew Shepard, a gay college student), *My Name is Rachel Corrie* (2005, about the American activist killed by Israeli forces in Gaza), *Called to Account* (2007, an indictment of Tony Blair for his support of the war in Iraq), and *Bradass87* (2013, about Chelsea Manning and Wikileaks).

30. Raymond Whitaker, "*Guantanamo—Honor Bound to Defend Freedom*, Tricycle, London," *The Independent*, May 30, 2004, accessed February 15, 2015, http://www.independent.co.uk/arts-entertainment/-dance/reviews/guantanamo-honor-bound-to-defend-freedom-tricycle-london-565362.html.

31. See C. D. Innes, "Toward a Post-Millennial Mainstream? Documents of the Times," *Modern Drama* 50, no. 3 (2007): 436.

32. Carol Martin, "Bodies of Evidence," *TDR* 50, no. 3 (2006): 12–13.

33. *The Exonerated*, by Jessica Blank and Erik Jensen, Culture Project, New York City, NY, September 29, 2012.

34. "The Exonerated," Culture Project, accessed July 9, 2015. http://cultureproject.org/highlights/exonerated/ (page removed).

35. Nicolas Bourriaud, *Relational Aesthetics*, trans. Simon Pleasance and Fronza Woods (Dijon: Les Presses du Réel, 2002); Shannon Jackson, *Social Works: Performing Art, Supporting Publics* (New York: Routledge, 2011).

36. Claire Bishop, *Artificial Hells: Participatory Art and the Politics of Spectatorship* (London: Verso, 2012).

37. Balme, *Theatrical Public Sphere*, 1–2.

38. More recently the Munich Kammerspiele has begun a series of free lectures, meals, and workshops designed for refugees, which take place on one of the studio stages

and appear to be more politically savvy and inclusive than the "town hall" event. See "Welcome Café," Munich Kammerspiele, accessed, April 10, 2017, https://www.muenchner-kammerspiele.de/en/staging/welcome-café.

39. Jacques Rancière, *The Emancipated Spectator*, trans. Gregory Elliott (London: Verso, 2009), 13.

40. Erika Fischer-Lichte, *The Routledge Introduction to Theatre and Performance Studies*, ed. Minou Arjomand and Ramona Mosse, trans. Minou Arjomand (New York: Routledge, 2014), 20.

1. HANNAH ARENDT: JUDGING IN DARK TIMES

1. *Beth Ha'am* can be translated either as the "People's House" or the "Nation's House": the word *Ha'am* has both class and national connotations (the common people, the Jewish people). In translating it as the "People's House," I follow Esther Grabiner, " 'Uniting the Nation's Various Limbs into a National Body': The Jerusalem People's House," in *Israel Studies* 20, no. 2 (2015): 76–109.

2. Grabiner, 76–109.

3. Hannah Arendt, *Eichmann in Jerusalem: A Report on the Banality of Evil* (New York: Penguin, 2006), 4.

4. Arendt, 5.

5. Susan Sontag, "Reflections on *The Deputy*," in *The Storm over the Deputy*, ed. Eric Bentley (New York: Grove, 1964), 117–18.

6. In his influential book *The Memory of Judgment*, Lawrence Douglas positions Arendt as an opponent of any form of theater within a courtroom. Douglas uses her as a "critical foil" to his own argument that Holocaust trials require stagings that go beyond the purely legal framework of the trials. Lawrence Douglas, *The Memory of Judgment: Making Law and History in the Trials of the Holocaust* (New Haven, CT: Yale University Press, 2001), 2. Shoshana Felman similarly juxtaposes her argument that "dramatic structures *can* be legally significant" (her emphasis) with Arendt, who "unambiguously discards the dramatic in the trial and denies it legal meaning." Shoshanna Felman, *The Juridical Unconscious: Trials and Traumas in the Twentieth Century* (Cambridge, MA: Harvard University Press, 2002), 161. On the tendency of critics and scholars to read Arendt's account of the trial as a condemnation of theatricality, see also Anson Rabinbach, "Eichmann in New York: The New York Intellectuals and the Hannah Arendt Controversy," *October* 108 (2004): 97–111; Michael Bachmann, "Theatre and the Drama of Law: A Theatrical History of the Eichmann Trial," *Law Text Culture* 14, no. 1 (2010): 94–116.

7. Arendt, *Eichmann in Jerusalem*, 9.

8. My reading of tragedy in this chapter follows closely the (neither entirely fair nor historically accurate) ways that Arendt and Brecht themselves define tragedy. Bonnie Honig's analysis of *Antigone* reveals the shortcomings of the simple equation of tragedy with fate, individual heroism, and humorlessness. See Bonnie Honig, *Antigone, Interrupted* (Cambridge: Cambridge University Press, 2013).

9. Arendt, *Eichmann in Jerusalem*, 6–9.

10. Tragedy, Arendt writes, "more than the other literary forms represents a process of recognition." Hannah Arendt, "On Humanity in Dark Times: Thoughts about Lessing," in *Men in Dark Times* (New York: Harcourt Brace, 1995), 20.

11. Arendt, *Eichmann in Jerusalem*, 52.

12. Arendt, 19.

13. Hannah Arendt, *On Revolution* (New York: Penguin, 1990), 88.

14. Hannah Arendt, "Quod Licet Jovi . . . Reflexionen über den Dichter Bertolt Brecht und sein Verhältnis zur Politik," *Merkur* 23, no. 7 (1969): 631. Unless otherwise noted, all translations are my own.

15. Arendt, *On Revolution*, 95.

16. Arendt, *Eichmann in Jerusalem*, 251. *The Diary of Anne Frank* was translated into German in 1950. A dramatic adaptation of the diary was performed in seven West German cities simultaneously in 1956 and became immensely popular. The play and productions of the time presented Anne Frank's life as a universal story, minimizing her Jewish identity and the question of German culpability. Arendt was not the only one to remark on its dangerous sentimentality. Adorno recounts a story of one woman leaving the theater and remarking, "At least they should have let *that* girl live." Torben Fischer and Matthias Lorenz, eds., *Lexikon der "Vergangenheitsbewältigung" in Deutschland: Debatten- und Diskursgeschichte des Nationalsozialismus nach 1945* (Bielefeld: Transcript, 2007), 107–8.

17. Susannah Young-ah Gottlieb, "Beyond Tragedy: Arendt, Rogat, and the Judges in Jerusalem," *College Literature* 38, no. 1 (2011): 45–56. Gottlieb shows how Arendt at once avoids using tragic tropes to understand the Eichmann trial while at the same time coming back to the idea of tragedy throughout the book. Gottlieb discusses Arendt's rejection of tragedy in relation to German philosophy (especially Nietzsche and Benjamin) and Yosal Rogat's *The Eichmann Trial and the Rule of Law*, which links the Eichmann trial to Athena's judgment in *The Eumenides*, but not in relation to contemporary theater.

18. Hannah Arendt, "Beyond Personal Frustration: The Poetry of Bertolt Brecht," in *Reflections on Literature and Culture*, ed. Susannah Young-Ah Gottlieb (Stanford, CA: Stanford University Press, 2007), 133.

19. Erdmut Wizisla, *Walter Benjamin and Bertolt Brecht: The Story of a Friendship* (New Haven, CT: Yale University Press, 2009), 111.

20. Elisabeth Young-Bruehl's biography states that Brecht and Arendt's initial meeting was during their time in Paris. Elisabeth Young-Bruehl, *Hannah Arendt: For Love of the World* (New Haven, CT: Yale University Press, 2004), 116.

21. Young-Bruehl, 136.

22. Detlev Schöttker and Erdmut Wizisla, eds. *Arendt und Benjamin: Texte, Briefe, Dokumente* (Frankfurt: Suhrkamp, 2006), 165.

23. Arendt published multiple versions of both essays ("What Is Permitted to Jove" and "Beyond Personal Frustration") in English and in German. Unless otherwise noted, my references are to the English versions reprinted in Arendt, *Reflections on Literature and Culture*.

24. Few studies have explored Arendt's relationship to contemporary theater techniques. Instead, work on Arendt has taken three main approaches to her use of theater. The first approach focuses on the relationship between Arendt's work and

the tradition of Greek tragedy (Halpern, Pirro). A second approach focuses on the metaphor of the "world stage" and the relationship between theater and reality (Curtis, Kottmann). The third approach focuses not on particular theater techniques so much as on performance and performativity (Butler, Cavarero, Honig, Villa). Cecilia Sjöholm's *Doing Aesthetics with Arendt* is rare in that it connects Arendt's aesthetics to avant-garde performance in 1960s and '70s New York. Judith Butler, *Notes Toward a Performative Theory of Assembly* (Cambridge, MA: Harvard University Press, 2015); Adriana Cavarero, *For More than One Voice: Toward a Philosophy of Vocal Expression*, trans. Paul Kottman (Stanford, CA: Stanford University Press, 2005); Kimberley Curtis, *Our Sense of the Real: Aesthetic Experience and Arendtian Politics* (Ithaca, NY: Cornell University Press, 1999); Richard Halpern, "Theatre and Democratic Thought: Arendt to Rancière," *Critical Inquiry* 37, no. 3 (2011): 545–72; Bonnie Honig, "Toward an Agonistic Feminism: Hannah Arendt and the Politics of Identity," in *Feminist Interpretations of Hannah Arendt*, ed. Bonnie Honig (University Park, PA: Penn State University Press, 1995): 135–66; Bonnie Honig, *Political Theory and the Displacement of Politics* (Ithaca, NY: Cornell University Press, 1993); Paul Kottman, *A Politics of the Scene* (Stanford, CA: Stanford University Press, 2008); Robert C. Pirro, *Hannah Arendt and the Politics of Tragedy* (Dekalb: Northern Illinois University Press, 2001); Cecilia Sjöholm, *Doing Aesthetics with Arendt: How to See Things* (New York: Columbia University Press, 2015); Dana Villa, *Arendt and Heidegger: The Fate of the Political* (Princeton, NJ: Princeton University Press, 1995).

25. Bertolt Brecht, "An die Nachgeborenen," in *Werke: Große kommentierte Berliner und Frankfurter Ausgabe*, ed. Werner Hecht, Jan Knopf, Werner Mittenzwei, and Klaus-Detlef Müller (Frankfurt: Suhrkamp, 1988), 12:85.

26. See David Luban, "Explaining Dark Times: Hannah Arendt's Theory of Theory," *Social Research* 50, no. 1 (1983): 215–48.

27. Brecht, "An die Nachgeborenen," 85.

28. Bertolt Brecht, "The Modern Theatre Is the Epic Theatre (Notes to the Opera *Aufstieg und Fall der Stadt Mahagonny*)," in *Brecht on Theatre: The Development of an Aesthetic*, ed. and trans. John Willett (New York: Hill and Wang, 1992), 37.

29. Bertolt Brecht, "Formal Problems Arising from the Theatre's New Content," in *Brecht on Theatre*, 227.

30. Arendt, "Beyond Personal Frustration," 137.

31. Walter Benjamin, "What Is Epic Theatre? [first version]," in *Understanding Brecht*, trans. Anna Bostock (New York: Verso, 1998), 12.

32. Benjamin, 4. Perhaps trying to save them from themselves, Arendt disputes both Benjamin's and Brecht's claims that Brecht is a dialectician in Hannah Arendt, introduction to Walter Benjamin, *Illuminations*, ed. Hannah Arendt, trans. Harry Zohn (New York: Harcourt, 1968), 15.

33. Arendt, *Men in Dark Times*, ix.

34. Hannah Arendt, *The Human Condition* (Chicago: University of Chicago Press, 1998), 188.

35. Arendt, 198.

36. See Arendt, 181–88.

37. Hannah Arendt, "Some Questions of Moral Philosophy," in *Responsibility and Judgment*, ed. Jerome Kohn (New York: Schocken, 2003), 90.

38. Arendt, 93–94.

39. Benjamin, "What Is Epic Theatre?," 153.

40. Arendt, *Eichmann in Jerusalem*, 228–29. In her personal letters about the trial, Arendt is strikingly chauvinistic about German Jews, expressing shock at the "Oriental mob" outside the courthouse and drawing comparisons between the judges, who represented the "best of the German Jewry," and Gideon Hausner, "a typical Galician Jew." It is, perhaps, no coincidence that Arendt singles out the articulacy of a witness who lived in Germany for over two decades. Arendt does not mention his language, but Grynszpan testified in Yiddish, presumably his native tongue. The clarity of his speech, as opposed to that of Hausner and other witnesses who tried to speak in their new language of Hebrew, is as much a sign of statelessness as of "purity of soul." Arendt is dismissive of the use of Hebrew at the trial, seeing it as part of the failed show-trial aspect of the proceedings and remarking on "the comedy of speaking Hebrew when everyone involved knows German and thinks in German." See Amos Elon, introduction to Arendt, *Eichmann in Jerusalem*, xviii.

41. Deborah Nelson, *Tough Enough: Arbus, Arendt, Didion, McCarthy, Sontag, Weil* (Chicago: University of Chicago Press, 2017), 54.

42. Arendt, *Eichmann in Jerusalem*, 231.

43. Arendt, 233. Her emphasis.

44. Arendt, 230.

45. See Bertolt Brecht, "Short Description of a New Technique of Acting Which Produces an Alienation Effect," in *Brecht on Theatre*, 138; Martin Puchner, *Stage Fright: Modernism, Anti-Theatricality, and Drama* (Baltimore: Johns Hopkins University Press, 2002), 143.

46. Benjamin, "What Is Epic Theatre?," 150.

47. Lida Maxwell, *Public Trials: Burke, Zola, Arendt, and the Politics of Lost Causes* (Oxford: Oxford University Press, 2015).

48. See Yasco Horsman, *Theaters of Justice: Judging, Staging, and Working Through in Arendt, Brecht, and Delbo* (Stanford, CA: Stanford University Press, 2011).

49. Arendt, *Eichmann in Jerusalem*, 287.

50. Excepts of the interview are published in Hannah Arendt, "Hannah Arendt: From an Interview," *New York Review of Books*, October 26, 1978, accessed February 27, 2017, http://www.nybooks.com/articles/1978/10/26/hannah-arendt-from-an-interview/. Arendt also quotes this passage in her essay "What Is Permitted to Jove" (253) as an example of Brecht's "extraordinary intelligence."

51. Arendt, "On Humanity," 6. Here, she is describing the way that Lessing uses laughter in his play *Minna von Barnhelm*.

52. Walter Benjamin, "The Author as Producer," in *Understanding Brecht*, 101.

53. Deborah Nelson argues that it was Arendt's tone in *Eichmann in Jerusalem* (particularly combined with her gender) rather than factual errors that resulted in the ad hominem attacks following its publication. Nelson makes the crucial point that it was because Arendt was so concerned about pain that she refused to write about pain sentimentally: "Arendt banishes suffering from the public realm in more

general terms, not because one can be indifferent to it, but because one cannot."
Nelson, *Tough Enough*, 52.

54. *The Trial of Adolf Eichmann: Record of the Proceedings in the District Court of Jerusalem* (Jerusalem: Trust for the Publication of the Proceedings of the Eichmann Trial, 1992), 3:1237.

55. Arendt, *Eichmann in Jerusalem*, 224.

56. Ariella Azoulay and Bonnie Honig make a compelling case for reading Arendt's account of K-Zetnik's testimony in a different way: not as an expression of derision but of respect. They note that while she does not endorse what he says, she does record his speech, while granting him the dignity of remaining silent about what took place after he fainted. By doing so, Arendt enacts a mode of care, *Tikkun Olam*, which is effaced by the binary between empathy and the law assumed by readers like Shoshana Felman. Ariella Azoulay and Bonnie Honig, "Between Nuremberg and Jerusalem: Hannah Arendt's *Tikkun Olam*," *differences* 27, no. 1 (2016): 64–65.

57. *The Deputy (Der Stellvertreter: Ein christliches Trauerspiel)* premiered in 1963 at the Freie Volksbühne in West Berlin, directed by Erwin Piscator. Within the next two years, it was produced widely across Europe and on Broadway. In response to the controversy surrounding the play, Eric Bentley edited a volume of essays about the play, *The Storm over the Deputy*. Susan Sontag's remarks on the Eichmann trial cited at the outset of the chapter are from an essay on *The Deputy* that she wrote for that volume.

58. Arendt, "Some Questions of Moral Philosophy," 59. She makes a similar argument about *The Deputy* in her postscript to *Eichmann in Jerusalem*. Arendt, *Eichmann in Jerusalem*, 295.

59. Arendt, *Eichmann in Jerusalem*, 374.

60. Judith Butler, "Hannah Arendt's Death Sentences," *Comparative Literature* 48, no. 3 (2011): 280–95.

61. Gottlieb, "Beyond Tragedy," 49.

62. Butler, "Hannah Arendt's Death Sentences," 284.

63. Azoulay and Honig, "Between Nuremberg and Jerusalem," 79.

64. See Ursula Ludz's fantastically thorough bibliography of Arendt's work in Hannah Arendt, *Ich will verstehen: Selbstauskünfte zu Leben und Werk*, ed. Ursula Ludz (Munich: Piper, 2005), 257–341.

65. Arendt, *The Human Condition*, 7.

66. Arendt, 179.

67. The speech was published as "On Humanity in Dark Times: Thoughts on Lessing" in *Men in Dark Times*, a book whose title is taken from the first line of Brecht's poem "To Those Born After." The conception of "the world" outlined in this speech accords with Arendt's biography of Rahel Varnhagen but is different from the way she uses "world" in *The Human Condition*. Seyla Benhabib points to the Lessing acceptance speech as Arendt's most thorough articulation of her conception of "the world," while Bonnie Honig argues for greater attention to the definition of "the world" in *The Human Condition* as created through work as well as action and composed of the web of relationships between things as well as people. Seyla Benhabib, *The Reluctant Modernism of Hannah Arendt* (New York: Rowman & Littlefield, 2000), 13; Bonnie Honig, *Public Things: Democracy in Disrepair* (New York: Fordham University Press, 2017), 38–39.

68. Arendt, "On Humanity," 30–31.

69. Arendt, 4–5.

70. Arendt, 31.

71. Erika Fischer-Lichte, *Kurze Geschichte des deutschen Theaters* (Tübingen: A. Francke, 1999), 109–10.

72. Friedrich Schiller, "The Stage as a Moral Institution," trans. John Sigerson and John Chambless, Schiller Institute, accessed February 28, 2017, https://www.schillerinstitute.org/transl/schil_theatremoral.html.

73. See Magda Romanska, introduction to *The Routledge Companion to Dramaturgy*, ed. Magda Romanska (London: Routledge, 2015), 2.

74. Arendt, "On Humanity," 6–7.

75. Hinrich C. Seeba, "Modern Criticism in Historical Context: 200 Years of Lessing Reception," in *A Companion to the Works of Gotthold Ephraim Lessing*, ed. Barbara Fischer and Thomas C. Fox (New York: Camden House, 2005), 342.

76. Hannah Arendt, *Origins of Totalitarianism* (New York: Harcourt Brace, 1968), 57–58.

77. Arendt, 61.

78. Arendt, *Eichmann in Jerusalem*, 134.

79. Arendt, "On Humanity," 17–18. We can see how closely tied this argument about Lessing is to Arendt's call for Jewish resistance during the Third Reich in the almost-identical language that she uses in a 1941 essay calling for the establishment of a Jewish army: "You can only defend yourself as the person you are attacked as." Hannah Arendt, *The Jewish Writings*, ed. Jerome Kohn and Ron H. Feldman (New York: Schocken, 2007), 137.

80. Arendt, "On Humanity," 18.

81. See Lisa J. Disch, "On Friendship in 'Dark Times,'" in Honig, *Feminist Interpretations of Hannah Arendt*, 285–312.

82. It is in Herder, not Lessing, that Arendt sees an interest not merely in toleration but in the emancipation of the Jews. Hannah Arendt, *Rahel Varnhagen: The Life of a Jewess*, ed. Liliane Weissberg, trans. Richard Winston and Clara Winston (Baltimore: John Hopkins University Press, 2000), 106.

83. Erika Fischer-Lichte, "Policies of Spatial Appropriation," in *Performance and the Politics of Space: Theatre and Topology*, ed. Erika Fischer-Lichte and Benjamin Wihstutz (London: Routledge, 2012), 223.

84. Fischer-Lichte, 229.

85. Arendt, *The Human Condition*, 187–88.

86. As Seyla Benhabib argues, Arendt's references to the Greek polis have distracted readers from the particularly modernist quality of her work. Benhabib's book focuses on the historical context of Arendt's philosophical approach (the influence of Existenz philosophy) and her experience of her German Jewish identity; Arendt's approach to theater must likewise be historically contextualized. See Benhabib, *The Reluctant Modernism*.

87. Halpern, "Theatre and Democratic Thought," 545–72. Richard Halpern tracks Arendt's departures from the historical practice of Greek theater but does not link these departures to the ways that Greek theater was being interpreted, cited, and reimagined through contemporary performance.

88. Michael Schwaiger, "Einbruch der Wirklichkeit: Das Theater Bertolt Brechts und Erwin Piscators," in *Bertolt Brecht und Erwin Piscator: Experimentelles Theater*

im Berlin der Zwanzigerjahre, ed. Michael Schwaiger (Vienna: Christian Brand-stätter, 2004), 10.

89. See Puchner, *Stage Fright*, 22–24.

90. Arendt, *The Human Condition*, 187–88.

91. Erika Fischer-Lichte, *The Routledge Introduction to Theatre and Performance Studies*, ed. Minou Arjomand and Ramona Mosse, trans. Minou Arjomand (New York: Routledge, 2014), 13.

92. Arendt, *The Human Condition* 183.

93. Arendt, *The Origins of Totalitarianism*, 335.

94. Rebecca Rovit, *The Jewish Kulturbund Theatre Company in Nazi Berlin* (Iowa City: University of Iowa Press, 2012), 3.

95. Rovit, 39–41. A review in the Zionist *Rundschau* condemned the choice of Lessing as assimilationist: "To use *Nathan* as a 'song of tolerance' is not doing Jews a service." It is not clear that the director, Kurt Singer, himself had any faith in the play's message of tolerance. Breaking with the tradition of presenting Nathan as an assimilated humanist, the Kulturbund production emphasized Nathan's ethnicity. Instead of ending with an embrace of the Jewish, Christian, and Muslim characters, as is written in the script, the production ended with Nathan alone onstage. The set designer of this production, Heinz Condell, fled Germany and went on to work at the Dramatic Workshop with Erwin Piscator, designing the set for *The Burning Bush*, which is discussed in the following chapter.

96. Quoted in Gerhard F. Probst, *Erwin Piscator and the American Theatre* (New York: Peter Lang, 1991), 37.

97. Manfred Braueneck, *Die Welt als Bühne: Geschichte des europäischen Theaters* (Stuttgart: J. B. Metzler, 2007), 5:470–71.

98. Arendt, *The Human Condition*, 232–33.

99. George Kateb, "Political Action: Its Nature and Advantages," in *The Cambridge Companion to Hannah Arendt*, ed. Dana Villa (Cambridge: Cambridge University Press, 2000), 130–48; Jürgen Habermas, "Hannah Arendt's Communications Concept of Power," in *Hannah Arendt, Critical Essays*, ed. Lewis Hinchman and Sandra Hinchman (Albany: State University of New York Press, 1994): 211–30; Hanna Fenichel Pitkin, "Justice: On Relating Private and Public," *Political Theory* 9, no. 3 (1981): 327–52.

100. See Honig, *Political Theory*.

101. See Honig, "Toward an Agonistic Feminism"; Butler, *Notes Toward a Performative Theory*.

102. Seyla Benhabib, "Ethics Without Normativity and Politics Without Historicity: On Judith Butler's *Parting Ways: Jewishness and the Critique of Zionism*," *Constellations* 20, no. 1 (2013): 150–63; Amy Allen, "Solidarity after Identity Politics: Hannah Arendt and the Power of Feminist Theory," *Philosophy and Social Criticism* 25, no. 1 (1999): 109.

103. Allen, 109.

104. In the German translation of *The Human Condition* (completed by Arendt, based on a first, rough translation by Charlotte Beradt), this distinction is not quite as neat. Arendt uses the terms *Handelnde* (or sometimes *Person*) and *handeln* (Nietzsche's terms are *Täter* and *Tat*). The German *Handelnde* does not have the same theatrical connotation as "actor," though *Handlung* (from *handeln*) means

"action" in the sense of dramatic action or plot. Hannah Arendt, *Vita activa oder Vom tätigen Leben* (Stuttgart: Kohlhammer, 1960).

105. Arendt, *On Revolution*, 48.

106. Karl Marx, *The Eighteenth Brumaire of Louis Napoleon* (London: Electric Book Company, 2001), 7.

107. Hannah Arendt, "The Concept of History," in *Between Past and Future: Six Exercises in Political Thought* (New York: Viking, 1961), 79.

108. Arendt, 43.

109. Arendt, *Eichmann in Jerusalem*, 85–86.

110. Arendt, 49.

111. Arendt, *On Revolution*, 103.

112. Arendt, 97.

113. Benjamin, "What Is Epic Theatre?," 2.

114. Nancy Fraser, *Justice Interruptus: Critical Reflections on the "Postsocialist" Condition* (New York: Routledge, 1997), 77–79.

115. Along similar lines, Zerilli distinguishes between the ability to identify and empathize with others (the ethical stance of "other-regard") with the "attempt to see from multiple standpoints in order to form a critical opinion" (the political practice of "representative thinking"). Linda M. G. Zerilli, *A Democratic Theory of Judgment* (Chicago: University of Chicago Press, 2016), 181.

116. Arendt's own writings on the civil rights and the black power movements reveal her failure to think beyond her own Eurocentric and racist assumptions. See Michael D. Burroughs, "Hannah Arendt, 'Reflections on Little Rock,' and White Ignorance," *Critical Philosophy of Race* 3, no. 1 (2015): 52–78; Kathryn T. Gines, *Hannah Arendt and the Negro Question* (Bloomington: Indiana University Press, 2014); Anne Norton, "Heart of Darkness: Africa and African-Americans in the Writings of Hannah Arendt," in Honig, *Feminist Interpretations of Hannah Arendt*, 247–61.

117. Arendt, *On Revolution*, 50.

118. Seyla Benhabib, "The Embattled Public Sphere: Hannah Arendt, Jürgen Habermas and Beyond," *Theoria* 44, no. 90 (1997): 18.

119. This is Butler's conception of the public in *Notes Toward a Performative Theory of Assembly* as—following Arendt—a space constituted through plural action and also—against Arendt—a space constituted through claims to the very infrastructural support and bodily requirements that make action possible.

120. Arendt, *Eichmann in Jerusalem*, 211.

121. Arendt, "Quod Licet Jovi . . . ," 638.

122. Young-Bruehl, *Hannah Arendt*, 150.

123. Walter Benjamin, "Commentaries on Poems by Brecht," in *Understanding Brecht*, 74.

124. Leora Y. Bilsky argues that *Eichmann in Jerusalem* is a call to incorporate reflective (aesthetic) judgment into trials of unprecedented crimes in "When Actor and Spectator Meet in the Courtroom: Reflections on Hannah Arendt's Concept of Judgment," *History and Memory* 8, no. 2 (1996): 137–73.

125. Arendt, *Eichmann in Jerusalem*, 137.

126. Arendt, "On Humanity," 31.

127. Hannah Arendt, *Life of the Mind*, ed. Mary McCarthy (New York: Houghton Mifflin Harcourt, 1991), 256.

128. Arendt, "Some Questions of Moral Philosophy," 140.

129. Hannah Arendt, "Franz Kafka, Appreciated Anew," in *Reflections on Literature and Culture*, 97.

130. Arendt, 96.

131. Walter Benjamin, "Conversations with Brecht," in *Aesthetics and Politics*, ed. Rodney Livingstone, Perry Anderson, and Francis Mulhern (New York: Verso, 1980), 90.

132. Benjamin, 90; Arendt, "Franz Kafka," 98.

133. Arendt, 108. *Amerika* was published posthumously in an edition by Max Brod. It is debatable whether this was Kafka's intended conclusion. It is also questionable whether it is, indeed, a happy ending. Howard Caygill disputes the readings given by Benjamin and Arendt, offering a compelling argument for a much darker reading of the Nature Theatre. See Howard Caygill, "The Fate of the Pariah: Arendt and Kafka's 'Nature Theatre of Oklahoma,'" *College Literature*, 38, no. 1 (2011): 1–14.

134. Walter Benjamin, "Franz Kafka: On the Tenth Anniversary of His Death," in *Illuminations*, 120.

135. Benjamin, 124–25.

136. Arendt, introduction to Benjamin, *Illuminations*, 18.

2. BERTOLT BRECHT: POETIC JUSTICE

1. Gary Jonathan Bass, *Stay the Hand of Vengeance: The Politics of War Crimes Tribunals* (Princeton, NJ: Princeton University Press, 2000), 202.

2. Bertolt Brecht, *Journal Amerika*, in *Werke: Große kommentierte Berliner und Frankfurter Ausgabe*, ed. Werner Hecht, Jan Knopf, Werner Mittenzwei, and Klaus-Detlef Müller (Frankfurt: Suhrkamp, 1988), 27:233.

3. Francine Hirsch, "The Soviets at Nuremberg: International Law, Propaganda, and the Making of the Postwar Order," *American Historical Review* 113, no. 3 (2008): 701–30.

4. Elisabeth Young-Bruehl, *Hannah Arendt: For Love of the World* (New Haven, CT: Yale University Press, 2004), 141.

5. "The Moscow Trials: A Statement by American Progressives," *New Masses*, May 3, 1938, 19.

6. Lion Feuchtwanger, *Moscow 1937: My Visit Described for My Friends*, trans. Irene Josephy (New York: Viking, 1937), 114.

7. Bertolt Brecht, *Tagebuch 1921*, in *Werke*, 26:216.

8. Feuchtwanger, *Moscow 1937*, 114.

9. Feuchtwanger, 128.

10. Feuchtwanger, 124.

11. Max Weber, *Economy and Society*, ed. Guenther Roth and Claus Wittich (New York: Bedminster, 1968).

12. Lida Maxwell uses the term "poetic justice" to describe "a dissident practice of truth-telling that reveals perspectives on events occluded by official narratives." Lida Maxwell, *Public Trials: Burke, Zola, Arendt, and the Politics of Lost Causes* (Oxford: Oxford University Press, 2015), 84. This type of poetic justice not only renarrates past events but also calls a public into being that might join in collective action against injustice. For Maxwell, both Zola's writing on the Dreyfus affair

and *Eichmann in Jerusalem* are examples of this type of poetic justice. Poetic justice in the sense that I use it here is not literary but rather theatrical: it takes place in a public space for an assembled audience.

13. Günther Anders, "Tagebuch 1944," in *Begegnungen mit Bertolt Brecht*, ed. Erdmut Wizisla (Leipzig: Lehmstedt, 2009), 167–75.

14. Bertolt Brecht, "The Street Scene: A Basic Model for Epic Theatre," in *Brecht on Theatre: The Development of an Aesthetic*, ed. and trans. John Willett (New York: Hill and Wang, 1992), 121–29.

15. Sergei Tretiakov, "Die Kunst ist ein Teil der Pädagogik," in Wizisla, *Begegnungen mit Bertolt Brecht*, 112–13.

16. Bertolt Brecht, "The Modern Theatre Is the Epic Theatre, (Notes to the Opera *Aufstieg und Fall der Stadt Mahagonny*)," in *Brecht on Theatre*, 38.

17. Stephen Parker, *Bertolt Brecht: A Literary Life* (New York: Bloomsbury, 2014), 357–58.

18. Parker, 370–71.

19. Walter Benjamin, "Conversations with Brecht," in *Aesthetics and Politics*, ed. Rodney Livingstone, Perry Anderson, and Francis Mulhern (New York: Verso, 1980), 97.

20. Bertolt Brecht, "Fünf Schwierigkeiten beim Schreiben der Wahrheit," in *Werke*, 22:81.

21. Quoted in Parker, *Bertolt Brecht*, 363.

22. Bertolt Brecht, "Popularity and Realism" in Livingstone, Anderson, and Mulhern, *Aesthetics and Politics*, 83.

23. Aesthetic opposition to socialist realism did not necessarily correlate with political opposition to the Moscow trials. Ernst Bloch, the prime defender of expressionism, also defended the Moscow trials, while Lukács was able to avoid publicly condoning the trials despite living in the Soviet Union. "Presentation I," in Livingstone, Anderson, and Mulhern, *Aesthetics and Politics*, 15.

24. Jochen Hellbeck, "With Hegel to Salvation: Bukharin's Other Trial," *Representations* 107 (Summer 2009): 64–65.

25. Ernst Bloch, "Bukharins Schlusswort," in *Vom Hasard zur Katastrophe: Politische Aufsätze aus den Jahren 1934–1939* (Frankfurt: Suhrkamp, 1972), 355.

26. Bloch, 352.

27. Quoted in Hellbeck, "With Hegel to Salvation," 72.

28. Feuchtwanger, *Moscow 1937*, 120.

29. Feuchtwanger, 123–24.

30. Benjamin, "Conversations with Brecht," 87–88. Emphasis in original.

31. US House Committee on Un-American Activities, Testimony of Berthold Brecht [sic], October 30, 1947, transcript, folder 4/2480, 9, Bertolt-Brecht Archiv, Berlin.

32. US House Committee, 12–17.

33. US House Committee, 34.

34. Brecht, *Journal Amerika*, 27:250.

35. Bertolt Brecht, "On the Formalistic Character of the Theory of Realism," in Livingstone, Anderson, and Mulhern, *Aesthetics and Politics*, 72. Emphases in original.

36. In this argument, Brecht follows Bloch's charge that Lukàcs's approach is mechanical, not dialectical—one of the same charges leveled against Bukharin during his

trial that same year. Ernst Bloch, "Discussing Expressionism," in Livingstone, Anderson, and Mulhern, *Aesthetics and Politics*, 21.

37. Brecht, "Popularity and Realism," 70.

38. Brecht, 84.

39. Benjamin, "Conversations with Brecht," 97.

40. Benjamin Bennett, *All Theater Is Revolutionary Theater* (Ithaca, NY: Cornell University Press, 2005), 58.

41. The example that Bennett gives is Galileo's writings, preserved and smuggled out of Italy by one of his pupils in Brecht's *The Life of Galileo*. Bennett, 61.

42. Brecht, *Journal Amerika*, 27:186.

43. Bertolt Brecht, *Der kaukasische Kreidekreis* in *Werke*, 8:185.

44. The play's first professional production took place in the United States in 1948 (directed, translated, and edited by Eric Bentley); the Berliner Ensemble production of 1954 was the first production of the original German text and the only production directed by Brecht himself.

45. During the protests, between sixty and one hundred civilians were either shot or run over by tanks. In the aftermath of the uprising, at least twenty other civilians were executed and some twelve to fifteen thousand more arrested. Gareth Dale, *Popular Protest in East Germany, 1945–1989* (London: Routledge 2005), 10.

46. Bertolt Brecht, *Journal Berlin*, in *Werke*, 27:349. Here, Brecht almost sounds like he is advocating for psychological identification between the actor and the role. The importance of Busch's experiences, though, is not that they enabled him to identify with the character, but that they allowed him to understand and represent the character, a slight but significant difference.

47. Brecht, *Der kaukasische Kreidekreis*, 159.

48. Gary Bruce argues that most accounts of the uprising overstate the importance of economic concerns and ignore the centrality of "legal insecurity" as a major cause. Gary Bruce, *Resistance with the People: Repression and Resistance in East Germany, 1945–1955* (Lanham, MD: Rowman and Littlefield, 2003).

49. Bruce, 227.

50. Stefan Brant, *The East German Uprising*, trans. Charles Wheeler (New York: Praeger, 1957), 83–84; Armin Mitter and Stefan Wolle, *Untergang auf Raten: Unbekannte Kapitel der DDR-Geschichte* (Munich: Bertelsmann, 1993), 76–77.

51. Brecht, *Journal Amerika*, 184.

52. Weber, *Economy and Society*, 243.

53. Weber, 980.

54. Elisabeth Hauptmann, "Recht austeilen in einer Gesellschaft, wo das Unrecht gesetzlich ist?," in program for *Der kaukasische Kreidekreis*, by Bertolt Brecht, Berliner Ensemble, Berlin, 1954, Bertolt-Brecht Archiv, Berlin. Unlike in the United States, German theaters typically publish substantial program books for each production, featuring essays, artwork, historical context, and substantial quotations from the play or other texts. The programs discussed in this book are not, in other words, atypically long or analytical.

55. Quoted in Tretiakov, "Die Kunst," 112–13.

56. Parker, *Bertolt Brecht*, 581.

57. Hans Bunge, "Tagebuch einer Inszenierung," folder 943, 73, Bertolt-Brecht Archiv.

58. Bunge, folder 944, 53.

59. Bunge, folder 944, 9.

60. Bunge, folder 944, 15.

61. Bunge, folder 944, 39.

> [BRECHT] SAGT: "Nein, das kann er nicht, im Lesen und Schreiben ist er zu
> ungeübt."
> BUSCH: "Natürlich kann er lesen und schreiben. Er führt mir ja während der
> Verhandlungen das Protokoll."
> BRECHT: "Ja—aber das ist hier ein illegales Lied. Das gibt man nicht aus der
> Hand."
> BUSCH: "Azdak sagt aber doch: Keine Furcht, man darf es hören, es hat einen
> beliebten Refrain!"
> BRECHT: "Ja—aber warum soll man es dann aufschreiben?"

62. Maria Lau, *Die Picasso-Rezeption in der DDR: Offizielle Wahrnehmung und Künstlerischer Dialog* (Peter Lang: Frankfurt, 2011), 39–40.

63. Parker, *Bertolt Brecht*, 563.

64. Parker, 581–85.

65. The poster also hung in Brecht's living room at the time of his death and can still be seen at the Bertolt Brecht Haus at 125 Chausseestraße in Berlin.

66. Parker, *Bertolt Brecht*, 505.

67. Alexander Dymschitz, "Über die formalistische Richtung in der deutschen Malerei," in *Tägliche Rundschau*, November 24, 1948, quoted in Lau, *Die Picasso-Rezeption*, 74.

68. Program for *Der kaukasische Kreidekreis*.

69. Parker, *Bertolt Brecht*, 561.

70. Bertolt Brecht, Letter to Walter Ulbricht, *Theater Heute* 6, no. 1 (January 1963): 12.

71. Bertolt Brecht, "Die Lösung," in *Werke*, 12:310.

72. Vasilii Sokolovskii, Vladimir Semyonov, and Pavel Yudin, report, "On the Events of the 17–19 June 1953 in Berlin and the GDR and Certain Conclusions from these Events," June 24, 1953, in *Uprising in East Germany 1953*, ed. Christian F. Ostermann (Budapest: Central European University Press, 2001), 274.

73. Brecht, *Der kaukasische Kreidekreis*, 8:185.

74. Brecht, 8:96–97.

75. Brecht, 8:99.

76. "Lenkt die Aufmerksamkeit der staatlichen Behörden auf ein zum Teil noch ungelöstes Problem," program for *Der kaukasische Kreidekreis*.

77. "Im Staatsrecht nennt man das Teilung der Gewalten," program for *Der kaukasische Kreidekreis*.

78. "Das Ergebnis der Diskussion wissen alle voraus, aber es wird erst gefunden." Bunge, "Tagebuch einer Inszenierung," folder 1122, 69, Bertolt-Brecht Archiv.

79. Günter Grass, *The Plebeians Rehearse the Uprising*, trans. Ralph Manheim (New York: Harcourt, Brace, 1966), 41.

80. Grass, 107.

81. Hannah Arendt, "What Is Permitted to Jove," in *Reflections on Literature and Culture*, ed. Susannah Young-Ah Gottlieb (Stanford, CA: Stanford University Press, 2007), 224–25.

82. Arendt, 231.

83. Arendt, 229–31.

84. Arendt, 255.

85. Arendt, 248–50.

86. Hannah Arendt, "Quod Licet Jovi . . . Reflexionen über den Dichter Bertolt Brecht und sein Verhältnis zur Politik," *Merkur* 23, no. 7 (1969): 638. This passage only appears in the German version of the essay.

87. Arendt, "What Is Permitted," 250.

88. Arendt, 336.

89. Brecht, "An die Nachgeborenen," in *Werke*, 12:85.

90. Hannah Arendt, *The Human Condition* (Chicago: University of Chicago Press), 246.

91. Arendt, "What Is Permitted," 254–55. Her emphasis.

92. See Bonnie Honig, *Political Theory and the Displacement of Politics* (Ithaca, NY: Cornell University Press, 1993).

93. As Elisabeth Hauptmann puts it, "Brecht complained about the regime, but like one would complain about family." Quoted in Thomas K. Brown, "Brecht and the 17th of June, 1953," *Monatshefte* 63, no. 1 (1971): 54.

3. ERWIN PISCATOR: THEATER AFTER AUSCHWITZ

1. Elisabeth Young-Bruehl, *Hannah Arendt: For Love of the World* (New Haven, CT: Yale University Press, 2004), 162.

2. Walter Benjamin, "Theses on the Philosophy of History," in *Illuminations*, ed. Hannah Arendt, trans. Harry Zohn (New York: Harcourt, 1968), 257–58. The first time that this famous excerpt from the "Theses" appeared in print was in Arendt's essay on Kafka. Gottlieb suggests that part of her motivation for writing the Kafka essay may have been the opportunity to publish at least this small excerpt from the essay. Hannah Arendt, *Reflections on Literature and Culture*, ed. Susannah Young-Ah Gottlieb (Stanford, CA: Stanford University Press), 307.

3. Benjamin, 257–58.

4. Quoted in Young-Bruehl, *Hannah Arendt*, 201.

5. Benjamin, "Theses," 255.

6. Young-Bruehl, *Hannah Arendt*, 95.

7. Freddie Rokem argues that Benjamin creates a "theatrical staging" in his "Theses on the Philosophy of History." Freddie Rokem, *Philosophers and Thespians: Thinking Performance* (Stanford, CA: Stanford University Press, 2010), 172.

8. Shoshana Felman, *The Juridical Unconscious: Trials and Traumas in the Twentieth Century* (Cambridge, MA: Harvard University Press, 2002), 11–12.

9. Although he is often credited as the first practitioner of both epic and documentary theater, Erwin Piscator has been neglected by scholars in favor of contemporaries like Bertolt Brecht and Vsevolod Meyerhold. His book *The Political Theatre* (*Das politische Theater*) has been out of print in both the United States and Germany for years, and the two English monographs on Piscator were both published in the late 1970s: John Willett, *The Theatre of Erwin Piscator* (New York: Holmes & Meyer, 1979); C. D. Innes, *Erwin Piscator's Political Theatre: The Development of Modern German Drama* (Cambridge: Cambridge University Press, 1977).

10. Erwin Piscator, *Schriften 2* (East Berlin: Henschelverlag, 1968), 158.

11. Erwin Piscator, *Das politische Theater* (East Berlin: Henschelverlag, 1968), 49.

12. Piscator, 49.

13. Kurt Pinthus, *8-Uhr Abendblatt*, Berlin, April 4, 1930, quoted in Innes, *Erwin Piscator's Political Theatre*, 137.

14. Piscator, *Das politische Theater*, 62.

15. Piscator's theoretical writing follows a similar principle. In lieu of a strong theoretical framework, Piscator's *The Political Theater* (*Das politische Theater*) is a sort of montage of theoretical reflections alongside excerpts from contemporary reviews (including ones that are highly critical of his work), earlier essays, and program notes.

16. Willett, *The Theatre of Erwin Piscator*, 90–95.

17. Piscator, *Das politische Theater*, 69–70.

18. Piscator, 74.

19. Erwin Piscator, "Bühne der Gegenwart und Zukunft" (1928), in *Schriften 2*, 36–37.

20. Wolfgang Drews, "Vorwort," in Piscator, *Das politische Theater*, 18–19.

21. Judith Malina, *The Piscator Notebook* (New York: Routledge, 2012), 23.

22. See Minou Arjomand, "Performing Catastrophe: Erwin Piscator's Documentary Theatre," *Modern Drama* 59, no. 1 (2016): 49–74.

23. See Gerhard F. Probst, *Erwin Piscator and the American Theatre* (New York: Peter Lang, 1991).

24. Innes, *Erwin Piscator's Political Theatre*, 68.

25. Malina, *The Piscator Notebook*, 41–43.

26. Federal Bureau of Investigation file on Erwin Piscator, released under a Freedom of Information Act request filed by Jay Ball.

27. See Innes, *Erwin Piscator's Political Theatre*; Thea Kirfel-Lenk, *Erwin Piscator im Exil in den USA, 1939–1951: Eine Darstellung seiner antifaschistischen Theaterarbeit am Dramatic Workshop der New School for Social Research* (East Berlin: Henschelverlag, 1984); Ilka Saal, "Broadway and the Depoliticization of Epic Theatre: The Case of Erwin Piscator," in *Brecht, Broadway and United States Theatre*, ed. Chris Westgate (Newcastle: Cambridge Scholars, 2007), 45–71; Willett, *The Theatre of Erwin Piscator*.

28. Rachel Rosenthal, email message to author, February 13, 2013.

29. Geza Herczeg, "The Story of 'The Burning Bush,'" in program for *The Burning Bush*, by Heinz Herald and Greta Herczeg, 1949, folder 169, Erwin Piscator Center, Akademie der Künste Archiv, Berlin (hereafter AdK).

30. Leonard Dinnerstein, *Antisemitism in America* (Oxford: Oxford University Press, 1994), 131–32.

31. Herczeg, "The Story of 'The Burning Bush,'" 2.

32. "The Dramatic Workshop Digest," folder 169, Erwin Piscator Center, AdK.

33. Program for *The Burning Bush*.

34. Program.

35. Program.

36. "Anti-Semitism in Hungary," folder 170, Erwin Piscator Center, AdK.

37. Program for *The Burning Bush*.

38. "Prologue," *The Burning Bush*, folder 170, Erwin Piscator Center, AdK.

39. This staging is discussed in chapter 1 and in that chapter's note 95.

40. "Prologue," *The Burning Bush*.

41. Christopher Bigsby, *Arthur Miller* (Cambridge: Cambridge University Press, 2009), 185.

42. The historical events of the list and the murals from *The Crucible* almost read like a repertoire of Piscator's wartime and postwar productions: Jesus (unfinished project with Peter Weiss); beheading of John the Baptist (Wilde's *Salome*, Florence, 1964); persecution of Christians (Shaw's *Androcles and the Lion*, West Berlin, 1964); Joan of Arc (Shaw's *Saint Joan*, Washington, DC, 1940); Giordano Bruno (unfinished project with Guntram Prüfer to be titled *The Temptation of Giordano Bruno* and to premiere in Kessel, c. 1959); Jacobin terror (Büchner's *Danton's Death*, West Berlin, 1956; Rolland's *Robespierre*, West Berlin, 1963); witch hunts (Miller's *The Crucible*); Spanish Inquisition (Schiller's *Don Carlos*, Munich, 1959), concentration camps (Hochhuth's *The Deputy*, West Berlin, 1963; Weiss's *The Investigation*, West Berlin, 1965); July 20th (Kirst and Piscator's *Uprising of the Officers*, West Berlin, 1966).

43. Program for *Hexenjagd* (The Crucible), by Arthur Miller, 1958, folder 304, 2–3, Erwin Piscator Center, AdK.

44. Benjamin, "Theses," 257.

45. Judith Butler, *Parting Ways: Jewishness and the Critique of Zionism* (New York: Columbia University Press, 2012), 113.

46. Walter Benjamin, *The Arcades Project*, trans. Howard Eiland and Kevin McLaughlin (Cambridge, MA: Harvard University Press, 1999), 463.

47. Erika Fischer-Lichte argues that the vacillation between frames of perception and understanding differentiates aesthetic from nonaesthetic modes of performance. See Erika Fischer-Lichte, *The Routledge Introduction to Theatre and Performance Studies*, ed. Minou Arjomand and Ramona Mosse, trans. Minou Arjomand (New York: Routledge, 2014), 164.

48. Michael Rothberg, *Traumatic Realism* (Minneapolis: University of Minnesota Press, 2000), 29.

49. Rothberg, 33.

50. Mikhail Bakhtin, *The Dialogic Imagination: Four Essays*, ed. Michael Holquist, trans. Caryl Emerson and Michael Holquist (Austin: University of Texas Press, 1981), 84.

51. William Hawkins, "'Burning Bush' Relives Historic Terror," *New York World Telegram*, December 17, 1949, 5.

52. Rebecca Schneider, *Performing Remains: Art and War in Times of Theatrical Reenactment* (New York: Routledge, 2011), 2.

53. Schneider, 10.

54. Hayden White, "The Value of Narrativity in the Representation of Reality," *Critical Inquiry* 7, no. 1 (1980): 6.

55. Michael Rothberg, *Multidirectional Memory: Remembering the Holocaust in the Age of Decolonization* (Stanford, CA: Stanford University Press, 2009), 3.

56. Theodor Adorno, "Cultural Criticism and Society," in *Prisms*, trans. Shierry Weber Nicholsen and Samuel Weber (Cambridge, MA: MIT Press, 1983), 34.

57. Christoph Weiß, *Auschwitz in der geteilten Welt: Peter Weiss und die 'Ermittlung' im Kalten Krieg* (St. Ingbert: Röhrig Universitätsverlag, 2000), 1:9.

58. See Rebecca Wittmann, *Beyond Justice: The Auschwitz Trial* (Cambridge, MA: Harvard University Press, 2005); Devin O. Pendas, *The Frankfurt Auschwitz Trial, 1963–65: Genocide, History and the Limits of the Law* (Cambridge: Cambridge University Press, 2006).

59. Wittmann, 6–7.

60. See Jeffrey Herf, "The 'Holocaust' Reception in West Germany: Right, Center, Left," *New German Critique* 19, no. 1 (1980): 30–52.

61. Jeffrey Herf, *Divided Memory: The Nazi Past in the Two Germanies* (Cambridge, MA: Harvard University Press, 1999), 183–84.

62. Quoted in Manfred Haiduk, *Der Dramatiker Peter Weiss* (Berlin: Henschelverlag, 1977), 286.

63. Bernd Naumann, *Auschwitz: A Report on the Proceedings Against Robert Karl Ludwig Mulka and Others Before the Court* (New York: Praeger, 1966). The translated English publication contains an introduction by Hannah Arendt.

64. The other two plays in this trilogy are *The Inferno* (which presents Dante's return to Florence as an allegory for postwar Germany and was only published posthumously) and *Song of the Lusitanien Bogey* (about Portuguese colonialism in Africa, which the Negro Ensemble Company premiered in the United States in 1968). Peter Weiss, "Gespräch über Dante," in *Rapporte* (Frankfurt: Suhrkamp, 1968), 144.

65. In his notebooks, Weiss connects Toffler to several women from his own life, most notably Lucie Weisenberger, whom he tried to marry in order to help her leave Theresienstadt, but who eventually perished in the camp. Jens-Fietje Dwars, *Und dennoch Hoffnung: Peter Weiss, Eine Biographie* (Berlin: Aufbau Verlag, 2007).

66. Heinrich Härtle, "Kommunistisches Auschwitztheater: Schaueprozeß oder Prozeßschaue—Spartakist Piscator und SED-Freund Weiss," *Deutsche Wochenzeitung*, October 29, 1965, reprinted in Weiß, *Auschwitz*, 2:652–55.

67. See Peter Weiss, *Notizbücher*, (Frankfurt: Suhrkamp, 1982), 1:389.

68. Joachim Kaiser, "Plädoyer gegen das Theater-Auschwitz," in Weiß, *Auschwitz*, 2:226.

69. Herman Naber pointed out in an article in *Die Zeit* that Kaiser was only one of many journalists to use the imagery of the "raped stage" to condemn *The Investigation*. Herman Naber, "Die 'Ermittlung' in der Presse," *Die Zeit*, October 29, 1965, accessed April 17, 2017, http://www.zeit.de/1965/44/die-ermittlung-in-der-presse.

70. Quoted in Weiß, *Auschwitz*, 1:233.

71. Günter Zehm, "Gehirnwäsche auf der Bühne," in Weiß, *Auschwitz*, 2:584.

72. Quoted in Weiß, *Auschwitz*, 1:267.

73. Hans Daiber, "Die Bühne als Tribüne: Plädoyer für ein Theater der Ermittlungen," in Weiß, *Auschwitz*, 2:341.

74. George Salmony, "Auschwitz-Drama uraufgefüht: Für wen ermittelte Peter Weiss?" in Weiß, *Auschwitz*, 2:478.

75. The reading was broadcast on television in the GDR; this is the only premiere performance for which I was able to find a video recording: "*Die Ermittlung*: Gemeinschaftssendung der Fernsehens der DDR und der Akademie der Künste der DDR."

76. Dieter E. Zimmer, "Die Lesung in der Volkskammer der DDR," in Weiß, *Auschwitz*, 2:662–64.

77. "Prominente vor der Premiere: BZA sprach mit dem Dramatiker Peter Weiss und Mitwirkenden an der heutigen Berliner Lesung," in Weiß, *Auschwitz*, 2:339–40.

78. Lothar Orzechowski, "'Die Ermittlung' in Dresden und Berlin," in Weiß, *Auschwitz*, 2:522–25.

79. Peter Weiss, *Die Ermittlung: Oratorium in 11 Gesängen* (Frankfurt Main: Suhrkamp, 2005), 194.

80. Manfred Nössig, "Ermittlung zur 'Ermittlung': Über einen Pressetod," *Theater der Zeit* 23 (1965): 4–5.

81. Michael Stone, "Rostock: "Die große Abrechnung," in Weiß, *Auschwitz*, 2:670–71.

82. Eo Plunien, "Oratorium über Auschwitz," in Weiß, *Auschwitz*, 2:405–6.

83. Wolfgang Ignée, "Schwierigkeiten, die Wahrheit zu spielen," in Weiß, *Auschwitz*, 2:508.

84. Program for *Die Ermittlung* (The Investigation), 1965, folder 146, Erwin Piscator Center, AdK. "Der Völkermord in Auschwitz war etwas Unvergleichbares, nicht zu fassen mit überkommenen Begriffen. Und nun gedenken wir gleichzeitig des Bestehens unserer Organisation, und mancher mag fragen, können wir nach Auschwitz überhaupt noch Feste in Deutschland feiern."

85. Program, 4. "Die trotz allen Geredes vom 'Befehlsnotstand' die Freiheit moralischer Entscheidung hatten."

86. Program, 4. Emphasis in the original. "Die Freiheit des Zuschauers angesichts der Fakten ist unbeschnitten: er kann seine eigene moralische Verantwortung ungehindert festlegen; er kann sich zum Zeugen oder gar zum Angeklagten machen; er kann zum Geschworenen werden, der zu *seinem* Urteil kommen will."

87. Program, 15. "Warum bleiben der Ausgang des Frankfurter Auschwitz-Prozesses und des Stückes *Die Ermittlung* unbefriedigend? Weil die Katharsie ausgeblieben ist: die Läuterung, Reinigung und Erhebung der Seele durch Reue und Mitleid. Und sie bleibt aus, weil die Reue der Täter ausgeblieben ist. Aber erst Reue erzeugt Verwandlung, Veränderung, sie erst verwandelt schlechte in gute Taten, schließt Wiederholungen aus—wird Maßstab künftiger Handlungen—ob sie nun geschehen in Vietnam, im Kongo oder in Indien."

88. Weiß, *Auschwitz*, 1:248.

89. Program, *Die Ermittlung*, 5. "Im Schillerschen Sinne als moralische Anstalt"; "Solange wir noch nicht wirklich mit unserer Vergangenheit abgerechnet haben, solange wir sie ausklammern wollen aus unserer Gegenwart und Zukunft . . . solange ist es die Aufgabe des politischen Theaters, das 'Unbewältigte' zu rekapitulieren. . . . So lange darf das Theater nicht unparteiisch und distanziert sein, selbst auf die Gefahr gewisser künstlerischer Unzulänglichkeiten. Und was unsere Lehrer uns immer sagten gilt auch hier: non scolae sed vitae discimus. Nicht für die Schule, sondern für das Leben lernen wir."

90. Willett, *The Theatre of Erwin Piscator*, 27.

91. Kirfel-Lenk, *Erwin Piscator*, 179.

92. Kirfel-Lenk, 179.

93. Program for *The Rally for Hope*, 1943, folder 443, Erwin Piscator Center, AdK.

94. Heinz Herald and Geza Herczeg, *The Burning Bush*, adapted by Noel Langley (New York: Shirley Collier Agency, 1947), 23. Emphasis in original.

95. Director's book, *The Burning Bush*, folder 171, 16, Erwin Piscator Center, AdK.

96. Director's book, 16. Handwritten underlining in original.

97. Wittmann, *Beyond Justice*, 69.

98. Wittmann, 82.

99. Wittmann, 150.

100. Wasserstrom's testimony about a child murdered by defendant Wilhelm Boger is transcribed in Wittmann, *Beyond Justice*, 88, and appears in *The Investigation* in the third canto, the "Song of the Swing." On Otto Wolken's testimony as the basis for Witness 3, see R. C. Perry, "Historical Authenticity and Dramatic Form: Hochhuth's 'Der Stellvertreter' and Weiss's 'Die Ermittlung,'" *Modern Language Review* 64, no. 4 (1969): 836.

101. See Sidra DeKoven Ezrahi, *By Words Alone* (Chicago: University of Chicago Press, 1982); Andreas Huyssen, "The Politics of Identification: 'Holocaust' and West German Drama," *New German Critique* 19, no. 1 (1980): 117–36; Alvin H. Rosenfeld, *A Double Dying* (Bloomington: Indiana University Press, 1980); Elie Wiesel, *Dimensions of the Holocaust: Lectures at Northwestern University* (Evanston, IL: Northwestern University Press, 1990); James E. Young, *Writing and Rewriting the Holocaust* (Bloomington: Indiana University Press, 1998). Several studies in the past decade have attempted to bolster *The Investigation*'s reputation. Robert Cohen argues that many of the accusations against Weiss are based on his essays rather than on the play itself. Christoph Weiß also points out that it was Weiss's political interviews and not *The Investigation* that gave the GDR occasion to use him for their own propaganda. More recently, Tammis Thomas's article in *Modern Drama* argues that *The Investigation* offers insights about the "gray zone" of coerced collaboration in Auschwitz. See Robert Cohen, "The Political Aesthetics of Holocaust Literature: Peter Weiss's *The Investigation* and Its Critics," *History and Memory* 10, no. 2 (Fall 1998): 43–67; Weiß, *Auschwitz*, 1:217; Tammis Thomas, "The Gray Zone of Victims and Perpetrators in Peter Weiss's *The Investigation*," *Modern Drama* 53, no. 4 (2010): 559.

102. Young, *Writing and Rewriting the Holocaust*, 72.

103. Young, 72.

104. Robert Cohen and Andreas Huyssen both read Weiss's lack of ethnic markers as a means to create a parable with applicability to anticolonial and social justice movements. Cohen, "The Political Aesthetics"; Huyssen, "The Politics of Identification."

105. Peter Weiss, *Rapporte 2* (Frankfurt: Suhrkamp, 1971), 270.

106. Weiss, *Die Ermittlung*, 21. The English translation leaves out the name, translating the line as "Before they were taken away / I always used to tell my family / You go right on buying from them / After all they are human too." Peter Weiss, *The Investigation*, in *Marat/Sade, The Investigation, and The Shadow of the Body of the Coachman*, ed. Robert Cohen, trans. Jon Swan and Ulu Grosbard (New York: Continuum, 1998), 129.

107. Robert Cohen, *Understanding Peter Weiss*, trans. Martha Humphreys (Columbia: University of South Carolina Press, 1993), 88.

108. Peter Weiss, *Peter Weiss in Gespräch*, ed. Rainer Gerlach and Mattias Richter (Frankfurt: Suhrkamp, 1986), 86.

109. Weiss, *Die Ermittlung*, 38.

110. Questions about the political implication of casting are not only important for thinking about *The Investigation* but also for thinking about contemporary

theater. The importance of casting in historical plays came to the fore recently with the decision of a director to cast Martin Luther King Jr. in Katori Hall's play *The Mountaintop* with a white actor. When she originally published her play, Hall took it for granted that directors would cast African American actors in the role of Martin Luther King Jr. In a play that bears witness to African American history, the decision of one director can commit, in Hall's words, "yet another erasure of the black body." The example of *The Mountaintop* (as well as the Stuttgart and East Berlin productions of *The Investigation*) shows that the director—as much as, if not more than, the playwright—has the capacity to either obscure or emphasize racial and ethnic difference and inequality based on casting and staging choices. Hall has since added a clause to the licensing agreement that unless she gives her consent to different casting choices, the roles must be cast with African American actors. See Katori Hall, "Playwright Reacts to the White Casting of MLK in *The Mountaintop*," *The Root*, November 9, 2015, accessed December 1, 2015, http://www.theroot.com/playwright-reacts-to-the-white-casting-of-mlk-in -the-mo-1790861704; Nolan Feeney, "*Mountaintop* Playwright Criticizes Casting of White Actor as Martin Luther King Jr. in Play," *Time*, November, 11, 2015, accessed December 1, 2015, http://time.com/4107990/white-actor-martin-luther -king-jr-mountaintop-katori-hall/.

111. Christoph Müller, "Es geht alles vorüber," in Weiß, *Auschwitz*, 2:597.

112. Hannah Arendt, *On Violence* (New York: Harcourt Brace, 1970), 65.

113. It is unclear whether audience members or viewers of the television broadcast would have known that those actors and participants were Jewish or had Jewish ancestry. Their ethnicity was neither mentioned in reviews in mainstream publications nor given in the staging materials from the production itself. The only mention of Jewish involvement in the East Berlin production that I could find came from a radical right publication that emphasized Jewish influence in promoting the play. Even this review, though, did not mention the particular actors involved but rather deployed the well-worn anti-Semitic rhetoric of the Nazi Party, linking Jews and Communism in a much more general way. See Härtle, "Kommunistisches Auschwitztheater," in Weiß, *Auschwitz*, 2:652–55.

114. Heinz Elsberg, "Piscators Inszenierung in Berlin," *Aufbau*, November 12, 1965, 32.

115. Hannah Arendt, *Eichmann in Jerusalem: A Report on the Banality of Evil* (New York: Penguin, 1963), 257.

116. Pendas, *The Frankfurt Auschwitz Trial*, 92.

117. "Notizen zu der Bekleidung," folder 684, 3, Erwin Piscator Center, AdK.

118. Ignée, "Schwierigkeiten," in Weiß, *Auschwitz*, 2:505.

119. Ignée, 2:508.

120. Michael Stone, "Hat *Die Ermittlung* das Publikum erreicht? Berlin: Piscators kalte Bilanz," in Weiß, *Auschwitz*, 2:668.

121. Stone, 2:669.

122. Elsberg, "Piscators Inszenierung," 32.

123. Dieter Hilderbrandt, "Ohne Applaus," in Weiß, *Auschwitz*, 2:426. The reviewer seems to mean "spectators" like you and I, and "they" not "it." Even after watching the production, the reviewer seems to have difficulty recognizing in Holocaust

survivors "people like you and I." "Die Zeugen . . . hocken vor dem Auditorium, gleichsam in der ersten Reihe, als seien es Menschen wie du und ich."

124. Program for *Die Ermittlung*, 17. "Auf der Bühne tritt der Mensch unmittelbar vor den Menschen hin. Kein Thema hat dies nötiger als das Thema der Entwürdigung des Menschen durch den Menschen."

125. Even though New York's Method acting schools in the 1940s–60s welcomed Jewish students and audiences, they were still marked by racial exclusions. A year before the premiere of *The Investigation*, James Baldwin had challenged the ways that Method acting systematically excluded black actors and marginalized the lived reality of black people in his 1964 play *Blues for Mister Charlie*. Shonni Enelow offers a brilliant analysis of the rehearsal process for this play and its place as a hinge in Baldwin's critique of liberal humanism in *Method Acting and Its Discontents: On American Psycho-Drama* (Evanston, IL: Northwestern University Press, 2015).

126. Hannah Arendt, *Origins of Totalitarianism* (New York: Harcourt Brace, 1968), 48. See the discussion of Arendt and *Nathan the Wise* in chapter 1.

127. Piscator, "Bemerkungen," folder 683, Erwin Piscator Center, AdK; "Notizen," folder 684, 3, Erwin Piscator Center, AdK. The image on the cover of this book is of one of the early models for the stage.

128. Ethel Schwiten, "Auschwitz—ein Fakten-Drama," in Weiß, *Auschwitz*, 2:532.

129. Stone, "Hat *Die Ermittlung*," in Weiß, 2:668.

130. Elsberg, "Piscators Inszenierung," 32.

131. Nössig, "Ermittlung zur 'Ermittlung,'" in Weiß, 2:877.

132. Müller, "Es geht," in Weiß, 2:597.

133. Müller, 2:597.

134. Stone, "Hat *Die Ermittlung*," in Weiß, *Auschwitz*, 2:669.

135. Survey, 1965, Erwin Piscator Center, folder 147, AdK.

Verehrter Theaterbesucher, bitte verlassen Sie die Aufführung nicht; versuchen Sie, durchzuhalten—wie es die Darsteller durch eine lange Probezeit getan haben, wie sie es jeden Abend tun. In welchem Verhältnis steht die Dauer eines solchen Abends zu jener unendlichen Fülle des Leidens, das über die Opfer des Hitler-Regimes gekommen ist?

Wenn Sie dennoch gehen wollen so bitten wir Sie herzlich, uns den Grund oder die Gründe dafür mitzuteilen.

Gehen sie fort,

Weil Sie dagegen sind, daß man jüdische Probleme auf der Bühne verhandelt? Ja—Nein

Weil Sie dagegen sind, daß man den Auschwitz-Prozeß auf die Bühne bringt? Ja—Nein

Weil die in der "Ermittlung" mitgeteilten Dinge Ihnen bereits bekannt sind? Ja—Nein

Weil Sie gelangweilt sind? Ja—Nein

Oder sind es Gründe anderer Art? Und welche?

Wir danken Ihnen für Ihre Angaben

Freie Volksbühne

Der Intendant.

136. Arendt, *Eichmann in Jerusalem*, 375.

137. "Die Ermittlung," *Morgenpost Berlin*, November 21, 1965, in Press Clippings, folder 147, Erwin Piscator Center, AdK.
138. Piscator, *Das politische Theater*, 17.

4. TRIALS IN NUREMBERG

1. The Vienna Burgtheater is the oldest German-speaking theater and the second-oldest theater in Europe. In 1776, Holy Roman Emperor Joseph II, whom Schiller admired as an Enlightenment monarch in "Theatre as a Moral Institution," named the Burgtheater (court theater) a Nationaltheater (national theater). Its current building, opened in 1888, is among the most imposing buildings of Vienna's Ringstrasse.

    Following the Anschluss, the Burgtheater was relatively quick to adapt its programming to suit the demands of the National Socialist regime. After the Second World War, the Burgtheater remained a very conservative institution, hardly influenced by the leftist political movements of 1968, until the 1970s. See Klaus Dermutz, *Das Burgtheater und die Wiener Identität: Kontinuität und Krisen, 1888–2009* (Vienna: Bibliothek der Provinz, 2010).
2. The IMT was an international tribunal, organized and presided over by the American, French, British, and Soviet powers. The IMT tried twenty-four major war criminals as well as ten organizations (including the SA, SS, National Socialist Party, and Gestapo) in a single trial. While the IMT is often referred to as *the* Nuremberg trial, it was followed by a series of other trials known as the Nuremberg Military Tribunals (NMT), which were prosecuted and judged by Americans. Schneider's *Trial in Nuremberg* is based on the IMT; the play and film *Judgment at Nuremberg*, discussed later in this chapter, are based on one of the NMT trials.
3. Review of *Prozess in Nürnberg*, *Express am Sonntag*, March 9, 1969, 3.
4. Review, 3. "Hervorragend, einfach hervorragend, der Mann weiß, worum es geht!"
5. Review, 3. "Es ist ein ganz miserables Werk. Der Nürnberger Prozess wäre doch ein herrlicher Stoff für einen Dramatiker. Der Autor (Wer hat das Ganze eigentlich geschrieben? Ein junger Deutscher, 1932 geboren? Na ja!) konnte leider nichts daraus machen. Mit ein bißchen Geschick hätte er aus dem Material eine ganz wunderbare Anklage gegen die Absurdität der Anklage gegen meine Person fertigen können!"
6. Review, 3–4. "Der Autor bringt mich in ein falsches Licht. Er will dem Publikum weismachen, daß ich in die Regierung Hitlers eintrat, um aufzurüsten. Das ist doch ein Unsinn! . . . Ich wollte die Arbeitslosigkeit bewältigen, deshalb mein Eintritt in die Regierung. Sie müssen bedenken, daß es damals 6,5 Millionen Menschen ohne Arbeit gab. Außerdem galt es in den dreißiger Jahren Deutschland vor dem Kommunismus zu retten. Es standen doch 230 nationalsozialistische Abgeordnete gegen 100 Kommunisten. Und nun frage ich sie: Wer hat die Arbeitslosigkeit gebändigt? Ich schaffte es als einziger in ganz Europa!"
7. Review, 4. "'Fürchten Sie sich nicht vor mir? Ich bin doch ein Kriegsverbrecher. Nein? Na endlich einmal eine, die keine Angst hat.'"
8. Review, 4. "Wenn Sie mich so fragen: Natürlich ich!"

9. Here, I follow Zerilli's argument, incorporating Arendt and Wittgenstein, that "what we need to grasp here is the extent to which our common sense of reality, the ordinary sense of objectivity, is *publicly* generated and sustained." Linda M. G. Zerilli, *A Democratic Theory of Judgment* (Chicago: University of Chicago Press, 2016), 30.

10. See Deborah Lipstadt, *History on Trial: My Day in Court with David Irving* (New York: Ecco, 2005), 259–60.

11. Carlo Ginsburg, *History, Rhetoric, Proof* (Hanover, NH: University Press of New England, 1999), 50.

12. The program for *Trial in Nuremberg*'s premiere production in East Berlin (October 15, 1967), noted that Soviet judge Nikitschenko wrote a dissenting opinion criticizing Schacht's release. Program for *Prozess in Nürnberg*, 1967, folder 506, Kurt-Meisel Archiv, Akademie der Künste Archiv, Berlin (hereafter AdK).

13. Tony Judt, "The Past Is Another Country: Myth and Memory in Postwar Europe," in *The Politics of Retribution in Europe: World War II and Its Aftermath*, ed. István Deák, Jan Gross, and Tony Judt (Princeton, NJ: Princeton University Press, 2000), 293–323.

14. Anna J. Merritt and Richard L. Merritt, eds., *Public Opinion in Semi-Sovereign Germany: The HICOG Surveys, 1949–1955* (Chicago: University of Illinois Press, 1980), 101.

15. The 1950 East German Waldheimer trials of prisoners from Soviet internment camps were widely seen as a Stalinist-style purge, with 3,432 convictions after trials lasting only about twenty minutes. Thomas Mann called the trials a "Blood Play" (*Blutschauspiel*) in a letter to Walter Ulbricht. See Wolfgang Eisert, *Die Waldheimer Prozesse—Der Stalinistische Terror 1950: Ein dunkeles Kapital der DDR Justiz* (Munich: Bechtle, 1993).

16. Annette Weinke, *Die Verfolgung von NS-Tätern im geteilten Deutschland: Vergangenheitsbewältigungen 1949–1969 oder; Eine deutsch-deutsche Beziehungsgeschichte im Kalten Krieg* (Paderborn: Ferdinand Schöningh, 2002), 76–82.

17. Devin O. Pendas, "Seeking Justice, Finding Law: Nazi Trials in Postwar Europe," *Journal of Modern History* 81, no. 2 (June 2009): 347–68.

18. These West German trials were, however, quite different from the IMT and the Eichmann trial in that they rejected the charges of crimes against humanity as ex post facto, and they also accepted the defense of acting on superior orders. For more on West Germany in the 1960s and the Frankfurt Auschwitz trial, see chapter 3.

19. *Trial of the Major War Criminals Before the International Military Tribunal* (Nuremberg: International Military Tribunal, 1947), 2:101.

20. Luke J. Stewart, "'A New Kind of War': The Vietnam War and the Nuremberg Principles, 1964–1968" (PhD diss., University of Waterloo, 2014), 111.

21. William F. Buckley, "The Nuremberg Doctrine Is Raised and It Was Just a Matter of Time," *Atlanta Journal*, September 25, 1965, 2; Bertrand Russell to Peter Weiss, September 3, 1966, folder 156, Peter Weiss Archive, AdK. Russell asked Peter Weiss to sign the letter in support of Mitchell, stressing its importance.

22. Richard A. Falk, *The Vietnam War and International Law* (Princeton, NJ: Princeton University Press, 1972), 3:478.

23. Stewart, "'A New Kind of War,'" 25.

24. Lewis Funke, "News of the Rialto: Shyre Moves: Three Projects Underway, Including 'Nuremberg Diary,'" *New York Times*, July 9, 1961, X1.

25. *The Andersonville Trial* (1959) is about the trial of a Confederate general accused of war crimes for the terrible conditions of the Andersonville prisoner-of-war camp, a thinly veiled allusion to the Nuremberg trials. It played on Broadway and was subsequently produced in West Germany (Schillertheater, 1960) and Tel Aviv (Te'atron ha-Kameri, 1971) and was adapted for television in both West Germany (ARD, 1972) and the United States (Hollywood Television Theatre, 1970). When the television version (starring Martin Sheen) was released in the United States in 1970, it was widely understood to be about using the Nuremberg precedent to judge America's war in Vietnam and, in particular, the My Lai massacre. Levitt went on to collaborate with Daniel Berrigan on another trial play, *The Trial of the Catonsville Nine*. In this play, one of the defendants accused of burning draft cards cites Nuremberg in his defense: "The United States in 1945 / supported the Nuremberg trials / I thought that was the finest precedent / this country ever set." Daniel Berrigan, *The Trial of the Catonsville Nine* (New York: Fordham University Press, 2004), 72–73; on the US television version, see Lewis Freedman, "How Far Is Andersonville from Vietnam?," *New York Times*, May 17, 1970, 107; on the German film and My Lai, see "Ein Blick voraus nach My Lai," *Die Zeit*, March 31, 1972. One German reviewer also linked the description of the Andersonville camp to the Siberian gulags; Henk Ohnesorge, "Gehorsam und Galgen: Der Andersonville-Prozess," *Die Welt*, March 25, 1972.

26. The findings of the most recent tribunal, the Russell Tribunal on Palestine, are online at http://www.russelltribunalonpalestine.com/en/ (accessed April 2, 2017).

27. Rolf Schneider, *Stücke* (East Berlin: Henschelverlag, 1970), 206.

28. Thanks to notes from the rehearsals, it is possible to reconstruct some of the key choices and discussions from this process. At the same time, it is likely that not all conversations (especially politically salient ones) were recorded: the notes likely reflect omissions and self-censorship. Notes from the rehearsal process are collected in folder 210, Inszenierungsdokumentation, AdK.

29. Schneider, *Stücke*, 108–9.

30. Schneider, 344.

31. Rolf Schneider, email correspondence with the author, November 15, 2017. "Das Verhältnis ist alt und ehrwürdig. Ein Gerichtsprozess ist auch Performance: mit festen Rollen, mit einer Dramaturgie, mit häufig ungewissem Ausgang, woraus sich eine natürliche Spannung ergibt."

32. Rebecca West, "Greenhouse with Cyclamens I," in *A Train of Powder* (New York: Viking Press, 1955), 3.

33. See Lawrence Douglas, *The Memory of Judgment: Making Law and History in the Trials of the Holocaust* (New Haven, CT: Yale University Press, 2001), 15–16.

34. Douglas, 15–17. The decision to focus on documentary evidence over witness testimony was part of Robert Jackson's chosen strategy. While others on the American prosecution team felt that witnesses would bring the proceedings greater human interest, Jackson was concerned that witness testimony could be more easily dismissed as propaganda than the documents created by the National Socialists themselves. Although it is possible that additional witness testimony would have brought human interest to the proceedings, it is not a given that witness

testimony would save the court from its boredom. Some of the tedium of the IMT was caused by the court's leniency with irrelevant testimony from defense witnesses out of concern that the court not be seen as silencing the defense.

35. Lawrence Douglas, "The Didactic Trial: Filtering History and Memory into the Courtroom," *European Review* 14, no. 4 (2006): 515.

36. Schneider, *Stücke*, 206.

37. Schneider email.

38. In doing so, Schneider also pushes the structure of the trial closer to the Anglo-American system because the lawyers reveal their evidence live during the trial rather than reading from submitted affidavits. Schneider also begins the prologue with a radically shortened version of Jackson's indictment, which is closer to an American-style opening statement. Compared to Continental trials, Schneider believes, a play of a trial structured along Anglo-American lines can, "with respect to dramaturgy, turn out even more spectacularly" ("die Dramaturgie betreffend, noch spektakulärer ausfallen"). Schneider email.

39. Ann Tusa and John Tusa, *The Nuremberg Trial* (New York: Skyhorse, 2010), 138.

40. Tusa and Tusa, 94.

41. Tusa and Tusa, 139.

42. Robert Jackson's opening statement positioned the tribunal as one part of an international effort to prevent future wars, which is closely connected to the founding of the United Nations. Crucially, he argued that the trial would make its organizers answerable in the future to the same standards that they used to charge the Germans at the IMT: "I am too well aware of the weaknesses of juridical action alone to contend that in itself your decision under this Charter can prevent future wars. . . . But the ultimate step in avoiding periodic wars, which are inevitable in a system of international lawlessness, is to make statesmen responsible to law. And let me make clear that while this law is first applied against German aggressors, the law includes, and if it is to serve a useful purpose it must condemn aggression by any other nations, including those which sit here now in judgment." *Trial of the Major War Criminals*, 2:153–54.

43. Mahmood Mamdani, "Beyond Nuremberg: The Historical Significance of the Post-Apartheid Transition in South Africa," *Politics and Society* 43, no. 1 (2015): 62.

44. Schneider's decision to give the court functionaries generic names while keeping the actual names of the defendants is similar to *The Investigation*. Where Schneider differs from Weiss, however, is in his choice to keep the names of the witnesses (as well as proper nouns like "National Socialism," "Auschwitz," and "Jew").

45. Hannah Arendt, *Eichmann in Jerusalem: A Report on the Banality of Evil* (New York: Penguin, 1963), 278.

46. By contrast, American courtroom plays and films of the era—among them, *To Kill a Mockingbird*, *Judgment at Nuremberg*, *The Andersonville Trial*, and *Inherit the Wind*—all have lawyers as their protagonists and cast the lawyers and judges with the most virtuosic actors. These differences in casting reveal how the roles played at Nuremberg continued to inform national identity.

47. Ulrich Engelmann, "Vom Stoff zum Stück, einige Bermerkungen zur Entwicklungsgeschichte von Rolf Schneiders *Prozess in Nürnberg*," 8, Inszenierungsdokumentation, AdK. "Die also Widerspruch zwischen dem politischen Informationswert

und den theatralischen Wirkung definieren läßt"; "Die Theaterwirkung ist gleich null."

48. Ulrich Engelmann, "Probennotate," 4, Inszenierungsdokumentation, AdK.

49. Engelmann, 4, 8.

50. Engelmann, 13–14. "Zu zeigen ist nicht nur eine Beweisführung, sondern die Demonstration einer Beweisführung."

51. Engelmann, 14.

52. Engelmann, 27. "Wie ein schlechter Schauspieler."

53. Engelmann, 13, 31.

54. Engelmann, 39.

> HEINZ: Schachts Argumente sind eigentlich doch wirklich sehr überzeugend. . . .
> DRINDA: Es wäre durchaus denkbar, daß ein echter Widerstandskämpfer sich wie Schacht verhalten hätte
> HEINZ: Wie soll man also seinen Argumenten die Überzeugungskraft nehmen?
> MEVES: Indem man zeigt, daß Schacht um die Überzeugungskraft seiner Argumente weiß und sie als Mittel einsetzt.
> DRINDA: Er muß ein 'Show' abziehen. . . .

55. Engelmann, 40. "Grundsätzlich darf Grosse also nicht Ehrlichkeit spielen, sondern 'Ehrlichkeit.' "

56. Engelmann, 43. "Wenn er schwört, die Wahrheit und nichts als die Wahrheit zu sagen, so spricht er keine Formel, sondern verspricht es. Bereits hier wird das erste Opfer im Gerichtssaal von den anderen differenziert."; "Das Verhör Suzkewers ist nicht verabredet. Das war nicht nötig. Suzkewer hat seinen Text nicht gelernt."

57. Douglas, *The Memory of Judgment*, 3.

58. Douglas, 2.

59. See Shoshana Felman, *The Juridical Unconscious: Trials and Traumas in the Twentieth Century* (Cambridge, MA: Harvard University Press, 2002).

60. Engelmann, "Vom Stoff," 10. "Wurden inspiriert"; "Korrekturen von politisch mißverständlichen Ausdrücken und Sentenzen"; "Eine durch geschickte Striche vorgenommene Aufwertung der Anklage gegenüber der Verteidigung"; "Eine Hebung der Rolle des sowjetischen Anklägers."

61. Schneider email.

62. Laura Bradley, *Cooperation and Conflict: GDR Theatre Censorship, 1961–1989* (Oxford: Oxford University Press, 2011), 39.

63. Schneider email. "Die SED als Staatspartei war allgegenwärtig, auch in den Köpfen. Sowohl die Dramaturgen als auch der Regisseur waren Parteimitglieder."

64. Engelmann, "Vom Stoff," 4.

65. Engelmann, 5. "Verfremdet so ständig das Bühnengeschehen."

66. Engelmann, 6. This framing closely resembles Günter Grass's play *The Plebeians Rehearse the Uprising*, which had premiered in West Berlin the previous year. In Grass's play, a group of actors based on Brecht's Berliner Ensemble are working on a production of Shakespeare's *Coriolanus* that begins to incorporate the contemporary events of the 1953 East German uprising.

67. Engelmann, 5. "Scheinbar nur redaktionelle"; "Ideologisch-ästhetischen Spielraums."

68. Engelmann, "Probennotate," 4.

69. Engelmann, 7.

70. "Stückfassung des Deutschen Theaters," 142. "Das Urteil war rechtskräftig; es gab keine Berufung dagegen; es wurde vollstreckt. Das Verfahren ist wiederholbar!"

71. Program for *Prozess in Nürnberg*, 20.

72. Schneider email. "Es ging mir, von Beginn an, um jenes völkerrechtliche Prinzip, das dem Nürnberger Prozess zugrunde liegt: Kriegsverbrechen, namens des Staates begangen, müssen juristisch geahndet werden.... Die einseitige Ausrichtung der Interpretation etwa auf die USA, wegen des Vietnamkriegs, habe ich aufseufzend hingenommen, in der begründeten Hoffnung, dass wache Zuschauer gleichermaßen an die Verbrechen Stalins und die Ereignisse 1956 in Ungarn denken."

73. Rolf Schneider, *Schonzeiten: Ein Leben in Deutschland* (Berlin: Be.bra, 2013), 114.

74. Schneider email. "Ich habe immer versucht, nicht nur in diesem Stück, hier etwas zurecht zu rücken."

75. Schneider, *Stücke*, 197.

76. Manfred Vogel, review of *Prozess in Nürnberg*, *Wochenpresse*, January 22, 1969, 12.

77. Ruediger Engerth, "Aktenstudium in Burgtheater: Rolf Schneiders 'Prozess in Nürnberg' in Wien ohne Wirkung," *Handelsblatt Düsseldorf*, January 20, 1969, folder 2005, Press Clippings, Dokumentation zum deutschsprachigen Theater, AdK.

78. "Prozess in Nürnberg—Dokumentarstück—2. Teil: Premierenmitschnitt der österreichischen Erstaufführung am Wiener Burgtheater (January 15, 1969)," Österreichische Mediathek, accessed June 12, 2017, https://www.mediathek.at/portaltre ffer/atom/17360287-3C9-000BE-000005A4-17354AB7/pool/BWEB/.

79. Schneider, *Stücke*, 169.

80. *Publikum* is not, however, the term that Habermas uses for the public sphere (*die Öffentlichkeit*).

81. See Christian Delage, *Caught on Camera: Film in the Courtroom from the Nuremberg Trials to the Trials of the Khmer Rouge*, trans. Ralph Schoolcraft and Mary Byrd Kelly (Philadelphia: University of Pennsylvania Press, 2014).

82. Delage, 129–57.

83. Richard Brust, "The Twenty-Five Greatest Legal Movies," *ABA Journal* (August 2008), accessed June 12, 2017, http://www.abajournal.com/magazine/article/the_25_greatest_legal_movies/. *Twelve Angry Men* (1952), *Witness for the Prosecution* (1957), *Compulsion* (1959), *Anatomy of a Murder* (1959), *Inherit the Wind* (1960), *Judgment at Nuremberg* (1961), *To Kill a Mockingbird* (1962), and *A Man for All Seasons* (1966); only *Witness for the Prosecution* is not based on an actual trial.

84. Robert G. Moeller, "How to Judge Stanley Kramer's Judgment at Nuremberg," *German History* 31, no. 4 (2013): 499.

85. Though set in 1925, *Inherit the Wind* is also an indictment of contemporary McCarthyism. The film *Inherit the Wind* was itself based on a 1955 Broadway play by Jerome Lawrence and Robert E. Lee. Kramer went on to produce a television series called *Judgment* for ABC that included dramatizations of the trial of Ethel and Julius Rosenberg and the court-martial of William Calley for My Lai atrocities. See Cecil Smith, "Kramer's Judgment: Designed to Provoke," *Los Angeles Times*, January 22, 1974, C1.

86. Moeller, "How to Judge," 503. In the screenplay, Mann changes the date of the trial from 1947 to 1948 in order to link the reluctance to try Nazi war criminals with the ramping up of the Cold War.

87. Moeller, 507.

88. See Paul A. Lombardo, *Three Generations, No Imbeciles: Eugenics, the Supreme Court, and* Buck v. Bell (Baltimore: Johns Hopkins University Press, 2008).

89. Moeller, "How to Judge," 500.

90. Moeller, 501.

91. See Erika Fischer-Lichte, *The Transformative Power of Performance*, trans. Saskya Iris Jain (New York: Routledge, 2008).

92. Freddie Rokem, *Performing History: Theatrical Representations of the Past in Contemporary Theatre* (Iowa City: University of Iowa Press, 2002), 192.

93. Quoted in Jennifer Frost, "Challenging the 'Hollywoodization' of the Holocaust: Reconsidering *Judgment at Nuremberg* (1961)," *Jewish Film and New Media* 1, no. 2 (2013): 140.

94. James Jordan, *From Nuremberg to Hollywood: The Holocaust and the Courtroom in American Fictive Film* (London: Vallentine Mitchell, 2016), 52. This can be true of a film screening even when the audience does not include celebrities. During some screenings of *None Will Escape*, for example, audiences cheered as they watched German soldiers massacre an entire Jewish community. This audience response turned a film that condemned the atrocities of Nazi Germany into an anti-Semitic rally.

95. Jordan, 115.

96. Philip Auslander, *Liveness: Performance in a Mediatized Culture* (London: Routledge, 1999), 113.

97. The organizers compromised on a hybrid system, with numerous affidavits and a long indictment submitted before the trial as well as live presentation of the evidence in court. Tusa and Tusa, *The Nuremberg Trial*, 77.

98. Norbert Ehrenfreund, *The Nuremberg Legacy: How the Nazi War Crimes Trials Changes the Course of History* (New York: Palgrave Macmillan, 2007), 7.

99. Torben Fischer and Matthias N. Lorenz, eds., *Lexikon der "Vergangenheitsbewältigung" in Deutschland: Debatten- und Diskursgeschichte des Nationalsozialismus nach 1945* (Bielefeld: Transcript, 2007), 24–25. Of the twenty-four individuals charged during the IMT, three were found not guilty. At the NMT, of the 185 people charged, thirty-five were found not guilty.

100. Fischer and Lorenz, 24.

101. See Nicholas Ridout, *Stage Fright, Animals, and Other Theatrical Problems* (Cambridge: Cambridge University Press, 2006).

102. See Dan Laob, "Theatrical Interpretation of the Shoah: Image and Counter-Image," in *Staging the Holocaust: The Shoah in Drama and Performance*, ed. Claude Schumacher (Cambridge: Cambridge University Press, 1998), 95–101. The play *Hannah Szenes* by Aharon Megged was first premiered by Habima in 1958 to celebrate the tenth anniversary of the State of Israel. The production was an unprecedented success and became a significant national production with special performances for soldiers and schools and on Holocaust Remembrance Day.

103. Schneider email.

104. Schneider email. "Eine melancholische Aura von Heimatlosigkeit."

105. Schneider email. "Sanft, doch entschieden widersprach."

106. Paul Hörbiger, as told to Georg Markus, *Ich hab für euch gespielt: Erinnerungen* (Munich: Herbig, 1980), 230–31.

107. Hörbiger, 247.

108. Hörbiger, 326.

109. Bonnie Honig, *Public Things: Democracy in Disrepair* (New York: Fordham University Press, 2017), 24.

CONCLUSION: ARCHIVES, LAW, AND THEATER TODAY

1. See Peggy Phelan, *Unmarked: The Politics of Performance* (New York: Routledge, 1993).

2. Diana Taylor, *The Archive and the Repertoire: Performing Cultural Memory in the Americas* (Durham, NC: Duke University Press, 2003), 19–20.

3. Rebecca Schneider, *Performing Remains: Art and War in Times of Theatrical Reenactment* (London: Routledge, 2011), 100.

4. Walter Benjamin, "Theses on the Philosophy of History," in *Illuminations*, ed. Hannah Arendt, trans. Harry Zohn (New York: Harcourt, 1968), 256.

5. Marianne Hirsch, *The Generation of Postmemory: Writing and Visual Culture after the Holocaust* (New York: Columbia University Press, 2012).

6. Amanda Hess, "Justice Through a Lens: A New Wave of Apps Offers Assistance—and Advice—for Citizens Capturing Police Wrongdoing on Camera," *Slate*, April 9, 2015, accessed March 20, 2017, http://www.slate.com/articles/technology/users/2015/04/copwatch_mobile_justice_and_other_apps_for_citizens_filming_police_encounters.html.

7. Alex Wagner, "To Live and Die on Facebook," *Atlantic*, July 11, 2016, accessed March 20, 2017, https://www.theatlantic.com/politics/archive/2016/07/to-live-and-die-on-facebook/490637/.

8. Directly after Officer Jeronimo Yanez shot Philandro Castile, Diamond Reynolds began to live stream the event on Facebook. As she explains what happened, we hear Yanez screaming at her as he points a gun into the car at her, her dying partner, and her four-year-old daughter in the back seat. Social media and cell phone cameras have even been used by victims to collect, disseminate, and preserve evidence of their own deaths. In March 2017, Rodney Hess live streamed his own death on Facebook as he was shot during a traffic stop. Wagner, "To Live and Die on Facebook"; Ralph Ellis, "Man Fatally Wounded by Deputy: Family Says Facebook Live Captured Chaos," *CNN*, March 19, 2017, accessed March 20, 2017, http://www.cnn.com/2017/03/18/us/facebook-live-killing-tennessee/.

9. Anna Deavere Smith, *Talk to Me: Listening Between the Lines* (New York: Random House, 2000), 19.

10. Hannah Arendt, *The Human Condition* (Chicago: University of Chicago Press, 1998), 187.

11. Anna Deavere Smith and Carl Weber, "Brecht's 'Street Scene—On Broadway, of All Places? A Conversation with Anna Deavere Smith," *Brecht Yearbook* 20 (1995), 59.

12. For an analysis of Smith's engagement with poststructural theories of race, see Debby Thompson, "'Is Race a Trope?': Anna Deavere Smith and the Question of Racial Performativity," *African American Review* 37, no. 1 (Spring 2003): 127–38.

13. See Shonni Enelow, *Method Acting and Its Discontents: On American Psycho-Drama* (Evanston, IL: Northwestern University Press, 2015).

14. Cherise Smith offers a different reading of Smith's virtuosity, warning that the power differential between Smith and some of the people she portrays means that her virtuosic portrayals empower her at the expense of her interview subject, who "risks becoming a puppet in Smith's hands." Cherise Smith, *Enacting Others: Politics of Identity in Eleanor Antin, Nikki S. Lee, Adrian Piper, and Anna Deavere Smith* (Durham, NC: Duke University Press, 2011), 161.

15. W. E. B. Du Bois, *The Souls of Black Folk* (New York: Dover, 1994), 2.

16. Smith, *Talk to Me*, 71.

17. Program for *Notes from the Field: Doing Time in Education*, American Repertory Theatre, Cambridge, MA, September 10, 2016.

BIBLIOGRAPHY

Adorno, Theodor. "Commitment." Trans. Francis McDonagh. *New Left Review I* 87–88 (September–December 1974): 75–89. Accessed June 11, 2017. https://newleftreview.org /I/87-88/theodor-adorno-commitment.

——. *Prisms*. Trans. Shierry Weber Nicholsen and Samuel Weber. Cambridge, MA: MIT Press, 1983.

Aeschylus. *The Oresteia*. Trans. Richard Lattimore. Chicago: University of Chicago Press, 1953.

Allen, Amy. "Solidarity after Identity Politics: Hannah Arendt and the Power of Feminist Theory." *Philosophy and Social Criticism* 25, no. 1 (1999): 97–118.

Anders, Günther. "Tagebuch 1944." In Wizisla, *Begegnungen mit Bertolt Brecht*, 167–75.

Andersen, Maxwell. *Joan of Lorraine*. New York: Dramatists Play Service, 1946.

Arendt, Hannah. *Between Past and Future: Six Exercises in Political Thought*. New York: Viking, 1961.

——. *Eichmann in Jerusalem: A Report on the Banality of Evil*. New York: Penguin, 2006.

——. "Hannah Arendt: From an Interview." *New York Review of Books*. October 26, 1978. http://www.nybooks.com/articles/1978/10/26/hannah-arendt-from-an-interview/.

——. *The Human Condition*. Chicago: University of Chicago Press, 1998.

——. *Ich will verstehen: Selbstauskünfte zu Leben und Werk*. Ed. Ursula Ludz. Munich: Piper, 2005.

——. Interview with Günter Gaus. *Zur Person*. Rundfunk Berlin-Brandenburg. October 28, 1964. http://www.rbb-online.de/zurperson/interview_archiv/arendt_hannah .html.

——. Introduction to *Illuminations*, by Walter Benjamin, 1–58. Ed. Hannah Arendt. Trans. Harry Zohn. New York: Harcourt, 1968.

——. *The Jewish Writings*. Ed. Jerome Kohn and Ron H. Feldman. New York: Schocken, 2007.

——. *Life of the Mind.* Ed. Mary McCarthy. New York: Houghton Mifflin Harcourt, 1991.

——. *Men in Dark Times.* New York: Harcourt Brace, 1995.

——. *On Revolution.* New York: Penguin, 1990.

——. *On Violence.* New York: Harcourt Brace, 1970.

——. *The Origins of Totalitarianism.* New York: Harcourt Brace, 1968.

——. "Quod Licet Jovi . . . Reflexionen über den Dichter Bertolt Brecht und sein Verhältnis zur Politik." *Merkur* 23, nos. 6–7 (1969): 527–42; 625–42.

——. *Rahel Varnhagen: The Life of a Jewess.* Ed. Liliane Weissberg. Trans. Richard Winston and Clara Winston. Baltimore: John Hopkins University Press, 2000.

——. *Reflections on Literature and Culture.* Ed. Susannah Young-Ah Gottlieb. Stanford, CA: Stanford University Press, 2007.

——. *Responsibility and Judgment.* Ed. Jerome Kohn. New York: Schocken, 2003.

——. *Vita activa oder Vom tätigen Leben.* Stuttgart: Kohlhammer, 1960.

Arjomand, Minou. "Performing Catastrophe: Erwin Piscator's Documentary Theatre." *Modern Drama* 59, no. 1 (2016): 49–74.

Auslander, Philip. *Liveness: Performance in a Mediatized Culture.* London: Routledge, 1999.

Azoulay, Ariella, and Bonnie Honig. "Between Nuremberg and Jerusalem: Hannah Arendt's *Tikkun Olam.*" *differences* 27, no. 1 (2016): 48–93.

Bab, Julius. "Die Botschaft der Kinder." *Aufbau*, June 11, 1943.

Bachmann, Michael. "Theatre and the Drama of Law: A Theatrical History of the Eichmann Trial." *Law Text Culture* 14, no. 1 (2010): 94–116.

Bakhtin, Mikhail. *The Dialogic Imagination: Four Essays.* Ed. Michael Holquist. Trans. Caryl Emerson and Michael Holquist. Austin: University of Texas Press, 1981.

Baldwin, James. *Blues for Mister Charlie.* New York: Dial, 1964.

Balme, Christopher. *The Theatrical Public Sphere.* Cambridge: Cambridge University Press, 2014.

Barish, Jonas. *The Antitheatrical Prejudice.* Berkeley: University of California Press, 1981.

Bass, Gary Jonathan. *Stay the Hand of Vengeance: The Politics of War Crimes Tribunals.* Princeton, NJ: Princeton University Press, 2000.

Benhabib, Seyla. "The Embattled Public Sphere: Hannah Arendt, Jürgen Habermas and Beyond," *Theoria* 44, no. 90 (1997): 1–24.

——. "Ethics Without Normativity and Politics Without Historicity: On Judith Butler's *Parting Ways: Jewishness and the Critique of Zionism.*" *Constellations* 20, no. 1 (2013): 150–63.

——. *The Reluctant Modernism of Hannah Arendt.* New York: Rowman & Littlefield, 2003.

Benjamin, Walter. *The Arcades Project.* Trans. Howard Eiland and Kevin McLaughlin. Cambridge, MA: Harvard University Press, 1999.

——. "Conversations with Brecht." In Livingstone, Anderson, and Mulhern, *Aesthetics and Politics*, 86–99.

——. *Illuminations.* Ed. Hannah Arendt. Trans. Harry Zohn. New York: Harcourt, 1968.

——. *Understanding Brecht.* Trans. Anna Bostock. New York: Verso, 1998.

——. *Versuche über Brecht.* Frankfurt: Suhrkamp, 1966.

Bennett, Benjamin. *All Theater Is Revolutionary Theater.* Ithaca, NY: Cornell University Press, 2005.

Bentley, Eric. *The Playwright as Thinker.* Minneapolis: University of Minnesota Press, 2010.

——. *Rallying Cries.* Washington, DC: New Republic, 1977.

——, ed. *The Storm Over the Deputy.* New York: Grove, 1964.

Berrigan, Daniel. *The Trial of the Catonsville Nine.* New York: Fordham University Press, 2004.

Bigsby, Christopher. *Arthur Miller.* Cambridge: Cambridge University Press, 2009.

Bilsky, Leora Y. "When Actor and Spectator Meet in the Courtroom: Reflections on Hannah Arendt's Concept of Judgment." *History and Memory* 8, no. 2 (1996): 137–73.

Bishop, Claire. *Artificial Hells: Participatory Art and the Politics of Spectatorship.* London: Verso, 2012.

Bloch, Ernst. "Discussing Expressionism." In Livingstone, Anderson, and Mulhern, *Aesthetics and Politics*, 16–26.

——. *Vom Hasard zur Katastrophe: Politische Aufsätze aus den Jahren 1934–1939.* Frankfurt: Suhrkamp, 1972.

Bourriaud, Nicolas. *Relational Aesthetics.* Trans. Simon Pleasance and Fronza Woods. Dijon: Les Presses du Réel, 2002.

Bradley, Laura. *Cooperation and Conflict: GDR Theatre Censorship, 1961–1989.* Oxford: Oxford University Press, 2011.

Brant, Stefan. *The East German Uprising.* Trans. Charles Wheeler. New York: Praeger, 1957.

Braueneck, Manfred. *Die Welt als Bühne: Geschichte des europäischen Theaters.* Stuttgart: J. B. Metzler, 2007.

Brecht, Bertolt. *Brecht on Theatre: The Development of an Aesthetic.* Ed. and trans. John Willett. New York: Hill and Wang, 1992.

——. Letter to Walter Ulbricht. *Theater Heute* 6, no. 1 (January 1963): 12.

——. "On the Formalistic Character of the Theory of Realism." In Livingstone, Anderson, and Mulhern, *Aesthetics and Politics*, 70–76.

——. "Popularity and Realism." In Livingstone, Anderson, and Mulhern, *Aesthetics and Politics*, 79–85.

——. *Theaterarbeit.* Dresden: VVV Dresdner Verlag, 1952.

——. *Werke: Große kommentierte Berliner und Frankfurter Ausgabe.* Ed. Werner Hecht, Jan Knopf, Werner Mittenzwei, and Klaus-Detlef Müller. Frankfurt: Suhrkamp, 1988.

Brittain, Victoria, and Gillian Slovo. *Guantanamo: Honor Bound to Defend Freedom.* London: Oberon, 2005.

Brown, Thomas K. "Brecht and the 17th of June, 1953." *Monatshefte* 63, no. 1 (1971): 48–55.

Bruce, Gary. *Resistance with the People: Repression and Resistance in East Germany, 1945–1955.* Lanham, MD: Rowman & Littlefield, 2003.

Brust, Richard "The Twenty-Five Greatest Legal Movies." *ABA Journal*, August 1, 2008. Accessed June 12, 2017. http://www.abajournal.com/magazine/article/the_25_greatest_legal_movies/.

Buckley, William F. "The Nuremberg Doctrine Is Raised and It Was Just a Matter of Time." *Atlanta Journal*, September 25, 1965.

Burroughs, Michael D. "Hannah Arendt, 'Reflections on Little Rock,' and White Igno-rance." *Critical Philosophy of Race* 3, no. 1 (2015): 52–78.

Butler, Judith. "Hannah Arendt's Death Sentences." *Comparative Literature* 48, no. 3 (2011): 280–95.

——. *Notes Toward a Performative Theory of Assembly.* Cambridge, MA: Harvard University Press, 2015.

——. *Parting Ways: Jewishness and the Critique of Zionism.* New York: Columbia University Press, 2012.

Cavarero, Adriana. *For More than One Voice: Toward a Philosophy of Vocal Expression.* Trans. Paul Kottman. Stanford, CA: Stanford University Press, 2005.

Caygill, Howard. "The Fate of the Pariah: Arendt and Kafka's 'Nature Theatre of Okla-homa.'" *College Literature* 38, no. 1 (2011): 1–14.

Chioles, John. "The 'Oresteia' and the Avant-Garde: Three Decades of Discourse." *Performing Arts Journal* 15, no. 3 (1993): 1–28.

Cohen, Robert. "The Political Aesthetics of Holocaust Literature: Peter Weiss's *The Investigation* and Its Critics." *History and Memory* 10, no. 2 (Fall 1998): 43–67.

——. *Understanding Peter Weiss.* Trans. Martha Humphreys. Columbia: University of South Carolina Press, 1993.

Conot, Robert. *Justice at Nuremberg.* New York: Harper, 1983.

Corrie, Rachel. *My Name is Rachel Corrie.* Ed. Alan Rickman and Katharine Viner. London: Nick Hern Books, 2014.

Curtis, Kimberley. *Our Sense of the Real: Aesthetic Experience and Arendtian Politics.* Ithaca, NY: Cornell University Press, 1999.

Dale, Gareth. *Popular Protest in East Germany, 1945–1989.* London: Routledge 2005.

Delage, Christian. *Caught on Camera: Film in the Courtroom from the Nuremberg Trials to the Trials of the Khmer Rouge.* Trans. Ralph Schoolcraft and Mary Byrd Kelly. Philadelphia: University of Pennsylvania Press, 2014.

Dermutz, Klaus. *Das Burgtheater und die Wiener Identität: Kontinuität und Krisen, 1888–2009.* Vienna: Bibliothek der Provinz, 2010.

Dinnerstein, Leonard. *Antisemitism in America.* Oxford: Oxford University Press, 1994.

Disch, Lisa J. "On Friendship in 'Dark Times.'" In Honig, *Feminist Interpretations of Hannah Arendt,* 285–312.

Dorst, Tankred. *Toller.* Frankfurt: Suhrkamp, 1968.

Douglas, Lawrence. "The Didactic Trial: Filtering History and Memory into the Court-room." *European Review* 14, no. 4 (2006): 513–22.

——. *The Memory of Judgment: Making Law and History in the Trials of the Holocaust.* New Haven, CT: Yale University Press, 2001.

Du Bois, W. E. B. *The Souls of Black Folk.* New York: Dover, 1994.

Dwars, Jens-Fietje. *Und dennoch Hoffnung: Peter Weiss, Eine Biographie.* Berlin: Aufbau Verlag, 2007.

"Ein Blick voraus nach My Lai." *Die Zeit,* March 31, 1972.

Eisert, Wolfgang. *Die Waldheimer Prozesse—Der Stalinistische Terror 1950: Ein dunkles Kapital der DDR Justiz.* Munich: Bechtle, 1993.

Ehrenfreund, Norbert. *The Nuremberg Legacy: How the Nazi War Crimes Trials Changes the Course of History.* New York: Palgrave Macmillan, 2007.

Ellis, Ralph. "Man Fatally Wounded by Deputy: Family Says Facebook Live Captured Chaos." *CNN.* March 19, 2017. Accessed March 20, 2017. http://www.cnn.com/2017/03/18/us/facebook-live-killing-tennessee/.

Elon, Amos. Introduction to *Eichmann in Jerusalem: A Report on the Banality of Evil,* by Hannah Arendt, vii–xxii. New York: Penguin, 2006.

Elsberg, Heinz. "Piscators Inszenierung in Berlin." *Aufbau,* November 12, 1965.

Enelow, Shonni. *Method Acting and Its Discontents: On American Psycho-Drama.* Evanston, IL: Northwestern University Press, 2015.

Engerth, Ruediger. "Aktenstudium in Burgtheater: Rolf Schneiders 'Prozess in Nürnberg' in Wien ohne Wirkung." *Handelsblatt Düsseldorf,* January 20, 1969.

Ezrahi, Sidra DeKoven. *By Words Alone.* Chicago: University of Chicago Press, 1982.

Falk, Richard A. *The Vietnam War and International Law.* Vol. 3, *The Widening Context.* Princeton, NJ: Princeton University Press, 1972.

Feeney, Nolan. "*Mountaintop* Playwright Criticizes Casting of White Actor as Martin Luther King Jr. in Play." *Time,* November 11, 2015. Accessed December 1, 2015. http://time.com/4107990/white-actor-martin-luther-king-jr-mountaintop-katori-hall/.

Felman, Shoshana. *The Juridical Unconscious: Trials and Traumas in the Twentieth Century.* Cambridge, MA: Harvard University Press, 2002.

Feuchtwanger, Lion. *Moscow 1937: My Visit Described for My Friends.* Trans. Irene Josephy. New York: Viking, 1937.

——. *Wahn, oder, Der Teufel in Boston.* Los Angeles: Pazifische Presse, 1948.

Fischer, Torben, and Matthias N. Lorenz, eds. *Lexikon der "Vergangenheitsbewältigung" in Deutschland: Debatten- und Diskursgeschichte des Nationalsozialismus nach 1945.* Bielefeld: Transcript, 2007.

Fischer-Lichte, Erika. *History of European Drama and Theatre.* Trans. Jo Riley. London: Routledge, 2002.

——. *Kurze Geschichte des deutschen Theaters.* Tübingen: A. Francke, 1999.

——. "Policies of Spatial Appropriation." In *Performance and the Politics of Space: Theatre and Topology,* ed. Erika Fischer-Lichte and Benjamin Wihstutz, 219–37. London: Routledge, 2012.

——. *The Routledge Introduction to Theatre and Performance Studies.* Ed. Minou Arjomand and Ramona Mosse. Trans. Minou Arjomand. New York: Routledge, 2014.

——. *The Transformative Power of Performance.* Trans. Saskya Iris Jain. New York: Routledge, 2008.

Fraser, Nancy. *Justice Interruptus: Critical Reflections on the "Postsocialist" Condition.* New York: Routledge, 1997.

Freedman, Lewis. "How Far Is Andersonville from Vietnam?" *New York Times,* May 17, 1970.

Frei, Norbert. *Adenauer's Germany and the Nazi Past: The Politics of Amnesty and Integration.* Trans. Joel Golb. New York: Columbia University Press, 2002.

Frost, Jennifer. "Challenging the 'Hollywoodization' of the Holocaust: Reconsidering *Judgment at Nuremberg* (1961)." *Jewish Film and New Media* 1, no. 2 (2013): 139–65.

Funke, Lewis. "News of the Rialto: Shyre Moves: Three Projects Underway, Including 'Nuremberg Diary.'" *New York Times,* July 9, 1961.

Gide, André, and Jean-Louis Barrault. *The Trial.* Trans. Leon Katz. New York: Schocken, 1964.

Gines, Kathryn T. *Hannah Arendt and the Negro Question*. Bloomington: Indiana University Press, 2014.

Ginsburg, Carlo. *History, Rhetoric, Proof*. Hanover, NH: University Press of New England, 1999.

Gottlieb, Susannah Young-ah. "Beyond Tragedy: Arendt, Rogat, and the Judges in Jerusalem." *College Literature* 38, no. 1 (2011): 45–56.

——. Introduction to *Reflections on Literature and Culture*, by Hannah Arendt, xi–xxxi. Ed. Susannah Young-ah Gottlieb. Stanford, CA: Stanford University Press, 2007.

Grabiner, Esther. "'Uniting the Nation's Various Limbs into a National Body': The Jerusalem People's House." *Israel Studies* 20, no. 2 (2015): 76–109.

Grass, Günter. *The Plebeians Rehearse the Uprising*. Trans. Ralph Manheim. New York: Harcourt Brace, 1966.

Habermas, Jürgen. "Hannah Arendt's Communications Concept of Power." In *Hannah Arendt, Critical Essays*, ed. Lewis Hinchman and Sandra Hinchman, 211–30. Albany: State University of New York Press, 1994.

——. *The Structural Transformation of the Public Sphere: An Inquiry into a Category of Bourgeois Society*. Trans. Thomas Burger with Frederick Lawrence. Cambridge, MA: MIT Press, 1991.

Haiduk, Manfred. *Der Dramatiker Peter Weiss*. East Berlin: Henschelverlag, 1977.

Hall, Katori. "Playwright Reacts to the White Casting of MLK in *The Mountaintop*." *The Root*, November 9, 2015. Accessed December 1, 2015. https://www.theroot.com /playwright-reacts-to-the-white-casting-of-mlk-in-the-mo-1790861704.

Halpern, Richard. "Theatre and Democratic Thought: Arendt to Rancière." *Critical Inquiry* 37, no. 3 (2011): 545–72.

Hauptmann, Gerhart. *Die Atridae-Tetralogie*. Frankfurt: Suhrkamp, 1949.

Hawkins, William. "'Burning Bush' Relives Historic Terror." *New York World Telegram*, December 17, 1949.

Hecht, Werner, ed. *Brecht im Gespräch: Diskussionen, Dialoge, Interviews*. Frankfurt: Suhrkamp, 1975.

Hellbeck, Jochen. "With Hegel to Salvation: Bukharin's Other Trial." *Representations* 107 (2009): 56–90.

Herald, Heinz, and Geza Herczeg. *The Burning Bush*. Adapted by Noel Langley. New York: Shirley Collier Agency, 1947.

Herf, Jeffrey. *Divided Memory: The Nazi Past in the Two Germanies*. Cambridge, MA: Harvard University Press, 1997.

——. "The 'Holocaust' Reception in West Germany: Right, Center, Left." *New German Critique* 19, no. 1 (1980): 30–52.

Hess, Amanda. "Justice Through a Lens: A New Wave of Apps Offers Assistance—and Advice—for Citizens Capturing Police Wrongdoing on Camera." *Slate*, April 9, 2015. Accessed March 20, 2017. http://www.slate.com/articles/technology/users/2015/04 /copwatch_mobile_justice_and_other_apps_for_citizens_filming_police_ encounters.html.

Hinchman, Lewis, and Sandra Hinchman, eds. *Hannah Arendt, Critical Essays*. Albany: State University of New York Press, 1994.

Hirsch, Francine. "The Soviets at Nuremberg: International Law, Propaganda, and the Making of the Postwar Order." *American Historical Review* 113, no. 3 (2008): 701–30.

Hirsch, Marianne. *The Generation of Postmemory: Writing and Visual Culture after the Holocaust*. New York: Columbia University Press, 2012.

Hochwälder, Fritz. *Holocaust: A Court for the Dead*. Trans. Ulrich Henry Gerlach and Ruth W. Gerlach. Riverside, CA: Ariadne Press, 2003.

Honig, Bonnie. *Antigone, Interrupted*. Cambridge: Cambridge University Press, 2013.

——, ed. *Feminist Interpretations of Hannah Arendt*. University Park: Penn State University Press, 1995.

——. *Political Theory and the Displacement of Politics*. Ithaca, NY: Cornell University Press, 1993.

——. *Public Things: Democracy in Disrepair*. New York: Fordham University Press, 2017.

——. "Toward an Agonistic Feminism: Hannah Arendt and the Politics of Identity." In Honig, *Feminist Interpretations of Hannah Arendt*, 135–66.

Hörbiger, Paul, as told to Georg Markus. *Ich hab für euch gespielt: Erinnerungen*. Munich: Herbig, 1980.

Horsman, Yasco. *Theatres of Justice: Judging, Staging, and Working Through in Arendt, Brecht, and Delbo*. Stanford, CA: Stanford University Press, 2011.

Hume, David. *An Enquiry Concerning the Principles of Morals*. Ed. J. B. Schneewind. Indianapolis: Hackett, 1983.

Huyssen, Andreas. "The Politics of Identification: 'Holocaust' and West German Drama." *New German Critique* 19, no. 1 (1980): 117–36.

Innes, C. D. *Erwin Piscator's Political Theatre: The Development of Modern German Drama*. Cambridge: Cambridge University Press, 1977.

——. "Toward a Post-Millennial Mainstream? Documents of the Times." *Modern Drama* 50, no. 3 (2007): 435–52.

Jackson, Shannon. *Professing Performance: Theatre in the Academy from Philology to Performativity*. Cambridge: Cambridge University Press, 2004.

——. *Social Works: Performing Art, Supporting Publics*. New York: Routledge, 2011.

Jordan, James. *From Nuremberg to Hollywood: The Holocaust and the Courtroom in American Fictive Film*. London: Vallentine Mitchell, 2016.

Judt, Tony. "The Past Is Another Country: Myth and Memory in Postwar Europe." In *The Politics of Retribution in Europe: World War II and Its Aftermath*, ed. István Deák, Jan Gross, and Tony Judt, 293–323. Princeton, NJ: Princeton University Press, 2000.

Kaplan, Brett Ashley. *Unwanted Beauty: Aesthetic Pleasure in Holocaust Representation*. Urbana: University of Illinois Press, 2007.

Kateb, George. "Political Action: Its Nature and Advantages." In *The Cambridge Companion to Hannah Arendt*, ed. Dana Villa, 130–48. Cambridge: Cambridge University Press, 2000.

Kaufman, Moisés, Leigh Fondakowski, Greg Pierotti, Andy Paris, Stephen Belber, and the Members of the Tectonic Theater Project. *The Laramie Project and The Laramie Project: Ten Years Later*. New York: Vintage, 2014.

Kingsley, Sidney. *Darkness at Noon: A Play Based on the Novel by Arthur Koestler*. New York: Random House, 1951.

Kipphardt, Heinar. *In der Sache J. Robert Oppenheimer: Ein szenischer Bericht*. Frankfurt: Suhrkamp, 1964.

Kirfel-Lenk, Thea. *Erwin Piscator im Exil in den USA, 1939–1951: Eine Darstellung seiner antifaschistischen Theaterarbeit am Dramatic Workshop der New School for Social Research*. East Berlin: Henschelverlag, 1984.

Kottman, Paul. *A Politics of the Scene*. Stanford, CA: Stanford University Press, 2008.

Kramer, Stanley, dir. *Inherit the Wind*. Hollywood, CA: Stanley Kramer Productions, 1961.

——, dir. *Judgment at Nuremberg*. Hollywood, CA: Roxlom Films, 1961.

Laob, Dan. "Theatrical Interpretation of the Shoah: Image and Counter-Image." In *Staging the Holocaust: The Shoah in Drama and Performance*, ed. Claude Schumacher, 95–101. Cambridge: Cambridge University Press, 1998.

Lau, Maria. *Die Picasso-Rezeption in der DDR: Offizielle Wahrnehmung und künstlerischer Dialog*. Frankfurt: Peter Lang, 2011.

Lawrence, Jerome, and Robert E. Lee. *Inherit the Wind*. New York: Ballantine Books, 2016.

Levitt, Saul. *The Andersonville Trial*. New York: Dramatists Play Service, 1961.

Lipstadt, Deborah. *History on Trial: My Day in Court with David Irving*. New York: Ecco, 2005.

Livingstone, Rodney, Perry Anderson, and Francis Mulhern, eds. *Aesthetics and Politics*. New York: Verso, 1980.

Lombardo, Paul A. *Three Generations, No Imbeciles: Eugenics, the Supreme Court, and Buck v. Bell*. Baltimore: Johns Hopkins University Press, 2008.

Luban, David. "Explaining Dark Times: Hannah Arendt's Theory of Theory." *Social Research* 50, no. 1 (1983): 215–48.

Malina, Judith. *The Piscator Notebook*. New York: Routledge, 2012.

Mann, Abby. *Judgment at Nuremberg*. New York: New Directions, 2002.

Mamdani, Mahmood. "Beyond Nuremberg: The Historical Significance of the Post-Apartheid Transition in South Africa." *Politics and Society* 43, no. 1 (2015): 61–88.

Martin, Carol. "Bodies of Evidence." *TDR* 50, no. 3 (2006): 8–15.

Marx, Karl. *The Eighteenth Brumaire of Louis Napoleon*. London: Electric Book Company, 2001.

Maxwell, Lida. *Public Trials: Burke, Zola, Arendt, and the Politics of Lost Causes*. Oxford: Oxford University Press, 2015.

Merritt, Anna J., and Richard L. Merritt, eds. *Public Opinion in Semi-Sovereign Germany: The HICOG Surveys, 1949–1955*. Chicago: University of Illinois Press, 1980.

Miller, Arthur. *The Crucible*. New York: Penguin, 1995.

Mitter, Armin, and Stefan Wolle. *Untergang auf Raten: Unbekannte Kapitel der DDR-Geschichte*. Munich: Bertelsmann, 1993.

Moeller, Robert G. "How to Judge Stanley Kramer's *Judgment at Nuremberg*." *German History* 31, no. 4 (2013): 497–522.

"The Moscow Trials: A Statement by American Progressives." *New Masses*, May 3, 1938.

Müller, Heiner. *Krieg ohne Schlacht: Leben in zwei Diktaturen*. Cologne: Kiepenheuer & Witsch, 1992.

Naumann, Bernd. *Auschwitz: A Report on the Proceedings Against Robert Karl Ludwig Mulka and Others Before the Court*. Ed. Hannah Arendt. New York: Praeger, 1966.

Nelson, Deborah. *Tough Enough: Arbus, Arendt, Didion, McCarthy, Sontag, Weil*. Chicago: University of Chicago Press, 2017.

Norton, Anne. "Heart of Darkness: Africa and African-Americans in the Writings of Hannah Arendt." In Honig, *Feminist Interpretations of Hannah Arendt*, 247–61.

Norton-Taylor, Richard, ed. *Called to Account: The Indictment of Anthony Charles Lynton Blair for the Crime of Aggression Against Iraq, a Hearing*. Devised by Nicholas Kent. London: Oberon Books, 2007.

Nössig, Manfred. "Ermittlung zur 'Ermittlung': Über einen Pressetod." *Theater der Zeit* 23 (1965): 4–7.

Ohnesorge, Henk. "Gehorsam und Galgen: Der Andersonville-Prozess." *Die Welt*, March 25, 1972.

Ostermann, Christian F., ed. *Uprising in East Germany 1953*. Budapest: Central European University Press, 2001.

Parker, Stephen. *Bertolt Brecht: A Literary Life*. New York: Bloomsbury, 2014.

Pendas, Devin O. *The Frankfurt Auschwitz Trial, 1963–65: Genocide, History and the Limits of the Law*. Cambridge: Cambridge University Press, 2006.

——. "Seeking Justice, Finding Law: Nazi Trials in Postwar Europe." *Journal of Modern History* 81, no. 2 (June 2009): 347–68.

Perry, R. C. "Historical Authenticity and Dramatic Form: Hochhuth's 'Der Stellvertreter' and Weiss's 'Die Ermittlung.'" *Modern Language Review* 64, no. 4 (1969): 828–39.

Phelan, Peggy. *Unmarked: The Politics of Performance*. New York: Routledge, 1993.

Pirro, Robert C. *Hannah Arendt and the Politics of Tragedy*. Dekalb: Northern Illinois University Press, 2001.

Piscator, Erwin. *Das politische Theater*. East Berlin: Henschelverlag, 1968.

——. *Schriften 2*. East Berlin: Henschelverlag, 1968.

Pitkin, Hanna Fenichel. "Justice: On Relating Private and Public." *Political Theory* 9, no. 3 (1981): 327–52.

"Presentation I." In Livingstone, Anderson, and Mulhern, *Aesthetics and Politics*, 15.

Probst, Gerhard F. *Erwin Piscator and the American Theatre*. New York: Peter Lang, 1991.

"Prozess in Nürnberg—Dokumentarstück—2. Teil: Premierenmitschnitt der österreichischen Erstaufführung am Wiener Burgtheater (January 15, 1969)." Österreichische Mediathek. Accessed June 12, 2017. https://www.mediathek.at/portaltreffer /atom/17360287-3C9-000BE-000005A4-17354AB7/pool/BWEB/.

Puchner, Martin. *The Drama of Ideas: Platonic Provocations in Theatre and Philosophy*. New York: Oxford University Press, 2010.

——. *Stage Fright: Modernism, Anti-Theatricality, and Drama*. Baltimore: Johns Hopkins University Press, 2002.

Rabinbach, Anson. "Eichmann in New York: The New York Intellectuals and the Hannah Arendt Controversy." *October* 108 (2004): 97–111.

Rancière, Jacques. *The Emancipated Spectator*. Trans. Gregory Elliott. London: Verso, 2009.

Review of *Prozess in Nürnberg*. *Express am Sonntag*, March 9, 1969.

Ridout, Nicholas. *Stage Fright, Animals, and Other Theatrical Problems*. Cambridge: Cambridge University Press, 2006.

Rokem, Freddie. *Performing History: Theatrical Representations of the Past in Contemporary Theatre*. Iowa City: University of Iowa Press, 2002.

——. *Philosophers and Thespians: Thinking Performance*. Stanford, CA: Stanford University Press, 2010.

Rolland, Romain. *Robespierre : Drame en trois actes et vingt-quatre tableaux*. Paris: A. Michel, 1939.

Romanska, Magda. Introduction to *The Routledge Companion to Dramaturgy*, ed. Magda Romanska, 1–15. London: Routledge, 2015.

Rosenfeld, Alvin H. *A Double Dying*. Bloomington: Indiana University Press, 1980.

Rothberg, Michael. *Multidirectional Memory: Remembering the Holocaust in the Age of Decolonization*. Stanford, CA: Stanford University Press, 2009.

——. *Traumatic Realism*. Minneapolis: University of Minnesota Press, 2000.

Rovit, Rebecca. *The Jewish Kulturbund Theatre Company in Nazi Berlin*. Iowa City: University of Iowa Press, 2012.

Saal, Ilka. "Broadway and the Depoliticization of Epic Theatre: The Case of Erwin Piscator." In *Brecht, Broadway and United States Theatre*, ed. Chris Westgate, 45–71. Newcastle: Cambridge Scholars, 2007.

Sartre, Jean-Paul. *No Exit and Three Other Plays*. Trans. Stuart Gilbert. New York: Vintage, 1989.

Schiller, Friedrich. "The Stage as a Moral Institution." Trans. John Sigerson and John Chambless. Schiller Institute. Accessed February 28, 2017. https://www.schillerinstitute.org/transl/schil_theatremoral.html.

Schneider, Rebecca. *Performing Remains: Art and War in Times of Theatrical Reenactment*. London: Routledge, 2011.

Schneider, Rolf. *Schonzeiten: Ein Leben in Deutschland*. Berlin: Be.bra, 2013.

——. *Stücke*. East Berlin: Henschelverlag, 1970.

Schöttker, Detlev, and Erdmut Wizisla, eds. *Arendt und Benjamin: Texte, Briefe, Dokumente*. Frankfurt: Suhrkamp, 2006.

Scott, George C., dir. *The Andersonville Trial*. Hollywood, CA: Community Television of Southern California, 1970.

Seeba, Hinrich C. "Modern Criticism in Historical Context: 200 Years of Lessing Reception." In *A Companion to the Works of Gotthold Ephraim Lessing*, ed. Barbara Fischer and Thomas C. Fox, 327–49. New York: Camden House, 2005.

Seghers, Anna. *Der Prozess der Jeanne d'Arc zu Rouen 1431: ein Hörspiel*. Leipzig: Reclam, 1985.

Shaw, Robert. *The Man in the Glass Booth*. New York: Grove Press, 1968.

Sjöholm, Cecilia. *Doing Aesthetics with Arendt: How to See Things*. New York: Columbia University Press, 2015.

Smith, Anna Deavere. *Talk to Me: Listening Between the Lines*. New York: Random House, 2000.

Smith, Anna Deavere, and Carl Weber. "Brecht's 'Street Scene'—On Broadway, of All Places? A Conversation with Anna Deavere Smith." *Brecht Yearbook* 20 (1995): 51–64.

Smith, Cecil. "Kramer's Judgment: Designed to Provoke." *Los Angeles Times*, January 22, 1974.

Smith, Cherise. *Enacting Others: Politics of Identity in Eleanor Antin, Nikki S. Lee, Adrian Piper, and Anna Deavere Smith*. Durham, NC: Duke University Press, 2011.

Sokolovskii, Vasilii, Vladimir Semyonov, and Pavel Yudin. Report, "On the Events of the 17–19 June 1953 in Berlin and the GDR and Certain Conclusions from these Events," June 24, 1953. In *Uprising in East Germany 1953*, ed. Christian F. Ostermann, 274. Budapest: Central European University Press, 2001.

Sontag, Susan. "Reflections on *The Deputy*." In *The Storm Over the Deputy*, ed. Eric Bentley, 117–23. New York: Grove, 1964.

Stewart, Luke J. "'A New Kind of War': The Vietnam War and the Nuremberg Principles, 1964–1968." PhD diss., University of Waterloo, 2014.

Schwaiger, Michael. "Einbruch der Wirklichkeit: Das Theater Bertolt Brechts und Erwin Piscators," in *Bertolt Brecht und Erwin Piscator: Experimentelles Theater im Berlin der Zwanzigerjahre*, ed. Michael Schwaiger, 9–15. Vienna: Christian Brandstätter, 2004.

Taylor, Diana. *The Archive and the Repertoire: Performing Cultural Memory in the Americas*. Durham, NC: Duke University Press, 2003.

Thomas, Tammis. "The Gray Zone of Victims and Perpetrators in Peter Weiss's *The Investigation*." *Modern Drama* 53, no. 4 (2010): 557–82.

Thompson, Debby. "'Is Race a Trope?': Anna Deavere Smith and the Question of Racial Performativity." *African American Review* 37, no. 1 (Spring 2003): 127–38.

Tretiakov, Sergei. "Die Kunst ist ein Teil der Pädagogik." In Wizisla, *Begegnungen mit Bertolt Brecht*, 103–18.

Tusa, Ann, and John Tusa. *The Nuremberg Trial*. New York: Skyhorse, 2010.

Villa, Dana. *Arendt and Heidegger: The Fate of the Political*. Princeton, NJ: Princeton University Press, 1995.

——, ed. *The Cambridge Companion to Hannah Arendt*. Cambridge: Cambridge University Press, 2000.

Vogel, Manfred. Review of *Prozess in Nürnberg*. *Wochenpresse*, January 22, 1969.

Wagner, Alex. "To Live and Die on Facebook." *Atlantic*, July 11, 2016. Accessed March 20, 2017. https://www.theatlantic.com/politics/archive/2016/07/to-live-and -die-on-facebook/490637/.

Weber, Max. *Economy and Society*. Ed. Guenther Roth and Claus Wittich. New York: Bedminster, 1968.

Weinke, Annette. *Die Verfolgung von NS-Tätern im Geteilten Deutschland: Vergangenheitsbewältigungen 1949–1969 oder; Eine Deutsch-Deutsche Beziehungsgeschichte im Kalten Krieg*. Paderborn: Ferdinand Schöningh, 2002.

Weiß, Christoph. *Auschwitz in der Geteilten Welt: Peter Weiss und die 'Ermittlung' im Kalten Krieg*. St. Ingbert: Röhrig Universitätsverlag, 2000.

Weiss, Peter. *Die Ermittlung: Oratorium in 11 Gesängen*. Frankfurt: Suhrkamp, 2005.

——. "I Come Out of My Hiding Place." *The Nation*, May 30, 1966.

——. *Marat/Sade, The Investigation, and The Shadow of the Body of the Coachman*. Trans. Jon Swan and Ulu Grosbard. New York: Continuum, 1998.

——. *Notizbücher*. Frankfurt: Suhrkamp, 1982.

——. *Peter Weiss in Gespräch*. Ed. Rainer Gerlach and Mattias Richter. Frankfurt: Suhrkamp, 1986.

——. *Rapporte*. Frankfurt: Suhrkamp, 1968.

——. *Rapporte 2*, Frankfurt: Suhrkamp, 1971.

West, Rebecca. *A Train of Powder*. New York: Viking Press, 1955.

Whitaker, Raymond. "*Guantanamo—Honor Bound to Defend Freedom*, Tricycle, London." *The Independent*, May 30, 2004. Accessed February 15, 2015. http://www .independent.co.uk/arts-entertainment/theatre-dance/reviews/guantanamo -honor-bound-to-defend-freedom-tricycle-london-565362.html.

White, Edgar. *Burghers of Calais in Black Drama*. Ed. James Vernon Hatch. Alexandria, VA: Alexander Street Press, 2002.

White, Hayden. "The Value of Narrativity in the Representation of Reality." *Critical Inquiry* 7, no. 1 (1980): 5–27.

Widdig, Bernd. "Cultural Dimensions of Inflation in Weimar Germany." *German Politics & Society* 32 (1994): 10–27.

Wiesel, Elie. *Dimensions of the Holocaust: Lectures at Northwestern University*. Evanston, IL: Northwestern University Press, 1990.

Willett, John. *The Theatre of Erwin Piscator*. New York: Holmes & Meier, 1979.

Wittmann, Rebecca. *Beyond Justice: The Auschwitz Trial*. Cambridge, MA: Harvard University Press, 2005.

Wizisla, Erdmut, ed. *Begegnungen mit Bertolt Brecht*. Leipzig: Lehmstedt, 2009.

——. *Walter Benjamin and Bertolt Brecht: The Story of a Friendship* (New Haven, CT: Yale University Press, 2009).

Wood, Elizabeth A. *Performing Justice: Agitation Trials in Early Soviet Russia*. Ithaca, NY: Cornell University Press, 2005.

Wouk, Herman. *The Caine Mutiny Court-Martial*. New York: Doubleday, 1954.

Young, James E. *Writing and Rewriting the Holocaust*. Bloomington: Indiana University Press, 1998.

Young-Bruehl, Elisabeth. *Hannah Arendt: For Love of the World*. New Haven, CT: Yale University Press, 2004.

Zerilli, Linda M. G. *A Democratic Theory of Judgment*. Chicago: University of Chicago Press, 2016.

ARCHIVES

Akademie der Künste Archiv, Berlin.
    Dokumentation zum deutschsprachigen Theater.
    Erwin Piscator Center.
    Inszenierungsdokumentation.
    Kurt-Meisel Archive.
    Peter Weiss Archive.
Arthur Miller Archive. Harry Ransom Center, University of Texas at Austin.
Bertolt-Brecht Archiv, Berlin.
Erwin Piscator Papers. Southern Illinois University Special Collections Research Center. Carbondale, Illinois.
The New School for Social Research.
Performing Arts Archive. New York Public Library.

FILES/TRANSCRIPTS

Federal Bureau of Investigation file on Erwin Piscator, released under a Freedom of Information Act request filed by Jay Ball.

Trial of the Major War Criminals Before the International Military Tribunal. Nuremberg: International Military Tribunal, 1947.

*The Trial of Adolf Eichmann: Record of the Proceedings in the District Court of Jerusa-
lem*. Jerusalem: Trust for the Publication of the Proceedings of the Eichmann Trial,
1992.

CORRESPONDENCE

Rosenthal, Rachel. Email correspondence with the author, February 13, 2013.
Schneider, Rolf. Email correspondence with the author, November 15, 2017.

INDEX

actors, 29, 37, 47–50; in epic theater, 28, 60, 65–66

Adler, Stella, 13, 101, 125, 134

Adorno, Theodor, 14, 108, 110, 135, 185n16

aesthetic experience, 108, 198n47

aesthetic judgment, 2–4, 15–16, 21, 52, 74, 92, 114, 178–79

aesthetic pleasure, 11, 14, 135

Anders, Günther, 11–12, 26, 59, 147

Andersonville Trial, The (play), 144, 206n25, 207n46

anticolonial movements, 12, 105, 114, 123

anti-Semitism, 5, 24, 40, 46, 100, 128, 134–35, 141, 154, 169; in Nazi Germany, 9–10, 12, 100, 160–61; in postwar East Germany, 159; in postwar West Germany, 112–14, 131–12; in the U.S., 102–3, 124

Arcades Project, The (Benjamin), 107–8

archives, 108–9, 171–72

Arendt, Hannah, 3, 5, 11–12, 93, 115, 130, 134–35, 170

Arendt, Hannah, theories of: action, 46; epistemology, 28; history, 6, 29, 48, 93–94; judgment, 7, 15–16, 34, 141; theater, 26–29, 43, 53, 67–68, 175, 185–86n24; thinking, 29, 35, 49

Arendt, Hannah, works of: *Between Past and Future*, 36; *Crisis of the Republic*, 36; *Eichmann in Jerusalem*, 4, 22–25, 27, 29–36, 40, 49, 51–53, 138, 151; "Franz Kafka, Appreciated Anew," 53; *The Human Condition*, 28–29, 36–37, 43–44, 47; *The Life of the Mind*, 36, 52–53; *Men in Dark Times*, 6–7, 27–29; *On Revolution*, 25, 36, 43, 47–50; *The Origins of Totalitarianism*, 10, 29, 40, 172; *Rahel Varnhagen*, 10, 40; "Some Questions of Moral Philosophy," 29; "Thinking and Moral Considerations," 37; "Thoughts on Lessing: On Humanity in Dark Times," 36–38, 47; "What is Permitted to Jove?" ("Quod Licet Jovi"), 36, 51, 88–92

Aristotle, 23, 26–28, 43

audience, 161; in a courtroom, 32; in a theater, 42, 61; participation, 96–99, 176; reception, 2–3, 13, 21, 29, 39, 43, 169

Auschwitz, 14, 34, 108, 113, 115, 122, 159, 160. *See also* Frankfurt Auschwitz Trial
avant-garde, 10–11, 13, 43, 99

Bakhtin, Mikhail, 108
Baldwin, James, 145, 181n5, 203n125
Ben-Ari, Raiken, 101, 134
Benhabib, Seyla, 47, 50, 188n67, 189n86
Benjamin, Walter, 12, 93, 135; and Brecht, 26, 28, 33, 51, 59, 62, 65
Benjamin, Walter, works of: *The Arcades Project*, 107–8; "Franz Kafka," 53–55; "Theses on the Philosophy of History," 93–94, 106, 171; "The Work of Art in the Age of Mechanical Reproduction," 11, 14
Berliner Ensemble, 67, 76, 79–81
Berliner, Martin, 122, 131–33
Between Past and Future (Arendt), 36
Bloch, Ernst, 64, 193n23, 193–94n36
Blücher, Heinrich, 93
Brecht, Bertolt, 3, 6–11, 25, 31–32, 43, 48, 50–51, 53–58, 66–67, 94–95, 155; as a director, 76–78, 86–87, 151; and epic theater, 26–28, 60–61, 96; theories of judgment, 7
Brecht, Bertolt, works of: *The Caucasian Chalk Circle*, 59, 67, 69–87, 116, 131, 172; *Fear and Misery in the Third Reich*, 90; *The Good Person of Szechuan*, 59–60, 90; "The Legend of the Origin of the Book Tao Te Ching," 51–52; *Life of Galileo*, 59, 89–90, 194n41; *Man Is Man*, 59–60; *The Measures Taken*, 59, 63, 66, 68–70, 76, 89; *The Resistible Rise of Arturo Ui*, 156; *The Rise and Fall of the City of Mahagonny*, 59–60; "The Solution," 83; "To Those Born After," 27, 91, 188n67; *The Threepenny Opera*, 44, 90; *The Trial of Lucullus*, 59, 79
Bukharin, Nikolai, 64–65
Burning Bush, The (play), 15, 94, 101–10, 125–27, 134, 136–37
Busch, Ernst, 71, 75–76, 81, 116

Butler, Judith, 35, 47, 106, 186–87n24, 191n119

casting, 116–18, 125, 127, 129, 131–35, 168, 174–75, 201n110
catharsis, 23, 25, 28, 123–24
Caucasian Chalk Circle, The (Brecht), 59, 67, 69–87, 116, 131, 172
censorship, 154, 158, 164–65
civil rights movement, 12
Cold War, 112, 116, 142–43, 163–64
comedy, 32–33
Communism, 11
Communist Party, 9, 57, 98, 100, 160; cultural policy of, 12, 59, 61–63, 78–84; in Germany, 8–9, 79, 140, 154
concentration camps, 51–52. *See also* Auschwitz
Condell, Heinz, 104, 190n95
Coriolanus (play), 87
courtroom dramas. *See* trial plays
Cripple, The (play), 96
Crisis of the Republic (Arendt), 36
Crucible, The (play), 104–10, 136–37

denazification trials, 143, 168
Denial (film), 141
Deputy, The (play), 34, 110–12, 147
Deutsches Theater Berlin, 146, 154, 167
Dessau, Paul, 102, 131, 136
Diary of Anne Frank (play), 25, 101, 111, 185n16
documentary theater, 14, 16–18, 94, 98, 101, 140, 155, 171, 173, 181n5
Douglas, Lawrence, 147–48, 153, 184n6
Dramatic Workshop, 13, 15, 101–2, 124
dramaturgy, 26–27, 39, 43, 77, 147, 149
Dreyfus Affair, 5, 102, 104
Du Bois, W. E. B., 176

Eichmann in Jerusalem (Arendt), 4, 22–25, 27, 29–36, 40, 49, 51–53, 138, 151
Eichmann trial, 2–3, 5, 22, 131, 143, 150, 158, 165. See also *Eichmann in Jerusalem* (Arendt)
epic theater, 11, 95. *See also* Brecht, Bertolt; Piscator, Erwin

estrangement effect, 28, 30, 87, 110
evidence, 140–42, 147–48, 161, 166,
    172–73, 206–7n34
Exonerated, The (play), 17–18

fascism, 6, 11, 27, 62, 142, 150, 158
Fear and Misery in the Third Reich
    (Brecht), 90
Felman, Shoshana, 94, 184n6
Feuchtwanger, Lion, 56–58, 61, 64
film, 102, 162, 166, 168, 173–74; and
    postwar trials, 161; and theater, 98–99
Fischer-Lichte, Erika, 21, 165, 198n47
forgiveness, 91–92
Frankfurt Auschwitz Trial, 2–3, 6, 111–13,
    127, 131, 143, 158. *See also* Auschwitz;
    Investigation, The (play)
"Franz Kafka" (Benjamin), 53–55
"Franz Kafka, Appreciated Anew"
    (Arendt), 53
Freie Volksbühne (West Berlin), 110,
    121–23, 137–38

Goethe, Johann Wolfgang von, 10, 39
Golden Doors, The (play), 125
Good Person of Szechuan, The (Brecht),
    59–60, 90
Grass, Günter, 87–88, 208n66
Greek tragedy, 23; chorus in, 35–36, 44;
    Great Dionysia Festival, 2–3, 36.
    See also *Oresteia, The* (play cycle)

Habermas, Jürgen, 50
Habima Theater (Tel Aviv), 167
Hannah Szenes (play), 167
Hauptmann, Elizabeth, 75, 87, 173,
    196n93
Heartfield, John, 96
Heinz, Wolfgang, 131, 151–52, 154
Herald, Heinz, 102
Herczeg, Geza, 102
Hiroshima bombing, 146
Hirsch, Marianne, 171–72
Holocaust, 13–14, 22, 24, 32–34, 45, 103,
    140, 148, 158; denial, 34, 141–42;
    representation, 14–15, 51, 110–211,
    114–16, 135–38, 154, 159–60

Honig, Bonnie, 35–36, 47, 170, 184n8,
    188n56
Hörbiger, Paul, 167–69
House Un-American Activities
    Committee Hearings, 5, 13, 66–67
Human Condition, The (Arendt), 28–29,
    36–37, 43–44, 47
humanism, 10, 40–42, 45, 134, 190n95
Hungarian Revolution, 143, 158
Hurwicz, Angelika, 131–34

Inherit the Wind (film), 163, 207n46,
    209n85
In Spite of It All! (play), 98–99
International Criminal Court, 145
In the Matter of J. Robert Oppenheimer
    (play), 19, 110, 147
Investigation, The (play), 111–13, 127–29,
    144, 147, 172, 207n44. *See also*
    Piscator, Erwin
Investigation, The, premiere
    productions of: East Berlin, 115–18,
    129–31, 136; Essen, 120–21, 136;
    London, 115; Munich, 115; Rostock,
    118–20, 136; Stuttgart, 115, 129–30,
    132, 136–37; West Berlin. *See also*
    Piscator, Erwin

Jackson, Robert, 143, 166, 206–7n34,
    207n42
judgment, 2–4, 32, 34, 176, 178; legal, 74,
    91, 142, 149; moral, 88–89, 150;
    political, 149–50; scenes in theater,
    2–4, 38, 61, 71, 155. *See also* aesthetic
    judgment
Judgment (television series), 209n85
Judgment at Nuremberg (film), 144,
    162–66, 204n2, 207n46
June 17 Uprising, 69, 71–73, 83, 87–88
justice, 21, 94, 173–74; economic, 74–75;
    ethical, 74–75, 81, 84, 150;
    performative, 145; poetic, 75;
    political, 150; postwar, 2–3, 143

Kafka, Franz, 53–55, 59, 67
Kant, Immanuel, 15, 52–53, 124
Kramer, Stanley, 144, 163

law, 1–4, 14, 21, 49, 52, 67, 73–75, 78,
    91–92, 145, 172–74
learning plays (*Lehrstück*), 60
"Legend of the Origin of the Book Tao
    Te Ching, The" (Brecht), 51–52
Lessing, Gotthold Ephraim, 10, 15. See
    also *Nathan the Wise* (play)
Levitt, Saul, 144
Life of Galileo (Brecht), 59, 89–90,
    194n41
Life of the Mind, The (Arendt), 36, 52–53
Lukács, György, 59, 62, 68, 81
lynching, 105, 164

Mamdani, Mahmood, 149–50
Man Is Man (Brecht), 59–60
Mann, Abby, 144, 163–64
Marx, Karl, 9, 47–48
masks, 49–50, 62–64, 66–68, 121
Measures Taken, The (Brecht), 59, 63, 66,
    68–70, 76, 89
Mehring, Walter, 125
Men in Dark Times (Arendt), 6–7,
    27–29
Merchant of Venice (play), 46
method-acting, 13, 49, 101, 134–35
Moscow Trials, 4–5, 8, 57–59, 63–65,
    68, 105
Munich Kammerspiele, 19–20, 115, 170,
    183–84n38

Nathan the Wise (play), 14, 38–40, 44–46,
    52, 74, 124, 134–35; Piscator's
    productions of, 45, 124
National Socialism, 8–10, 12–13, 79, 140,
    150, 158
New York Dramatic Workshop. *See*
    Dramatic Workshop
Nietzsche, Friedrich, 10, 47, 190n104
None Shall Escape (film), 162
Nono, Luigi, 115, 135–38
Nuremberg Diary (Gilbert), 144, 151
Nuremberg trials, 2–3, 5–6, 56–57, 94,
    139, 145, 147, 159, 166, 204n2; defense
    at, 73, 130; precedent of, 142–44,
    149–50, 158. See also *Judgment at*

Nuremberg (film); *Trial in
    Nuremberg* (play)

On Revolution (Arendt), 25, 36, 43,
    47–50
Oresteia, The (play cycle), 1–2, 35–6, 42
Origins of Totalitarianism, The (Arendt),
    10, 29, 40, 172

participatory art, 16, 18–20, 179
performativity, 1–2, 47, 145, 152, 175
persona, 29, 49–50
Perry Mason (television series), 162
Picasso, Pablo, 79–80, 85–86
Piscator, Erwin, 6–15, 18, 43, 62, 95;
    theory of epic theater, 95–99, 196n9
Piscator, Erwin, productions of: *§218*, 97;
    The Burning Bush, 15, 94, 101–10,
    125–27, 134, 136–37; *The Cripple*, 96;
    The Crucible, 104–10, 136–37; *The
    Golden Doors*, 125; *In Spite of It All!*,
    98–99; *The Investigation*, 110, 120–25,
    131–38; *Nathan the Wise*, 45, 124; *The
    Robbers*, 100; *Thunder Over
    Gotland*, 100
pity, 23–25, 28–29, 125
police brutality, 172–74, 178
postwar trials, 2–3, 5, 71–73, 123, 143–44,
    147–49, 182, 205n18
Proletarian Theater (Berlin), 95–96
public realm, 2, 7, 15, 19, 21, 37–38, 44, 47,
    50–52, 192n12; and theater, 161, 170,
    172, 179
purges, Stalinist, 12, 60, 63, 89, 100,
    143, 158

racism, 103, 128, 131, 164
Rahel Varnhagen (Arendt), 10, 40
Rancière, Jacques, 21
realism, 42, 58–59, 62–63, 65;
    psychological, 27, 49–50, 101;
    socialist, 12, 62, 68, 78–82
reenactment, 44, 109
refugees, 7, 12, 26, 51–52, 55, 93, 170
Regietheater (director's theater), 42–43
Reinhardt, Max, 42–43, 167–68

relational aesthetics, 18. *See also* participatory art

resistance, 27, 31–32, 41, 52–55, 118–20, 154–55, 168–69

Richard III (play), 155

Rise and Fall of the City of Mahagonny, The (Brecht), 59–60

Resistible Rise of Arturo Ui, The (Brecht), 156

Robbers, The (play), 100

Rokem, Freddie, 165, 196n7

Rosenthal, Rachel, 101

Rothberg, Michael, 108, 110

Russell, Bertrand, 144–45

Russell Tribunals, 145, 157–58

Sacco and Vanzetti trial, 104

Sartre, Jean-Paul, 144–45

Schacht, Hjalmar, 139–40, 142, 152, 160–61, 163, 167–69

Schiller, Friedrich, 10, 15; *The Robbers*, 100; "Theater as a Moral Institution," 39, 124, 204n1

Schneider, Rebecca, 109, 171

Schneider, Rolf, 6, 146–48, 158–59, 167

§218 (play), 97

Shakespeare, William: *Coriolanus*, 87; *Merchant of Venice*, 46; *Richard III*, 155

show trials, 4, 23, 112, 118

Six-Dar War, 142, 161

Smith, Anna Deavere, 173–79

Socrates, 61, 104–5

"Solution, The" (Brecht), 83

"Some Questions of Moral Philosophy" (Arendt), 29

Sontag, Susan, 23, 69

Stalinism, 13, 161; purges, 12, 60, 63, 89, 100, 143, 158. *See also* Moscow Trials

Stanislavski, Konstantin, 50, 79, 101, 151

Stranger, The (film), 162

Sutzkever, Abraham, 152, 161, 167–69

Taylor, Diana, 171

That Justice Be Done (1945 film), 161

"Theater as a Moral Institution" (Schiller), 39, 124, 204n1

theatricality, 4, 14–18, 23, 48, 58, 65, 94, 96, 99, 108; in theater, 110, 114–15, 121, 137, 151–53

"Theses on the Philosophy of History" (Benjamin), 93–94, 106, 171

"Thinking and Moral Considerations" (Arendt), 37

"Thoughts on Lessing: On Humanity in Dark Times" (Arendt), 36–38, 47

Threepenny Opera, The (Brecht), 44, 90

Thunder Over Gotland (play), 100

Till, Emmett, 5, 164

To Kill a Mockingbird (novel/play), 164, 207n46

"To Those Born After" (Brecht), 27, 91, 188n67

Trial in Nuremberg (play), 6, 142–43, 145, 148–50, 163, 165–66; productions in East Berlin, 146–48, 151–59, 205n12; productions in Vienna, 139–40, 160–61, 167

Trial of Lucullus, The (Brecht), 59, 79

Trial of the Catonsville Nine, The (play), 206

trial plays, 1–3, 6, 147, 150, 162, 166–67, 171, 181–82n5

Verboten! (film), 162

Verfremdungseffekt. See estrangement effect

Vienna Burgtheater, 46, 139, 167, 169–70, 204n1

Vietnam War, 142, 144–45, 156, 158, 206n25

virtuosity, 2, 4, 36, 46, 49–50, 92, 174–76

Wagner, Richard, 10, 43

Weber, Max, 59, 74

Weigel, Helene, 67, 116, 131

Weiss, Peter, 6, 18, 113–14, 128–29, 205n21. See also *Investigation, The* (play)

West, Rebecca, 147

"What is Permitted to Jove?" ("Quod Licet Jovi") (Arendt), 36, 51, 88–92

White, Hayden, 109–10

white supremacy, 142, 177

witch hunts, 104

witnesses, 29, 49, 172–73; in postwar trials, 29–30, 112, 127, 147, 166, 187n40, 206n34; in theater, 60–61, 117–23, 127–38, 150–51, 160, 165–66, 169

"Work of Art in the Age of Mechanical Reproduction, The" (Benjamin), 11, 14

World War I, 7–9, 95, 148

World War II, 8, 72, 134

Zerilli, Linda, 7, 182n14, 191n115, 205n9

Zola, Émile, 102, 192–93n12

Printed in the USA
CPSIA information can be obtained
at www.ICGtesting.com
JSHW020536021223
53138JS00001B/3

9 780231 187794